Collective Intelligence and Digital Archives

Digital Tools and Uses Set

coordinated by
Imad Saleh

Volume 1

Collective Intelligence and Digital Archives

Towards Knowledge Ecosystems

Edited by

Samuel Szoniecky
Nasreddine Bouhaï

WILEY

First published 2017 in Great Britain and the United States by ISTE Ltd and John Wiley & Sons, Inc.

ISTE Ltd
27-37 St George's Road
London SW19 4EU
UK

www.iste.co.uk

John Wiley & Sons, Inc.
111 River Street
Hoboken, NJ 07030
USA

www.wiley.com

Library of Congress Control Number: 2016957668

British Library Cataloguing-in-Publication Data
A CIP record for this book is available from the British Library
ISBN 978-1-78630-060-7

Contents

Chapter 3. From the Digital Archive to the Resource Enriched Via Semantic Web: Process of Editing a Cultural Heritage.

Lénaïk LEYOUDEC

Chapter 4. Studio Campus AAR: A Semantic Platform for Analyzing and Publishing Audiovisual Corpuses

Abdelkrim BELOUED, Peter STOCKINGER and Steffen LALANDE

Chapter 7. On Knowledge Organization and Management for Innovation: Modeling with the Strategic Observation Approach in Material Science   207

Sahbi SIDHOM and Philippe LAMBERT

Ecosystems of Collective Intelligence in the Service of Digital Archives

1.1. Digital archives

The management of digital archives is crucial today and for years to come. It is estimated that every 2 days, humanity produces as much digital information as was produced during the two million years that preceded our existence. In addition to this human production is the information that machines continuously produce. With the cost of digital memory becoming ever cheaper, most of this information is stored in vast databases. In 2025, all of these "big data" will constitute nearly eight zettabytes (trillions of gigabytes) [SAD 15]. In our age, there are very few human activities that do not generate digital archives; each day we feed digital workflows even outside our use of computers, telephones or other digital devices. It is enough for us to turn on a light, run errands, take public transport or watch television to produce digital traces that, for the most part, will never be accessible to us, but which are compiled, indexed and calculated in server farms and management centers.

The status of these digital archives is obviously not the same when dealing with the tweet sent automatically by a cow, the digitization of a course by Gilles Deleuze or the 3D modeling of the Citadelle Laferrière near Cap-Haïtien. Even if these archives are ultimately composed of a set of 0s and 1s and are therefore formally comparable to one another, their

Chapter written by Samuel SZONIECKY.

importance is not equivalent and they particularly vary according to space, time and actor contexts that are faced with this information. The tweet sent by a digital device in relation to a cow's activities[1] is probably not important for most of us, but for the milk producer who wants to follow his herd's movements to correlate the milk composition with the pastures grazed, it is important to know that a certain pasture has an influence on the amount of fat in the milk. Similarly, a certain passage in Gilles Deleuze's courses where he speaks of the importance as a fundamental criterion seems to some people like an almost meaningless phrase while it takes on very great importance for the researcher interested in the relationship between ethics and ontology, but also for the reader of these lines who at this very moment is thinking about this concept just by the fact that they are reading it:

> "What does that mean, this category? The important. No, it is agreed; that is aggravating, but it is not important. What is this calculation? Isn't it that? Isn't it the category of the remarkable or the important that would allow us to establish proportions between the two intransigent meanings of the word proportion? Which depends on and results from the intensive part of myself and which rather refers to the extensive parts that I have[2]."

These proportions between the inner-being and the outer-having are quite easily transposed into the domain of digital archives. Due to their dynamic, upgradeable and interactive characters, digital archives are ecosystems where each element can be analyzed in terms of existence made up of "intensive parts" and "extensive parts". The example of the digitization of the fort at Cap-Haïtien sheds light on the importance of digital archives that illustrate this "intensive/extensive" double dimension that Deleuze emphasizes to show the correlation between an exterior dimension connected to having and the material, and an interior dimension connected to being and the immaterial. In the case of this historic monument classified as a UNESCO World Heritage Site, digital archiving is the chance to develop both a material and immaterial heritage in one of the poorest countries in the world. The creation of an international research program focusing on the issues of augmented realities, the teaching and education of students on these issues, and the mobilization of artists for the innovative use of these technologies are three examples of immaterial heritage development. At the

---

1 http://criticalmedia.uwaterloo.ca/teattweet/
2 http://www2.univ-paris8.fr/deleuze/article.php3?id_article=24

same time, these activities allow for consideration of material heritage development through the implementation of an economy that uses these digital archives to create new services aimed at tourists on cruises passing by this country. Here, the impact of the digital archive goes beyond the scope of a company or that of knowledge by having repercussions on the whole economy of a country through a joint development of material and immaterial heritage.

Consequently, the fundamental issue of digital archives consists in examining their importance at both the material and the immaterial level in order to estimate their relevance in terms of balance between the finality of the digitization process and the uses made of it. Given the breadth that digital archives take on today and their impact on our lives, we must examine the importance of these archives at both the personal and the collective level. These investigations can only be done through long-term collective work that must take place through a pooling of analyses and the constitution of a collective intelligence capable of lending humanity the means to avoid handing over to machines the full responsibility of semantic choices necessary for the interpretation of archives [CIT 10]. Solutions already exist or are being developed as initiatives taken by the W3C to harmonize information management practices; others remain to be discovered from a technical, epistemological, political or ethical point of view.

1.2. Collective intelligence

It is rather trivial to explain what collective intelligence is through the anthill analogy [FER 97] or all other insect societies [PEN 06]. This conception leads to a very partial vision of the phenomenon of collective intelligence and brings about a questionable ethical position in the case of human organizations. The conception of a collective intelligence modelled on insect societies tends to reduce the human participant in this intelligence to a simple and basic being, whose entire complexity must be removed to make each individual react like the whole. As Bernard Stiegler remarks, therein lie the stakes of a war for control of societies through symbols [STI 04]. Furthermore, it is one of the recurring criticisms vis-à-vis collective intelligence that would only be intelligent in name, and would only serve to centralize memory to better control it without allowing new knowledge to emerge [MAY 06].

What sets humans apart from ants is their ability to reflect on the information flows in their interior and thus express a reflective conscience [LEV 11]. As Yves Prié explains, reflexivity is the ability to get back in touch with oneself in order to construct from memory representations allowing the regulation of one's actions [PRI 11]. This definition, which places reflexivity in an individual context, can nevertheless be understood in a collective framework as well, where individuals share their reflexivity to work collectively in accordance with the consciences of each individual. There we find the basic principles of a science that aims to elaborate a consensus and allows us to define collective intelligence as the sharing of reflexivity in order to complete an action that could not be done by a single person.

But before they can benefit from this collective "ability to act" [RAB 05], the actors must agree to direct their personal interests towards an altruistic sharing of their will. This is possible by formalizing and sharing knowledge while also accepting their validation by collective constraints in order to make the task interoperable and reusable for a community. All of the difficulty of collective intelligence remains in this ability of individuals to agree to restrain their own expressions through formalism, for it quite often challenges habits of reflection. They must not deceive themselves about the primary motivations of humans, which do not necessarily go in the direction of the ethical development of harmonious collaboration. As Yves Citton states, sometimes it is necessary to use tricks to make practices evolve and to anchor them in new social organizations [CIT 08]. It is rather indicative to see that research conducted by Anita Woolley to define a collective intelligence factor confirms that the abandonment of selfish interests in favor of an altruistic approach increases a group's capacity for collective intelligence. In fact, it shows that each individual's intelligence has far less impact than the social sensibility of a group's members, allowing them to listen and not monopolize the discussion in particular [WOO 10].

The issue of restraining individual intelligence in favor of completing a collective action today goes through technical devices and particularly through graphic interfaces that will formalize semiotic systems whose goal is to facilitate individual expression in correlation with the constraints necessary for sharing that expression. The use of a computer language like WIKI is a clear example of going through this constraint to facilitate the interoperability of an individual expression and completing an encyclopedia's project. These collective intelligence projects do not stop at one computer language; they bring with them an entire knowledge ecosystem at the heart of which these projects will be able to develop through the successive completion of the individual actions.

1.3. Knowledge ecosystems

These are the solutions to these issues that we are going to analyze by taking concrete examples in domains as diverse as corporate innovation or personal archives, but which also have in common the use of collective intelligence to exploit digital archives. To provide a strong coherence to the diverse examples and to handle all of the complexity of the issues they present, we will analyze the solutions following the analogy of ecosystems. In these solutions, which implement collective intelligence approaches in relation to the use of digital archives, we will see how these practices can be analyzed by understanding information not as inert objects but as autonomous beings that develop distinctive ways of life [LAT 12].

The goal of our proposed model consists of developing a generic method for analyzing the ecosystems of knowledge that make up a complex universe of simultaneously complementary and antagonistic relationships between a multitude of human, mechanical, institutional, conceptual, documentary, etc. relationships. With this model, we hope to provide researchers with the means to describe their fields of research and the arguments they defend through the modeling of informational beings. The goal is to be able to render analyses interoperable through the automatic comparison of these beings. To achieve comparative analyses of these ecosystems, we model the informational beings by crossing the Gille Deleuze's Spinozan logical principles [DEL 68] with those of Philippe Descola [DES 05]. Concerning Deleuze, we return to the three dimensions of existence (extensive parts, relationships, essences) correlated with three types of knowledge (shocks, logic, intuition). As for Descola, we use the ontological matrices that characterize the relationships between physicalities and interiorities. More specifically, we focus on the analogy ontology that actually corresponds to the case of digital archives and collective intelligence, given digital physicalities' unlimited transformational capacity and the multiplicity of interiority relationships proposed by collective intelligence:

> "This continued struggle between a vertiginous ocean and relationship networks, always in the process of multiplying their connections, strictly defines analogism, a word that wonderfully summarizes and paints our objective world, our cognitive tasks, our subjective dreams, and the groups that are born today and will do the politics of the future." [SER 09, p. 85]

With the help of these principles, we form unique representations that we describe as monads. They are made up of four groups: documents, actors, concepts and relationships. Within each group, the elements maintain relations of differential semantics [BAC 07, p. 142] following the relative position of an element in relation to two axes, that of the father and the brother in a tree.

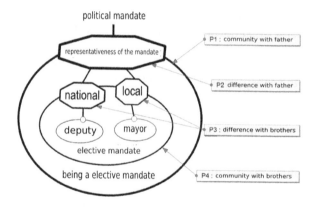

Figure 1.1. *Principles of differential semantics*

The levels defined by the position of the elements in a tree of father–son hierarchies put in contact with the element number in each group gives a precise metric of the monad. This metric allows the level of complexity of a being to be known in order to automatically compare interpretations that cover the same documents, the same actors and the same concepts. We call this metric the Existential Complexity Index (ECI), and we are developing a tool to automatically calculate this index using modeling of a being.

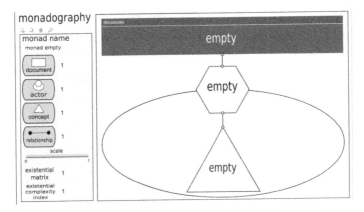

Figure 1.2. *Modeling an empty being*

Each monad and the associated ECI is a unique description of the state of an ecosystem of knowledge at a given moment for a given person. This state gives a particular perspective on the ecosystem; it does not seek exhaustivity, but rather the expression of an interpretation that serves to support arguments and creates the potential for controversies from which the consensus necessary for collective action may emerge.

1.4. Examples of ecosystems of knowledge

1.4.1. *Modeling digital archive interpretation*

The research conducted in the field of digital humanities produces new archive sources that are challenging the division traditionally used by historians and the literati to distinguish between "primary" sources, those produced by the object of study, and "secondary" sources, those produced by research activity. The use of digital technologies leads to the creation of "secondary" archives in the form of databases that, if they are accessible and interoperable, automatically become new "primary" sources for a reflexive analysis of research activities or for other researchers studying the same field. The creation of these digital archives and, more specifically, the durable dimension of their use, conditions the researcher's task by putting an emphasis on the formalization of the task in such a way that it becomes open, interoperable and lasting. This scientific imperative is imposed upon researchers more and more by the simple fact that they work on projects where the digital dimension is central, as it guarantees financing. The question then arises, how can this data be produced and made visible without being an expert in computer science or knowledge engineering?

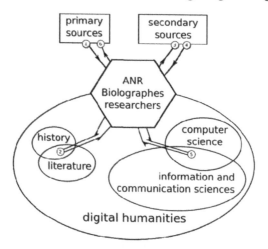

Figure 1.3. *Recursive cycle of sources*

Muriel Louâpre and Samuel Szoniecky aim to tackle this question by analyzing the task performed in the framework of the ANR Biolographes project. This very concrete terrain allows for examination of the nature of digital archives produced by research to extract the special features particular to the field of human science. After a presentation of the digital practices implemented in this type of research, the specific case of visualization methods is dealt with by a review of the primary tools available on the Web in order to critique the epistemological and practical limits. Using the same body of data, the authors show the utility of these tools for quickly testing the coherence of data, for visualizing networks, or for multiplying the approaches and defining new research perspectives. Finally, they reflect on a generic method for modeling influence networks using a prototype developed specifically to help researchers describe their interpretations so that they are interoperable with other perspectives. The goal of this process is to provide cognitive cartographies serving as an aid for the elaboration of a scientific consensus.

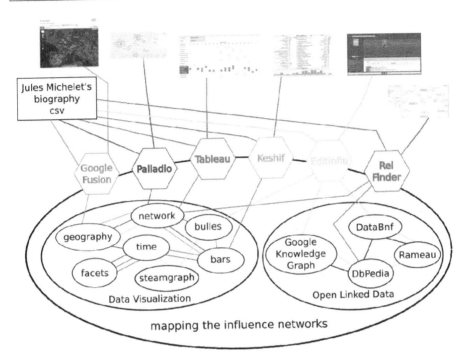

Figure 1.4. *Mapping the influence networks. For a color version of the figure, see www.iste.co.uk/szoniecky/collective.zip*

From these reflections emerges the result of a sometimes-difficult dialogue between researchers coming from different fields of expertise. Faced with the digital "black box", digital models can be imposed upon researchers whose needs in terms of information processing are too often not explained concretely. Even if the lure of a button that can simply be pushed to obtain the relevant information starts to disappear after disappointments and frustrations during the dialogue with the machine, the lack of knowledge engineering training remains flagrant at times. Beyond knowing what the machine can do, it is important for humanities researchers who use digital technology to understand in what way they also bring reorganization to the collective task and research practices.

1.4.2. Editing archives via the semantic web

As we explained above, there are multiple examples of digital archive creation and they not only concern the field of research, but also cultural heritage. Lénaik Leyoudec is interested in the process of editing these digital archives, wondering about the possibilities of preserving the meaning and intelligibility of heritage documents. To explore these issues, he references the differential semantics defended by Rastier [RAS 01] and Bachimont [BAC 07] (Figure 1.1) to deduce an interpretive approach that can be broken down into three consecutive phases: semiotic analysis, document validation method and architext editing. As with the propositions of Muriel Louâpre and Samuel Szoniecky, Lénaik Leyoudec emphasizes the interpretation of the digital archive and the need to equip this process in order to preserve it in the best way possible.

In the framework of an experiment on various audiovisual funds that possess "semiotic objects" belonging to the "private cinema" register, a precise analysis of the cinematographic structure shows how the interpretive approach allows the definition of "memory indicators" at different levels, depending on whether there is interest in a specific plan (micro), a related plan (meso) or all of the segments (macro). This first level of semiotic analysis is enriched by an analysis of the cinematographic indicators specific to family films to bring about the emergence of "perceptive saliences" like so many "memorial diegeses" that will serve as the basis for archive editing. The editing principle proposed goes through the transcription of memory indicators into as many annotations that will define a generic typology: "person", "place", "object", "date" and "activity". What is being played at in this stage of editing is the mobilization of *Linked Open Data* resources like Wikidata.

Fortified by this ambition, a digital device is developed to respond specifically to the needs of family film editing. Devised as an ecosystem of "écrits d'écrans" bringing a semiotic polyphany into play, this tool accompanies the user in the interpretation process by facilitating document annotation. Particularly through a timeline representing the sequences of audiovisual flow, it allows the construction of a graphic in the form of networks for navigation between the categories, a research interface to find the annotations and a device for linking categories with the *Linked Open Data* resources.

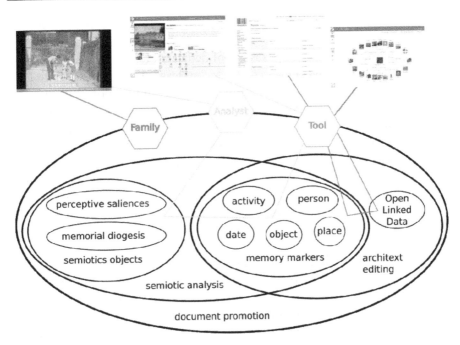

Figure 1.5. *Editing the archives via the semantic web. For a color version of the figure, see www.iste.co.uk/szoniecky/collective.zip*

Numerous questions were raised by this experiment, matching general issues concerning digital archives and the place of collective intelligence in its validation. One of the primary issues concerns the preservation of the document's integrity. Each edition of the document, each interpretation, modifies the primary resources, sometimes by enriching it and sometimes by altering it. Archaeologists know well that as the dig moves forward, they destroy sources of information. Conversely, digital technology allows continuous archiving of resources and their annotations; everything can be preserved. But is this really the most important thing? Is it better to enrich digital memories or to stimulate humans' interpretive experience? If preference is given to the latter approach, it is clearly not necessary to preserve everything for the simple fact that nothing exhausts humans' interpretive capacity, as is shown by the multitude of interpretations for a single book over millennia or a simple sunrise.

1.4.3. *A semantic platform for analyzing audiovisual corpuses*

The previous solution proposes a tool dedicated to the analysis of family films by using *Linked Open Data* to increase the interoperability of interpretations; other researchers are working on similar tools with the aim of facilitating the subjective appropriation of audiovisual data to transform them into a meaningful object. The ANR Studio Campus AAR[3] project has allowed for the development of a tool dedicated primarily to academia and research that increasingly uses audiovisual data as research and educational material. In this context, archives are devised as a *hub* serving as a reference between different communities that form communication ecosystems and lead to a semiotic turning point given the specificity of activities concerning these data.

Structured like foliage of outlines oscillating between the content and the expression, the semiotics of the audiovisual data spreads out according to genres (fiction, documentaries, etc.) and a compositional hierarchy that imposes organization structures and restricts interaction with the data. To describe this system of signs, this tool's creators use the landscape analogy to define a metalanguage and methods of description. In doing so, they make the concrete management of audiovisual data analysis, publication and reediting activities possible.

The Studio Campus AAR sets out to accompany users following two complementary perspectives, the activities of construction and those of audiovisual data appropriation. These activities are made up of steps, themselves structured into procedures that will serve as the basis for orchestrating the data rewriting practices at the thematic, narrative, expressive, discursive and rhetorical levels. These writing/rewriting operations mobilize complex cognitive operations in an intercultural context of re-coverage.

Devised as a software infrastructure based on cognitive and semiotic approaches, this tool aims to provide actors in the audiovisual world with the means to deal with a document in order to transform it into an intellectual resource for cultural education, research and mediation. To achieve this, the solution is organized around an RDF database and a work environment proposing the functionalities necessary for activities of re-coverage: addition

---

3 For more information about the project, see http://campusaar.hypotheses.org/. To access the experimental Campus AAR portal, see http://preprod.campus-aar.armadillolab.fr/campus/

of an archive, analysis with an ontology, management of individuals, publication/republication, research, modeling the discourse universe.

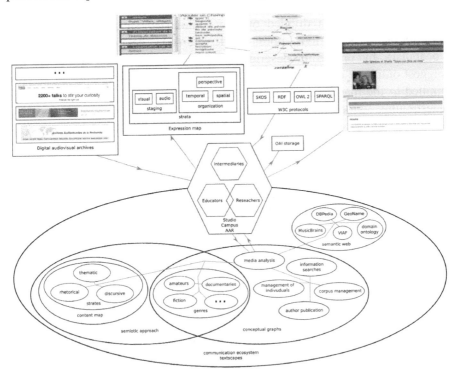

Figure 1.6. *Studio Campus AAR*

At the heart of this platform, knowledge graph editing constitutes a crucial point, particularly for giving those not specialized in knowledge engineering the means to model and analyze the corpuses with languages originating from works of the W3C like RDF, OWL2 and SPARQL. The means of achieving this consist of providing examples of ontology or ontological structures in the form of patterns defining restriction trees. Once the graphs are edited, they can be resolved following different argumentation algorithms that automatically analyze the corpus to deduce content suggestions. The graphical representation of a knowledge graph is another challenge that the Studio Campus AAR is trying to tackle, particularly to reduce the complexity of editing and to respond to the criteria of simplicity, adaptability, dynamism and reusability.

There are various applications of these knowledge graphs that cover all needs through audiovisual analysis. First of all, the media analysis, which consists, for example, of describing the subjects mentioned in the document in the form of strata divided on the audiovisual steam's timeline. This description uses various ontological reference documents and SKOS vocabulary by proposing description patterns via dynamic formulas that suggest ontology entities while the user is typing. These principles are also applied to the management of individuals who will be gathered for faceted questioning, which completes the information search applications via SPARQL requests. Some other applications of this tool to be mentioned are the management of corpuses and author publication.

To finish, Studio Campus AAR offers a complete platform for analyzing audiovisual documents by means of knowledge graphs using formal reference languages (RDF, OWL2, SKOS, etc.) that make the analyses produced durable and interoperable. In this sense, this tool illustrates the work necessary for the formalization of digital archives, so that these will provide knowledge allowing collective intelligence to be developed.

1.4.4. *Digital libraries and crowdsourcing: a state-of-the-art*

Even before being able to promote digital archives, they must first be created by digitizing sources that have not yet been digitized. This task, very simple when the source is recorded directly using digital tools like a word processor or a digital camera, becomes much more difficult when the sources come from a library, or the increase in volume and sometimes their fragility make it difficult to go from an analog to a digital version, and more still the exploitation of digital data that cannot yet be understood by machines. Mathieu Andro and Imad Saleh introduce an original typology of the collective intelligence solutions that can be put into practice to optimize this task through analysis of the notion of "crowdsourcing" and how it is practiced in libraries.

"Crowdsourcing" literally means mobilizing the masses as a resource to carry out a task, but there are different definitions according to whether outsourcing, conscious involvement, volunteering, collaboration, etc. are considered. Whatever the case may be, these practices can be considered to go very far back in time, for example, connecting them to the appeals made in the 18th Century to resolve scientific problems like determining the longitude of a boat at sea; also, the conceptual origins of this notion find their roots in socialist, Marxist, anarchist, humanist or liberalist ideologies, ideologies that actually place the debate in the political domain, particularly on questions of the "uberization" of libraries.

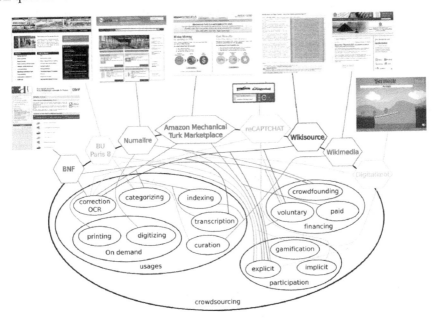

Figure 1.7. *Crowdsourcing in libraries. For a color version of the figure, see www.iste.co.uk/szoniecky/collective.zip*

To analyze these collective collaboration practices, categorizing according to the degree of participant engagement offers a non-negligible quantitative criterion, but one that can be enriched by other, more qualitative criteria. The authors propose, for example, differentiating the implicit practices like gamification or ludification, which consists in appealing to participants' desire to play. "Crowdfunding" constitutes one of the other large categories of "crowdsurfing", where participation is essentially financed like digitization or on-demand printing, for example, which makes it possible to have players pay for a part of the hard work done.

In libraries, there are various challenges of externalizing micro-tasks to Internet users. In addition to reducing costs for correcting errors made by optical character recognition (OCR) tools, these practices would allow the collection to be reedited so as to enrich the existing indexes at the book level with more precise categorization at the page or even the sentence level. However, the management of libraries is not always open to outside participation, especially the devaluing of employees' jobs, particularly their expertise in categorizing and indexing. Among the other difficulties that halt the development of these collective intelligence projects, we can include the employment of a person dedicated to stirring communities often perceived as useless, the low quality of production and the poor reintegration into information systems, and the difficult evaluation of these projects.

It can be seen here that "crowdsourcing" projects in libraries focus on various issues that allow a better understanding of the relationships between digital archives and collective intelligence. Despite all of these difficulties and the fact that the masses are not always very sensible, "crowdsourcing" is nevertheless a practice that brings about numerous innovations in the fields of technology, economics, politics and even personal development. Let us hope that these experiences will lead to concrete solutions so that we may better coexist in hyper-connected societies.

1.4.5. *Conservation and promotion of cultural heritage*

Human activities leave numerous material and immaterial traces that together make up the cultural heritage whose durable and interoperable promotion is today going through knowledge modeling. To do this, the community of this domain has developed formal languages that take the form of metadata norms like the Dublin Core, LIDO, MODS, EDM, etc. These are completed through the use of controlled vocabularies like KOK, SKOS, RAMEAU, etc. by lexical databases like Wordnet and by ontologies like CIDOC CRM. However, four primary difficulties make knowledge modeling for cultural heritage difficult: the acquisition of data, knowledge modeling, usage and interoperability.

Concerning the acquisition of data, the problem of balance between the complexity of heritage objects, the complexity of implicit expert knowledge and the complexity of formal languages must be resolved. For example, it is often difficult for experts who have their own vocabularies and systems of description to use ontologies whose organization and way of working are different. To facilitate this communication between implicit user knowledge and formal knowledge, it is possible to model ontological paths that will guide the user in the formal description of his or her knowledge. Another way to perform this task consists of automating data input through automatic language processing technology or through the integration of different data sources. In this case, the problems of contradictory data must nevertheless be managed through the use of a named graph.

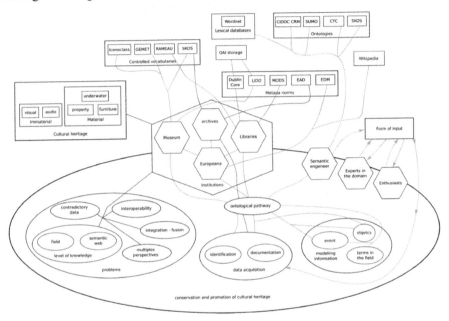

Figure 1.8. *Conservation and promotion of cultural heritage*

The diversity of approaches for modeling information is a central issue. Depending on whether the models come from the field of museums, libraries or archaeology, the approaches are different and the harmonization of these is not always clear. There are methods for automatically calculating the approximation between various formal models that for some use the extension of basic ontological classes and for others appeal to thesauri to enrich the terms in the field.

User profiles condition the uses that will be made of the computer system for the conservation and promotion of cultural heritage. These uses will evolve according to their level of knowledge of the semantic web's technologies, their expertise in the domain and the nature of the terminology. The interfaces of visualization and interaction with information from then on become a fundamental issue so that collective intelligence can be developed effectively. If they are too complex, the tool will not be used; if they are too simple, they will not serve the users' needs.

As there are multiple ways of describing knowledge, interoperability becomes a challenge, particularly according to the structuring choices that will be made. Even if there are also tools to compare these different structures, the first solution to this type of problem consists of using knowledge models with an elevated level of conceptualization like the OAI-PHM protocol.

Here again, we can see that the use of formal languages undoubtedly contributes to the emergence of a collective intelligence through the qualities of durability and interoperability that semantic technology brings about. Nevertheless, their implementation often remains difficult, is constrained and demands that users adapt their practices. To facilitate this appropriation of semantic technologies, a new actor appears who, by modeling semantic pathways, builds the bridge between ontological complexities and those of experts or enthusiasts in a domain.

1.4.6. *Modeling knowledge for innovation*

The examples that we have just dealt with show how digital technology can help with the implementation of a collective intelligence and facilitate the task of researchers by giving their analyses a durable and interoperable character. The solution that we now present aims to structure the skills offered through a knowledge model extracted from digital archives that researchers create to respond to evaluation demands like those of AERES. The goal here is not limited to accompanying a research task, but rather foresees a prospective dimension by using the model to deduce recommendations for decision makers who, in this case, are not document analysts but rather interpreters of these analyses whose task is to finalize a decision, especially in terms of investment in an innovation. The information system that is developed will allow a real-time evaluation of research activities through a continuous enrichment of experiment returns or the addition of new knowledge.

In this case, digital technologies, notably automatic language processing, are used to create synergies between the world of research and the socio-economic world. The primary goal is to provide decision makers with information about the skills available in a field so as to be able to respond more efficiently to proposal requests and thus develop a network of innovation involving all the actors in an economic ecosystem. To do this, the researchers form the hypothesis that a field ontology allows the automatic extraction of specific information allowing a laboratory's operating fields by means of a cognitive redaction model. This process follows a three-point methodology.

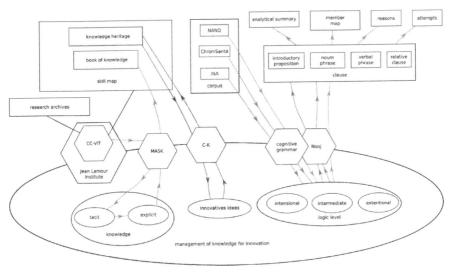

Figure 1.9. *Management of knowledge for innovation*

The first step in this methodology consists of the adaption of Knowledge Management processes to construct the formal descriptions of the organizations that the research will focus on. This stage adopts the outlines of the MASK method, which aims to structure knowledge by adapting it to the C-K theory of innovation to organize the accumulation of knowledge for innovation.

The second step consists of exploiting the digital corpus, thanks to automatic language processing technologies, in order to extract information with a high profit margin. To do this, researchers adopt a morpho-syntactic analysis strategy to extract "organic units" and construct a cognitive grammar from different fields of experimentation.

Finally, the third step aims to organize the information in a class hierarchy in order to structure a skill offer and construct a field ontology. Thanks to the morph-syntactic "patterns" of automatic processing tools, it is possible to construct dictionaries and class hierarchies, and to use them in the analysis of an organism's activities over time or at a given moment in order to identify its skills and expertise in the framework of innovative projects to detect weak signs of a theme, thanks to dictionaries and grammars designed during this research.

1.5. Solutions

These solutions, as numerous as they are diverse, tend to provide an image of incoherence from which no order or expectation can be extracted. However, as chaos, there is definitely order if distance is taken in order to carry out an analysis of the overall arrangement of these solutions. At the systemic level, it can be seen that all of these solutions aim to make the connections that informational existences maintain with one another. In this sense, we can speak of information ecosystems and, using this analogy with a living system, better understand the complexity of the contexts and analyses necessary for understanding them.

From these ecosystemic analyses, it stands out that each of the examples presented seeks to implement formal languages, in most cases issuing from Open Linked Data, which allow an interoperable and durable formalization of the relationships between the documents, actors and concepts. In these modeling tasks that are expressed in the notions of "patterns", "ontological pathways", "digital monads" or "morpho-syntactic patterns", we discern what we call "semantic grains", that is to say, the generic formalization of semantic potential. These grains carry a dynamic algorithm that guides the user in the cognitive maelstrom of digital archives by making connections between the documents, actors and concepts. It is from this continuous growth of semantic potential that the user can construct his or her interpretation by selecting the connections that seem well suited to then share the fruit of these reflections.

Even if the analogy is a bit audacious, it clearly shows the challenges of research on collective intelligence and digital archives and that can be summarized in a few questions. Do semantic grains have a DNA? Who are the creators of semantic grains? Semanticist-engineers? Biologist-cognition specialists? Can digital archives be promoted, just as a garden is cultivated? Through these questions, what is generally at stake is the ability of human–machine interfaces to make the complexity of formalisms accessible to those who do not specialize in computer engineering without losing the details of expertise in a field.

1.6. Bibliography

[BAC 07] BACHIMONT B., *Ingénierie des connaissances et des contenus: Le numérique entre ontologies et documents*, Hermes Science-Lavoisier, Paris, 2007.

[CIT 08] CITTON Y., "Entre l'économie psychique de Spinoza et l'inter-psychologie économique de Tarde", in *Spinoza et Les Sciences Sociales: De La Puissance de La Multitude À L'économie Des Affects*, Editions Amsterdam, Paris, 2008.

[CIT 10] CITTON Y., *L'avenir des humanités: Economie de la connaissance ou cultures de l'interpétation*, La Découverte, 2010.

[DEL 68] DELEUZE G., *Spinoza et le problème de l'expression*, Éditions de Minuit, Paris, 1968.

[DES 05] DESCOLA P., *Par-delà nature et culture*, Gallimard, Paris, 2005.

[FER 97] FERBER J., *Les systèmes multi-agents: vers une intelligence collective, Informatique, intelligence artificielle*, InterEditions, Paris, 1997.

[LAT 12] LATOUR B., *Enquêtes sur les modes d'existence: Une anthropologie des Modernes*, La Découverte, 2012.

[LEV 11] LÉVY P., *La sphère sémantique: Tome 1, Computation, cognition, économie de l'information*, Hermes Science-Lavoisier, 2011.

[MAY 06] MAYERE A., "L'intelligence collective: une notion en chantier", *Intelligence collective Rencontre 2006*, Presses de MINES, 2006.

[PEN 06] PENALVA J.-M., *Intelligence collective*, Presses de MINES, 2006.

[PRI 11] PRIÉ Y., Vers une phénoménologie des inscriptions numériques. Dynamique de l'activité et des structures informationnelles dans les systèmes d'interprétation (HDR), University Claude Bernard – Lyon I, 2011.

[RAB 05] RABARDEL P., "Instrument subjectif et développement du pouvoir d'agir", *Modèles Du Sujet Pour La Conception: Dialectiques, Activités, Développement*, Octarès Éditions, Toulouse, 2005.

[RAS 01] RASTIER F., CAVAZZA M., ABEILLÉ A. (eds), *Sémantique pour l'analyse. De la linguistique à l'informatique*, Masson, Paris, 2001.

[SER 09] SERRES M., *Ecrivains, savants et philosophes font le tour du monde*, Editions Le Pommier, Paris, 2009.

[SAD 15] SADIN E., *La vie algorithmique: Critique de la raison numérique.* Editions L'échappée, Paris, 2015.

[STI 04] STIEGLER B., *De la misère symbolique: Tome 1. L'époque hyperindustrielle*, Editions Galilée, 2004.

[WOO 10] WOOLLEY A.W., CHABRIS C.F., PENTLAND A. *et al.*, "Evidence for a collective intelligence factor in the performance of human groups", *Science*, vol. 330, pp. 686–688, 2010.

2

Tools for Modeling Digital Archive Interpretation[1]

In theory, digital archives allow SSH researchers to multiply previously unthinkable systematic approaches. However, if systematic surveying of archival collections is one of the operations familiar to historians, which allows us to imagine their conversion to digitally assisted quantitative approaches in the not so distant future, the question is quite different for researchers working in the field of the arts, who frequently have a solitary hermeneutical approach and for whom all syntheses emerge from a vast personal erudition. Less inclined towards quantitative approaches, also aware that no enumeration could summarize an esthetic experience, these researchers have long regarded the computer's initial forays into literary analysis (the Hubert de Phalèse group) or discourse analysis (the MOTS laboratory ENS Saint-Cloud) warily. While sociologists and geographers were inventing tools to understand the diffusion and mutation of polemics in the media [CHA 03], to visualize and put phenomena anchored in a place of study in perspective, literary specialists grasped new tools much later, accompanying the slow opening up of their reference institution, the National Library of France, to data sharing.

Chapter written by Muriel LOUÂPRE and Samuel SZONIECKY.
1 This chapter expands upon and completes the work performed for the conference ISKO-Maghreb 2015; see https://hal.archives-ouvertes.fr/hal-01220142/document.

Yet the use of digital tools in the framework of the social sciences and more specifically the humanities (literature, history, philosophy, etc.) has become more than an option in recent years. It has become an obligation, given the degree to which research-financing agencies are basing the allocation of funds on the use of tools guaranteeing a "production" not limited to the development of books and symposia, but including the delivery of databases that can be exploited by others. This demand for long-term exploitation of research by-products on projects that are inevitably limited in time has come with the provision of increasingly important quantities of information made available through the opening of digital archive depots, so computer tools are being invested with a growing importance at each step of scientific work: definition of sources, analysis methodology, editing and circulation of research documents, etc., and this to the point of decentering projects and destabilizing researchers hesitating between a fantasized vision of miraculous computer tools (the dream of the button-press) and worry in the face of a pragmatic order they have no hold over and which seems to devalue their skills, or worse, the system of values on which this skill is founded.

In this regard, the cooperation experiment performed with researchers of literary history seems opportune for highlighting the real possibilities and the equally real tensions between letters and data, or more precisely, the literary and digital worlds. In fact, literary history is among all classes of literature the one that is logically the closest to historic issues and for which it would thus be easiest to adopt these tools (supposing a form of professionalization in the sense of defining the practices that even historians have not yet mastered: the craftsman remains the master model).

The experiments performed with these researchers thus allow us to establish the foundations of a reflection on the roads and dead-ends of digital archive exploitation in the social sciences around three axes: how do literary historians exploit these archives, with what tools, borrowed or *ad hoc*, what exchanges with other specialists, and above all else, the impact of this eruption of data grouped in a field until now dominated by a personal relationship to the source and a traditional model of meaning production. We will see that beyond technical issues, this evolution promotes representations, and that the epistemological issues of these tools demanding a very different structuring of researcher cooperation cannot be underestimated.

2.1. What archives are we speaking of? Definition, issues and collective intelligence methods

2.1.1. *Database archives, evolution of a concept and its functions*

At the heart of historical practices, archives have long been defined as traces, set apart from collections created in a joint way and to serve an identified goal. As unconscious by-products of an activity, archives consequently required of the researcher the patient task of appropriating its constitution mechanisms, for these mechanisms conditioned the value of truth that could suitably be attached to each type of data.

With the appearance online of vast corpuses rarely structured and often aggregated of data, the nature of the archive is changing, as is its methods of use. Here, we could duplicate the well-known bibliographical couple of "primary" and "secondary" sources: similarly for archives, there is a "primary" archive, produced by the process or institution studied, and the secondary archive, which would be the product of exploiting the first while studying this process or institution. Thus, the notion of archives henceforth covers not only data produced by the organizations during their function (for example, editing house publication data, etc.), but also vast corpuses of data assembled in the scope of a research project that, without creating proper collections, are already the result of a selection process and have a structure of their own. For all that, these collections that we will speak of "become archive", in the sense that they are intended to be deposited, afterward, in the maelstrom of accessible databases: they will then become archives for others, in the sense of a by-product, this time from previous research activity.

Will these second-order "archives", which aggregate data in their various degrees of maturity, remain subject to the same usage norms as others? For the historian, the researcher's first gesture when faced with an archive is, in the words of Michel de Certeau, to "redistribute space", that is, to set apart, reassemble and reorganize data that had been produced by others in another order. This restructuring of the archive remains necessary to the extent that our subjects in social sciences are only indirectly and partially susceptible to a quantitative approach: the categories are not self-evident; they are almost always constructed, and as such, arguable. A clear example would be that of genre approaches: the tenet formulated by the ANR Euterpe team (2007–2011) to study the scientific poems published between 1792 and

1906 should assume a stabilized genre that in reality evolved over the course of the century between didactic poetry with scientific content, poems inspired by technology and the philosophy of science. It was thus necessary to compile a list of generic criteria assuring the coherence of the corpus, criteria that will necessarily bias later reutilizations by projects that do not closely handle the question of genre, but are solicitous of popularization, for example, or of relationships between science and the arts.

The first singularity of digital exploitation of archives in social sciences will therefore often be the very constructed character of its subjects, which curtails their fungibility. They do, however, have the advantage, vis-à-vis first-level archives, of explicitly demonstrating their categories, which facilitates the understanding of their structures and allows for the elaboration of reutilization strategies.

This wide redefinition of the notion of archives is not our doing: it follows a tendency particular to digital practices, where archiving, deposit and registration converge, to the point of becoming synonymous by the grace of Windows menus, and where the notion of information consequently seems to fuse with the prestigious "archive". If this extension of the term under the pressure of digital uses can be lamented because it blunts its precision and thus its efficacy, we must admit that the power ("arkheion") often identified with the archive lingers there, producing the same pragmatic effects. It reminds us of Derrida evoking the etymology of archives, as much a start as a commandment, in his reflection on the dark side of archives: because archives are the sources of the historical account: "No one ever renounces – and this is the unconscious itself – the appropriation of power over the document, over its detention, its retention or its interpretation. But who ultimately has the authority over the institution of the archive?" [DER 95, pp. 15–16]. The question is singularly pertinent in France, where the National Archives are associated with the reorganization of the Nation, both lending to the revolutionary break in which they institute a new order, and to the "arkhê", a real box in which the repressed of this young nation are locked up (we can think of the famous "Armoire de fer", an iron cabinet in Louis XVI's former apartments, the true heart of the national archives where the first laws of the Constituent Assembly and essential items from the Ancien Régime, notably those from Joan of Arc's trial and Louis XVI, are preserved).

There is no better way to present the symbolic impact of archives and the articulation between a hidden past, repressed in Derridean analysis, and a present power that the mastery of this past creates. What remains of this power in "digital archives"? For Dietmar Schenk, archivist historian and author of an archive theory who recently spread to the digital world, secret and power continue to characterize the fantasy of the digital archive [SCH 14b, SCH 13]: "in the systems of digital data processing, power, technology, and organization are very strongly interconnected factors; the quantities of information thusly managed often surpass understanding – archives can become anxiogenic, as their contents, from a strictly quantitative point of view, exceed the limits of the imaginable and evade our sight; it is in this way that the old type of secret archives as they existed in the princely states at the start of our modernity has become the archetype of an imaginary approach of the most modern information storage companies. Picturing the archive in terms of 'power' is in tune with the experience that many people have with new technological media with which they are not yet familiarized [...]" [SCH 14a, p. 39].

It is precisely this anxiogenic character that seems to reappear in the humanist uses of digital archives, despite their open, democratized character, which would seem to distance the very idea of control and power. In fact, researchers fear not the archive itself, but that there is no possible access to these archives except through intercession of those who can make it speak, in such a way that the interposition of a sort of computational "black box" poses numerous problems, both technical and epistemological, that we will try to approach through a practical case, that of our research within a multidisciplinary team, the ANR/DFG "Biolographes" team. Before dealing with special cases, however, it is only right to complete this exploration of the notion of archives with an overview of the methods and tools available to researchers in the humanities to exploit these mysterious archives.

2.1.2. *The exploitation of digital archives in the humanities*

There are diverse methods of exploring archives offered to humanists, and they engage, as was just said, in more or less profound cooperation with computer scientists; they may also concern different procedures according to which are proposed:

– the exploration of textual corpuses (primary archives, therefore in plain text);

– the exploitation of databases structured by researchers themselves;

– the exploitation of data from bibliographic tools used by these same researchers during their work (secondary archives).

The analysis of corpuses in plain text was the first computer-assisted method of analysis for literary researchers: the disciplinary proximity between literary researchers and linguists, the obligation of the former to know the basics of the latter's discipline to pass the agrégation encouraged cooperation *a priori*. This is not the place to retell the story of the encounter between textual analysis and literary research, but we will be permitted to remind the reader that these initial experiences left a lasting mark on the representations of humanists: the vision of a computer science that could only with difficulty find what could be deduced much more quickly from a reading informed by the knowledge of a scholar. Counts of occurrences, co-occurrences, collocations and all the finer functions made available by the various available tools of textometry (of recent note, TMX, a new product from an ANR at the ENS Lyon, but also Iramuteq, just to mention the most well-known examples) proved to be much more pertinent to the study of vast journalistic corpuses than for dealing with very formally elaborated texts, also less extensive, and where a sophisticated syntax could very well nullify the orientations that were believed to have been detected in the lexicon. To be pertinent in researchers' eyes, computerized tools had to offer help in the face of tasks that an individual could not perform alone: their use was thus reserved to the study of very important corpuses, like genre studies, of which it can be said, incidentally, that they contributed to rekindle them, together with the institutional injunction to undertake complicated team projects to justify loans. These supercorpuses falling under history or media communication more often than literature, it should come as no surprise that historians of literature and publishing are overrepresented in these tasks, and thus in our examples. The example of the Prelia project could be given, devoted to the socio-editorial field of small symbolist magazines at the end of the 19th Century, and rare case of a project run by a literary specialist who knew how to code, or even the super-database of literary correspondence from the Enlightenment devised at Stanford, "Mapping the Republic of Letters", and at the root of the Palladio tool which will be at issue again later.

Finally, we have essentially alluded here to the limits of research in plain text by assuming that these "archives" are established and exploitable, yet with a simple attempt to work with slightly older documents digitized by the National Library of France, it is easily understood that this enormous mass of data is not subject to automatic processing: the limits of the OCR used and the complexity of the organization of pages in certain publishing formats particularly complicate the data: this is thus the case of randomly placed scholarly apparatuses, but also in the case of 19th Century press, the mere existence of the "feuilleton", an important place for narrative experimentation at the time and one that shows up on ordinary pages, but separated from the top of the page by a borderline that is difficult for algorithms to interpret. There is worse: we have worked together on a Franco-German project implying the constitution of a vast bilingual corpus of war stories: if the indexing of the named entities was surmountable by the French team, the use of Fraktur font, particularly troublesome for OCR, by German publishers at the time meant detouring through a specialized structure that (even academically) would sharply increase the price of the project.

Most often, in order to produce interesting results, the "corpuses" accessible en masse for processing in plain text must first become true archives: here again, we find the break gesture characterizing archiving according to Derrida, the separation gesture according to de Certeau, and which allows the corpus to be structured and made exploitable. Of course, it is tempting to exploit "loose" corpuses, especially when Google makes simple tools like the NGram viewer available to us, but the opacity of Google's methods for establishing and structuring these corpuses makes the results difficult to evaluate except in terms of frequency [PEC 11].

The humanists who wish for rigorous analyses but dreamed that computer science would do the job also find themselves faced with indexing troubles: yet if these issues are familiar to researchers in information sciences, the humanists, who are rarely trained in indexing, do not know the TEI and do not have the resources around them that would allow them, for example, to index the "named entities" that they often need. The arduousness of indexing tasks is undoubtedly the reason that most archives exploited by humanists are databases that are already established or created over the course of the project. Most of the time, studies give rise to tabulated databases, subject to various treatments, extractions and visualizations (in the best of cases, as loose "studies" of ".doc" files are often the first intention, etc.).

Among many others, we can cite the example of the database being created by the ambitious ANR Anticipation ("Anticipation. Scientific futuristic novels at the turn of the 19th Century (1860–1940)", directed by Claire Barel-Moisan, 2014–2018), which we have been able to follow as "technical consultancy" for the program. This database strives not only towards a descriptive goal (integrating the narrative structure and characters of the futuristic stories studied, the structuring thus being proposed by categories originating in narratology) but also towards a hermeneutic goal, for the metapoetic indicators coexist with the description of the texts. As with other projects, the time it takes to create the database is such that it is possible for the first results on a "complete" corpus or one considered as such not to be accessible until the end of the program, the group members producing numerous and incidentally interesting "Ancien Régime" analyses in this time, fed by gathering the already-acquired records that consequently remain at the stage of preparatory notes[2]. This gap between research time and institutional program time is an obstacle common to many humanist projects. Requiring long reflection to fix the framework of the studies, and supposing that almost the entire corpus has been scrutinized so that the expected powerful quantitative descriptions can be considered, these databases are forcibly disconnected from the time of the researchers, who must produce in this period to justify their financing, of which they are less a tool than a product, just as an administrative archive can be. Here we see the reappearance of this trait particular to the digital archive: it is also often, if not more so, the trace of a research task rather than an autonomous resource exploited by researchers (as bibliographical notes would be). This difference in time between the moment of program financing and that of finally delivering an exploitable database draws attention to the need to think beforehand about the way that this database will exist once the financing is over, but also about its interoperability: in order that what has become "an archive" in the literal sense of the word may be used by other researchers, it is once again necessary for it to be accessible online, on a durable server. The program's server generally stops with the financing, and the university laboratory sites only offer fragile guarantees if they are not backed by national organizations. The archiving offer from TGIR Huma-Num[3] responds hereafter to this need: it is again necessary to know the device and anticipate the time needed to implement it.

---

2 Again, this ANR has not only profited from a rapid start, thanks to the anticipation of technical questions, but also from the closeness of certain researchers on the team with programming colleagues working in the same IUT (French Polytechnic University).
3 http://www.huma-num.fr/

The exploitation of an archive made up of bibliographic bookmarks like those that a data-harvesting tool like Zotero[4] can provide, or Diigo[5] to a lesser degree, shows the same character of secondary archives, a character just as quantitative, but much more spontaneous. It assumes that researchers tag or index the works or citations found on the Internet, even in real libraries in the case of Zotero: by then recovering the data in CSV format, visualizations based on this library or tags associated with it by the researcher can be produced. In this specific case, usage evolves towards a sort of folksonomy: without computer skills, users add information, and this true archive that is a bibliographic database gathered in a shared library benefitting from everyone's studies becomes a material just as precious as that of databases. We can foresee the exploitation of the themes of these bibliographic notes, thanks to visualization tools implemented for Zotero, such as Paper Machine[6]. This tool offers quality visualizations including Sankey diagrams, and its use is well documented by an efficient tutorial. In practice, the difficulty lies in involving researchers and not just in a generation that has made little use of bibliographic indexing tools: if history faculties start educating their students in the use of bibliographic tools, literary specialists are still wondering about their utility for them, and it should be noted that their use is hardly commonplace or spontaneous, such that "I have to start using Zotero" is one of the favorite phrases heard around various projects at the end of each presentation of its virtues. We have implemented this technology for another project aiming, among other things, to detect mentions of an author, Jacques Delille, in writings after his death in 1813 in order to study his trace in French publications, that is, the evolution of the fame of a person who was, during his life, the equivalent of an Ancien Régime Victor Hugo and whose reputation very quickly became the complete opposite over the course of the century. Furthermore, the use of these bibliographic tools allows us to start filling the RDF database created by the University of Basel's Digital Humanities Lab[7].

---

4 https://www.zotero.org/
5 https://www.diigo.com
6 http://papermachines.org/
7 The "Reconstructing Delille" project is financed by the Swiss National Science Foundation, but it benefits from the rare existence of a structure dedicated to the digital humanities, which has created a platform of RDF databases called Salsah and whose first sizeable project was a HyperHamlet, a sort of database for reuses of Shakespearean verses in the works of more than 3,000 authors. See http://www.hyperhamlet.unibas.ch/

2.1.3. *The specific case of visualization tools*

Finally, among the vast set of digital tools made available to researchers, special attention must be paid to visualization tools, in which we have become particularly interested in our own work. This choice had a purpose: it neutralized the humanist's suspicion regarding an ostensibly quantitative approach like that of statistics; it also had an even more strategic goal: it offered the possibility of making people appreciate the hermeneutic plus-value of technology. The specificity of data visualization is in fact allowing for a purely visual grasp of the corpus' elements, favoring the detection of similarities, pattern regularities or, to the contrary, anomalies, which can be interpreted thanks to subsequent exploration of the legend, or at least will allow the creation of interpretation guidance, if not new research. This pre-attentive perception brought to light in 1985 by Anne Triesman thus quite certainly underpins the hermeneutic productivity of visualization. Jean-Marie Schaeffer completed this observation by associating precisely our ability to interpret with the existence of a categorical wandering in that pre-attentive phase: it allows approximations, often based only on graphic forms, to operate without effort and without considering the categories of the things represented (this link to the category comes in during a second phase with the exploitation of the legend and data tags). Jean-Marie Schaeffer attributes the richness of artistic experience generally to what he calls a "delayed categorization": it is the fact that the object read or seen resists the immediate assimilation that categorization would allow, or at least the fact that it offers a space, or "elbow room", which is the source of creativity. In the face of data visualization, in the same way, categorization loses evidence and frees the associative power of wandering attention.

To provide a very simple example, the researchers in the ANR Euterpe group knew from experience at what stages peaks in the publication of scientific poetry came about during the 19th Century, and without the aid of visualization, they could indicate three successful periods for the genre with little risk of error through mere familiarity with the corpus. However, the visualization revealed to them a pattern, that of a series of ebbs and flows, we could say, going in and out of fashion, a process that visibly stalls after 1872 (and not in 1871 as an effect of the tightening of publication in a country at war as may have been expected, that year instead seeing a proportional increase in poetic writings in global editorial production).

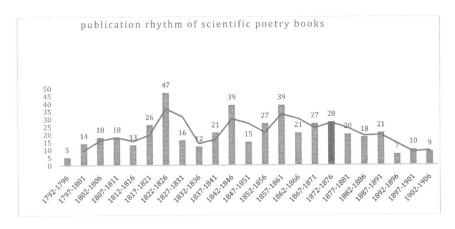

Figure 2.1. *Publication rhythm of scientific poetry books*

For historians who wondered about the reasons for the virtual disappearance of the genre after the 1910s, this simple diagram provides an alternative route: the closing decade is in fact the end of a breakdown process that began in 1872–1876, at the moment when the usual upswing in the cycle is clearly stopped. The question is thus no longer what happens in 1890, but rather what happens around 1874? Another question, or rather another field of knowledge for the researcher, is that if 1890 is known as the theater of a profound crisis for bookstores (therefore, an explanation not particular to the genre studied), the immediate post-war period, on the other hand, sees large debates over the causes of the French defeat in the face of German science, which makes science both a desired power and the privilege of the hated and reviled victors. Immediately, through visualization, there is another possible story, even well-founded and verifiable, for which the researcher is grateful to the tool, whatever native mistrust he may have.

These approaches through visualization have been introduced in literary history by the comparatist Franco Moretti, who used resources from Stanford to produce visualizations that allow new questions to be posed about known corpuses, and about data that is not necessarily quantitative, but which has a distinguishing feature of spatialization, in the absence of geolocalization. Both powerful and evocative, the images of this work have given rise to new perspectives, even if the polemics were heated, even in the researcher's circle. They form a reference, as this was the first time that a researcher led, sponsored a visualization project [MOR 08].

Among these visualizations, we became particularly attached to those allowing for the representation of influence networks, for the reasons mentioned above. The tools that we experimented with did not meet the criteria that we counted on, particularly in terms of the expression of researchers' point of view. In order to provide a more effective tool, we have come up with a digital device primarily dedicated to the expression and sharing of these points of view. The principle consists of modeling researchers' arguments in interoperable semantic graphs in the shape of a network between documents, actors and concepts of relation to a given time and location. With this tool, we aim to go beyond the tools available today by offering a generic method for analyzing digital archives and developing collective intelligence processes understood as:

"The ability of human groups to collaborate on the intellectual stage to create, innovate, and invent. This ability can be applied to any level, from small work groups to the human species by going through networks of all sizes." [LEV 10, p. 105]

2.2. Digital archive visualization tools: lessons from the Biolographes experiment

In the scope of the ANR Biolographes project (2012–2016)[8], bringing French and German researchers together under the direction of Gisèle Séginger (University of Marne-la-Vallée) and Thomas Klinkert (University of Zurich), we aim to represent networks gathering French-language literary specialists and naturalists from the 19th Century.

On a broader front, "Biolographes" seeks an understanding of the methods of interaction between knowledge of the living, popularization and texts considered literary, particularly at a time when the use of literary form is not yet foreign to the scholarly world and where a vast territory of "literary communication" [VAI 06] spreads out with aims not exclusively esthetic or informative. Similarly, the objects of science still occupy the

---

8 http://biolog.hypotheses.org/

spare time of so-called literary men, in such a way that the participation of the enlightened hobbyist in the scientific debates of the time is still frequent enough for the literary man not to be immediately discredited upon bringing up these subjects. A canonical example would be the invention of the "Alpine" subject by literary texts (Haller's didactic poem *The Alps* (1732) and Rousseau's *New Heloise*, in particular), texts whose considerable popularity elicits the calling of naturalist-explorers. This singularity of the 19th Century prevents all thoughts of relationships between science and literature in the simple form of influence, and limits us to more sophisticated approaches than the description of "relationships" oriented by the scholar towards literature that would put the scientific material into words. We would thus hope to explain what circulated between our different scientific or literary poles and how: in fact, it quickly appeared that ideas and concepts could circulate as well as words (even concepts reduced to the rank of keywords) and that vectors of this movement were just as much people, called to exchange in real life or by mutual correspondence, as texts, magazines or books that responded to one another. The team, quite extensive, initially gathered 10 German and 12 French researchers from different universities reaching as far as Switzerland, including doctoral candidates. Only three of them, coming from the Euterpe project, had experience in the creation and exploitation of digital archives.

The project's first gesture, symbolically, was therefore to create a "stratified" online chronology (we used a simple tool, Preceden) that provided an initial tool, admittedly brief, allowing for the visualization of concurrences or, on the other hand, profound differences; it was then necessary to find out if they were significant – in fact, the existence of delaying effects, even the persistence of an old order, had been foreseen starting in the pre-project phase. This first action demonstrates the need to bring the researchers together, as it happens, the team's science historians, long before work, in the collection phase, while they show themselves to be more voluntary as final users of the assembled data. It is their disciplinary skill that had to be leaned upon to assess the importance in a given field of a certain event, a certain publication, a certain name that seemed obscure to non-specialists and which holds special meaning for experts.

The second task was to complete the bibliography with a list of magazines likely to serve as an intermediary between specialists and laypeople and that were then analyzed. The digital tool, initially planned exclusively for the visualization of sociability networks, from then on seemed to need to take on an unexpected importance, for the data to be correlated, already abundant, was spreading across a spatial, even geographic plane, but also a diachronic plane. The project then saw a sort of "digital turn", if we may call it that, for it seemed that only digital tools could truly respond to the initial attempts, and the skills of two specialists were called upon, one in information sciences, Samuel Szoniecky, the other in automatic language processing, Philippe Gambette, as well as a postdoctoral student with the same training.

The first difficulty of this type of project for non-specialists consists of identifying the tools that will maximize the yield of the required investments – understood as investments in human time. As said, one of the reasons for success resides in the involvement of researchers in the assembly of data and the use of visualization tools: it is therefore important to bring the researchers together and make them aware of the tools' potential. At this stage, every presentation of progress also falls under communication. Moreover, we hoped that the team could seize the tools, which excluded powerful but dreary tools like R, or libraries like d3.js that assume JavaScript skills. After reflection, we also excluded Gephi, a very widespread tool, but one which looks austere and requires graphic work to improve the visualizations obtained and make them fully convincing, which we did not want to do at an experimental stage.

As a first step, we tested tools available on the Web with the data from a spreadsheet created by Muriel Louâpre to identify the points of contact between the knowledge of the living and a central author for these issues, successful historian and popularizer of science Jules Michelet. It was a matter of locating the direct and indirect relationships with scholars or professionals of popularization by qualifying the relationship (contact in-person, by letter, through books, etc.); we also integrated geographic or institutional contact spaces and locations, speculating about the advantage of having maps of exchanges available over the long term for all the writers in the corpus (places of residence, institutions, vacations).

2.2.1. *Tools for testing*

The tool Google Fusion[9] at first allowed us to consolidate the data from the spreadsheet and to test various methods of representation. Thanks to this tool, it is rather easy to "play" with the data to test the pertinence of the representations.

Figure 2.2. *Map of the locations visited by Jules Michelet. For a color version of the figure, see www.iste.co.uk/szoniecky/collective.zip*

This map shows the locations visited by Jules Michelet as well as the frequency of these visits: the brighter and redder the location is, the more the location is visited. The interest of this map is to quickly evaluate the activity zones of this person or, conversely, the places he did not visit. Clearly, this visualization lends nothing to a Michelet expert, who has memorized his journeys and his vacations, and most of us expected to see Normandy appear often in the locations visited by Flaubert, Maupassant, Michelet, etc., but in general, it is rather the establishment of relationships in maps concerning lesser-known actors who may lead to the appearance of unexpected cross referencing. The following representation, also with Google Fusion, aims to characterize the types of relationships in association with the location of the stay.

---

9 To read the Google Fusion documents, see https://goo.gl/Tm83jp.

Figure 2.3. *Relationship between the types and locations of stays (1st attempt). For a color version of the figure, see www.iste.co.uk/szoniecky/collective.zip*

This first visualization work makes the researchers aware of the potential inconsistencies in the data, particularly in terms of duplications, unusable information or ambiguity in the choice of categories. For example, the difference between "journey" and "stay" had to be made explicit to understand that in the former, it was a question of a voyage supposing short says in each town, while in the latter, one of real, long-term moves, in a new space allowing more than quick visits to foreign scholars, for example.

Google Fusion thus proved to be an excellent "pre-test" tool, despite the questionable esthetic of its visualizations, highlighting the weaknesses of certain categories, and allowing the quick and easy correction of the initial database, which was supposed to provide a model for the other datasets.

2.2.2. Tools for visualizing networks: DBpedia, Palladio

The visualization of networks is generally a decisive exercise thanks to the Gephi software. Reluctant to use Gephi, as was said, because the immediate readability of the visualizations seemed insufficient and counterproductive in terms of popularization of the digital tool vis-à-vis our colleagues, we also reproached it for not giving us the information that interested us the most, knowing the nature of the relationship in question. All the same, we sought to quickly visualize our data to verify popular beliefs and discover new paths, so we had two tools: the first, Palladio[10], like Google Fusion, allows us to test representations online using datasets. The same kinds of map and network representations are found with the additional functionality of gathering a chronology for data exploration.

Devised with the specific view to equip researchers in digital humanities, Palladio is developed by Humanities + Design laboratory at Stanford University[11]. It was created in the scope of a program similar to our own, as it dealt with the visualization of intellectual networks using European correspondences. Palladio is thus ideal for the visualization and multidimensional discovery of relationships in time and space. To create a Palladio project, the users upload their data in a spreadsheet file or CSV or in the form of a query in SPARQL format (for advanced users). Once a user has created a Palladio project, he can save the project locally, for no data is stored on Palladio servers. The user can then distribute and share his or her project or upload it to Palladio again for continued development.

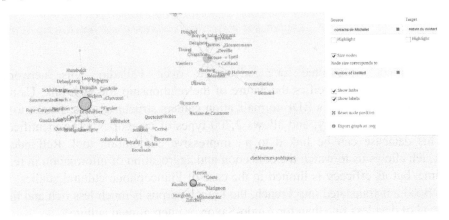

Figure 2.4. *Palladio network representation*

10 URL for the tool: http://palladio.designhumanities.org
11 Online: http://hdlab.stanford.edu/tools/

However, as K. Gallant explains, "Palladio does not have the most intuitive of interfaces, and the documentation could be more robust" [GAL 14]. In fact, it is a rather long and difficult process to get a more detailed grasp of this tool, especially for modeling relationships between different tables. Similarly, we did not manage to link our data with SPARQL, though this functionality may prove to be useful.

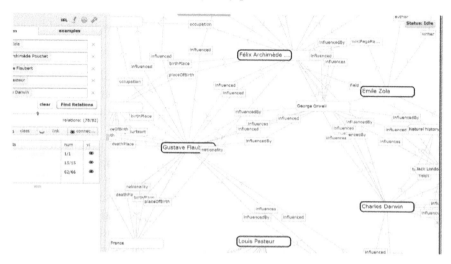

Figure 2.5. *RelFinder, Wikipedia's structured data exploration tool. For a color version of the figure, see www.iste.co.uk/szoniecky/collective.zip*

RelFinder presented one advantage over Palladio: this network construction tool specifies the nature of the relationship for each link. Using DBpedia, Wikipedia's RDF formalization gathers structured data, thanks to a hand-written ontology, and allows 2,700 types of categories to be identified. This database can be linked to an impressive exploration tool, RelFinder, which allows us to watch the collection and aggregation of information in real time, but its efficacy is limited in the case of Francophone cultural studies: if DBpedia is translated into French, the French corpus is much less rich and the level of data less fine than for Anglo-Saxon or international culture.

2.2.3. *Multi-purpose tools (Keshif, Table)*

For more advanced visualizations, we can resort to tools allowing us to vary the types of visualizations and thus to test their productivity directly using a single data sheet. Tools like Keshif or Tableau additionally offer more esthetically advanced graphic models, thus closer to the results desired for a publication or presentation.

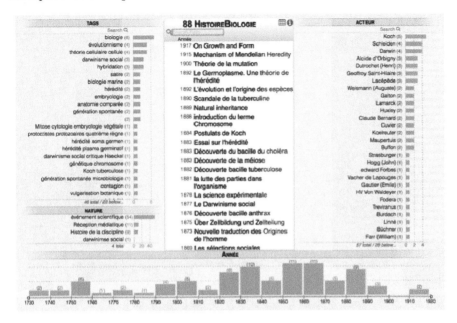

Figure 2.6. *Keshif faceted browser*

Keshif[12] is a computer library written in JavaScript allowing data navigation following thematic, geographic, chronologic, etc. facets. Each facet is interconnected with the others, which allows for rapid filtration of the information to obtain data on complex issues. Easily adjustable, this library quickly offers researchers an interface for manipulating their data. The possibilities with Keshif are quite extensive; however, they are only accessible from the moment that the data are perfectly structured, which is not the case at this stage in the project. Furthermore, the use of this library requires the involvement of a web developer to model the different facets.

Having noticed the great efficacy of the tools used in a business setting to help managers visualize data and pass on dashboards, we therefore chose to leave the domain of researchers' favorite tools to experiment with this

12 URL to the library: http://keshif.me/

admittedly expensive, but pragmatic software. At first, it was the free version, Table Public, which was used to create the visuals below.

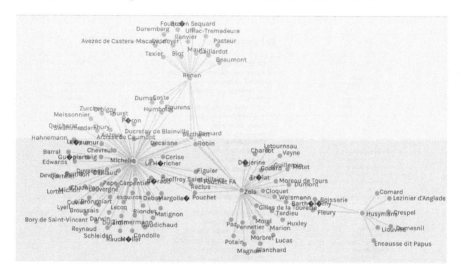

Figure 2.7. *Table, a Gephi-like software for data visualization*

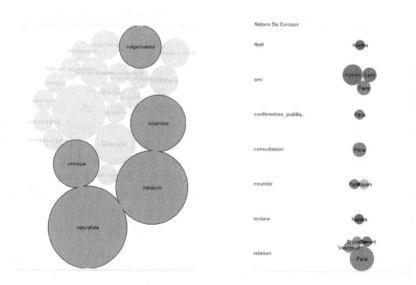

Figure 2.8. *Table – a wide variety of graphics for refining readings of relationship types*

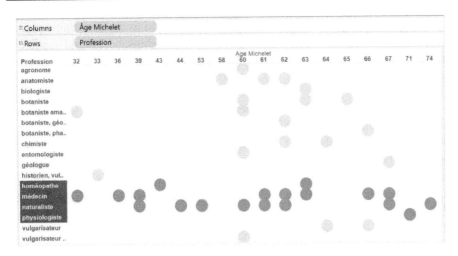

Figure 2.9. *The specialties of the scholars visited throughout his life*

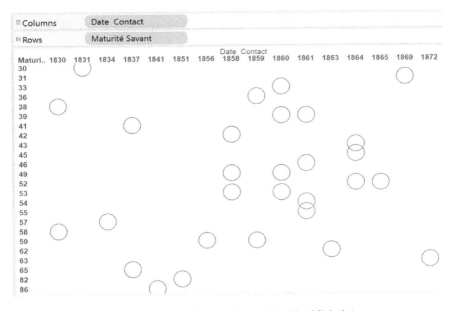

Figure 2.10. *Are the scholars visited by Michelet young researchers or old authorities of renown?*

On the left-hand side Figure 2.8, we can see a chart of the scholarly professions visited by Michelet broadly, the most important of which have been emphasized (the grayed-out chart is an artifact due to an error in data retrieval); to the right, the same data have been linked to the historian's places of residence to create a specialization of the relationships, social and academic in Paris, familiar and less elevated (popularizers, hobbyists) at his summer residence in Hyères.

These experiments show the permanence of a familiarity with certain classic disciplines, those of knowledge generalists (doctors, naturalists, physiologists), but also that over time, and particularly from the moment when he becomes interested in popularization, our author drew closer to researchers much younger than himself and who were more at a stage of knowledge production than the eminent researchers before them. It was therefore no longer the certainty of knowledge validated by time, by the dynamics of the research, of the discovery, that he could inspire in his popularization works.

All the visualizations above were produced with the same dataset by simply modifying the facets and the format choices. The visual interface makes the experiment much easier, even if it requires a bit of attention towards the nature of the data used.

These different tools, particularly rich and easy to use, allow researchers to perform their own experiments when it comes to visualization. However, we wanted a more sophisticated tool for the team, one that would combine the richness of Gephi and a sort of fractal character: considering that the level of detail in our possession was not the same for different others, we wanted to post these levels of detail and make them interoperable to escape the problem frequently encountered with the original spreadsheet: its inability to consider a large number of simultaneous variables like space and time.

2.3. Prototype for influence network modeling

The tools that we tested were presented to the researchers to familiarize them with three fundamental points:

– choosing a shared vocabulary to categorize the influences;

– the interoperability of the vocabulary, particularly in terms of spatial–temporal or conceptual references or those concerning people;

– preserving and sharing the points of view of each member so that a consensus emerges from disputes.

Based on these three points, we came up with a prototype for influence network modeling.

2.3.1. *Categorization of relationships*

To estimate the shared vocabulary and to minimize the tedious job of data cleaning (deletion of duplicates, incorrect date or location formats, incorrect spelling), we set up a Google form[13] to give researchers the means to choose the categories that seemed important to them in four main fields:

– actor categories;

– location categories;

– relationship categories;

– notion categories.

The data harvested[14] allowed different researcher profiles to be represented according to the name and quality of categorization choices:

Figure 2.11 is a matrix that correlates the researchers (columns) and the categories (rows) whose colors correspond to categorical fields. Even if the printed version does not allow a detailed view of the choices made by the researchers, it broadly shows that there are various points of view on the useful categories for modeling the influences between literature and biology. From a project management perspective, the visual allows the discovery of each researcher's specific interests, thus to better anticipate certain researchers' misunderstandings or refusals to commit, as well as to establish work groups based on shared perspectives, for example. On the level of collective reflection, this representation gives researchers the possibility of comparing the categories that they use to express their points of view, to spread them to the other researcher, and thus to bring about the reflective process necessary for the arrival to a scientific consensus.

13 URL to the form: https://goo.gl/fkB56K
14 URL to the data harvested: https://goo.gl/3YRch6

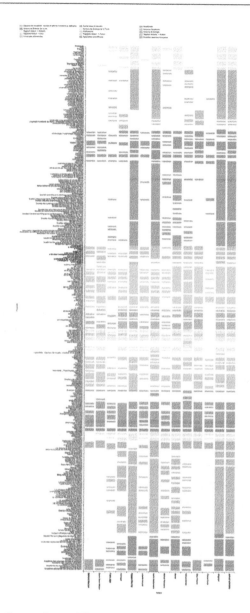

Figure 2.11. *Comparison of the categorization choices among researchers[15].*
For a color version of the figure, see www.iste.co.uk/szoniecky/collective.zip

15 URL of the category choice representation: http://gapai.univ-paris8.fr/jdc/public/biolographes/
comparecat, made with the help of the JavaScript library http://dimplejs.org/.

2.3.2. *Assisted influence network entry*

Once this task of familiarization with the collective categorization was finished, we developed a prototype tool to model the influence relationships between documents, actors and concepts. The goal is to assist researchers in the expression of their perspectives so that these are interoperable with the standards of Open Linked Data (DBpedia, data.bnf, Google Knowledge Graph, ISNI, etc.). In this first version, we were not seeking to automatically extract interpretations of documents by using automatic language processing (ALP) algorithms; rather, we were manually editing arguments in the form of a graph. During a second phase, we will work on the exploitation of these graphs to simulate disputes that we will present these to the researchers for validation. We aim to set up a learning cycle between the researchers and the algorithms where the perspicacity of the former is confronted with the computational reason [PAR 16] of the latter.

We used the choices made by the researchers to determine the categories that interest them (see section 2.3.1) to create "sieves", which are so many filters allowing the elimination of menu items that are not relevant for such and such researcher. By simplifying the menus in this way, the tool's users build their influence networks with their own categories while keeping them interoperable with those of the other researchers. In this way, users model the influence networks by graphically editing the spatial and temporal relationships between documents, actors and concepts. In doing so, they contribute to the mapping of the economy of affects [CIT 08] in a given time and space.

The actor retrieval form, for example, helps the researcher categorize an actor that he wants to add to an influence network by searching for his ISNI number [ANG 12]. After retrieving the actor's name, the user starts the search in Data BNF to display the list of results sent by the SPARQL query. From this list, he can evaluate the person who corresponds to what he is looking for by displaying the information for each item on the list. Once his choice has been validated, the interoperability information (ISNI, VIAF, idArk, etc.) is connected to the actor who is from then on linked to the Open Linked Data.

Figure 2.12. *Edit Influ: addition of an actor reference*

This same form also uses the Google Knowledge Graph[16] API to find the occurrences in DBpedia that correspond to the request that the research expressed in the form of a chain of characters. All that remains to be done then is to select the line in the list that corresponds to the sought after person to automatically obtain those long-lasting, interoperable references.

Other forms are available to recover the information concerning a conceptual reference. In this case, we ask the DataBNF service to display a list of keywords from the Rameau[17] reference database. The researcher chooses the term from the list that he wishes to add to his reference database or whose relationships he wants to explore in Rameau. For this second need, a semantic cartography in the form of a Sankey diagram[18] allows him to browse through the concepts to find a connected term, be it more precise or more generic. This system of choice through browsing can take place from a reference database other than Rameau, for example, the SKOS reference source made available by UNESCO[19] or even the knowledge object database available in the SYMOGIH[20] project.

---

16 https://developers.google.com/knowledge-graph/
17 For more information, see http://rameau.bnf.fr/
18 See https://en.wikipedia.org/wiki/Sankey_diagram
19 See http://skos.um.es/unescothes/?l=en
20 For an explanation of the project, see http://symogih.org/

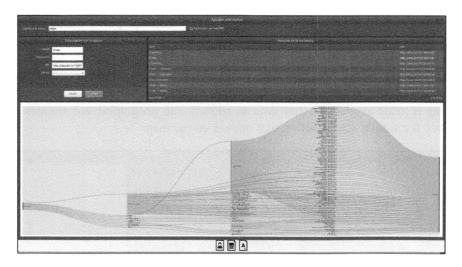

Figure 2.13. *Edit Influ: addition of a conceptual reference*

A form is specially dedicated to document research. It serves to find the works used by the researcher in the BNF catalogue. It also provides the possibility to divide the document into as many fragments as necessary to model an interpretation of such and such line of a work or such and such part of a table, for example.

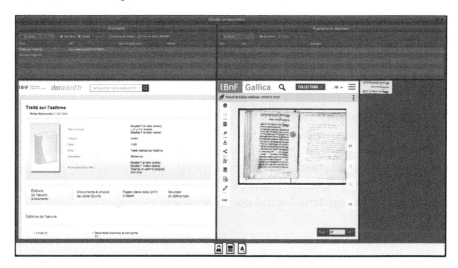

Figure 2.14. *Edit Influ: addition of a reference to a document*

The three object types (documents, actors, concepts) that make up the generic modeling paradigm are compared to a fourth object type: relationships. For this type, we have also developed a specific form that particularly allows the definition of spatial–temporal references to the relationships that exist between the other objects. To help the researcher, a map is made available to translate an address into geographic coordinates or even the simple manipulation of a marker on the map.

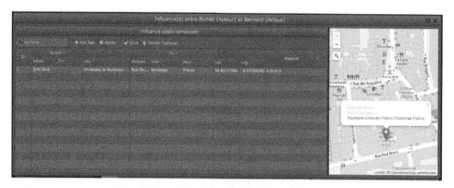

Figure 2.15. *Edit Influ: addition of a relationship*

We are continuing the development of this web application with the Paragraphe[21] laboratory's internal resources and the help of researchers from the Biolographes program. All of the computer sources used are available on GitHub[22] in order to open the project to other participants and create a community allowing the development of new functionalities as well as user tests with interested researchers through influence network modeling.

2.4. Limits and perspectives

The tools we have just presented offer numerous advantages, but they do not solve the fundamental issue concerning the exploitation of digital archives in social science research from the perspective of both their relevance and the epistemological consequences of their uses.

---

21 http://www.paragraphe.info/
22 https://github.com/samszo/jardindesconnaissances/tree/master/application/views/scripts/ed
itinflu

2.4.1. *Epistemological conflicts*

In light of these experiments, we observe that the dialogue between the "computer scientists" and the "humanists" still remains difficult. If the former has a tendency to implement solutions and methods showing the power of machines, the latter sees in this power the means to free themselves from the wearisome tasks necessary for exploring their corpus and finding the proof to confirm their hypotheses as fast as possible. With the risk of fatal disenchantments when they realize that the machine only updates already-known data, the "qualitative" expertise of a specialist often compensates, in fact, for the more empirical character of his approach. From there, the risk of turning away from approaches that have been accosted by the bias of tools that are inadequate because they were initially thought up for quantitative disciplines. The same Biolographes team was thus able to test Treeclouds[23] [GAM 14], a collocation visualization model in the form of a very seductive tree, originating from genomics where "language" sequences are bereft of connotation and avoid the complexities of discourse pragmatics. The results were, unsurprisingly, rather disappointing, applied to literary texts well understood by the researchers. If the Treeclouds are ill-adapted to literature, this is not necessarily the case for critical articles, and their use can instead be considered and will be tested in the aforementioned Delille project.

It should be noted that the impression of limited Treecloud productivity for their project, while widely shared, did not arouse formalized criticism from the participants, which says a lot about the sidestep strategies in multidisciplinary research groups and their reluctance to appear reactionary in the face of the novelty proposed (and socially personified, etc.) by computer scientists. SHS researchers are also wary of the "positivism" of tool-using approaches; they also feel that they have more to lose than to gain by engaging themselves in processes that they have not completely mastered. In most cases, they will have to rely on the skills of "others", whose language they do not at all understand and whose quality and validity they cannot evaluate with certainty in their own field. This hesitation is easily seen when the researchers see each other proposing computerized approaches based on very different epistemological presuppositions, and we have seen recurring debates between supporters of TAL and TIC, one group valuing the tool and the infallible character of complicated systematic counts (but with what utility?), the others demanding that they all rely on the

---

23 http://treecloud.univ-mlv.fr/

researchers' expertise to develop light, pragmatic approaches (not thorough in the eyes of the former). Among the two, the literary specialists were tossed between a tedious approach in their eyes, but one crowned by a scientism ventured on the machine, and a more mixed and therefore accessible approach, but one rendered suspect by its efforts towards openness and communication (the seduction of the image against the precision of the number!). The indecision about means of evaluation, when we leave its skill area, can be anxiogenic and cause them to wait for others to open the best routes. Furthermore, it is a more important criterion of scientific identity than vigilance in the face of its own field of expertise: in a world of research largely structured by CNU disciplinary sections and the obligation to be specialized in order to lead a viable career, despite all the official appeals for interdisciplinarity, a good researcher must hesitate to work on projects that do fall within his field of expertise.

However, certain approaches like the archive representations we mentioned allow for an expansion of its field of analysis without falling into speculation, and it is undoubtedly one of the most striking contributions of digital archives. In fact, one researcher is familiar with his corpus, but by leaning on well-exploited archives, he can find points of reference to propose a hypothesis by going outside his primary field of expertise without actually falling into dangerous speculation. It is a matter of using the digital archive to "equip a process of investigation", to use the words of a sociologist who pioneered these practices [CHA 03]. Typically, being a Michelet specialist means knowing that he visited science popularizers, and it may have been noted that some of them knew other writers from the same Normand circle, but it will be necessary to visualize and compare the network of scholars visited by the writers, fanned out by specialty, to discover that this position as a scientific ambassador is very important for all the writers who dealt with science after 1850, undoubtedly more important than the relationships with eminent figures. Is this importance going to grow over the century, as the writer moves away from the social poles associated with the bourgeoisie, salons and academies? This is a hypothesis that can be tested, as the archives provide a point of reference to become detached without giving into speculation and to propose a spread of hypotheses without giving up the real one.

This type of approach explains why the digital exploitation of archives is particularly well adapted to the exploration of vast corpuses, particularly when we know little about them. This was the case for the Euterpe project, of which no member could initially say that he was a specialist in the subject, as it was a matter of unearthing texts that had been completely forgotten by literary history and whose existence was but a supposition. Over the course of the collective task, it became clear that the point of reference provided by the digital analysis also allowed them to distance the received ideas, and even more surely the categories derived from theories that cover the real more than they reveal it. The case was presented where two researchers worked in parallel on the characteristics of the authors of scientific poems, one using visual archive processing, the other by defining "actor categories" *a priori*, based on predicated strategies one could effectively find out in some outstanding poets biography (this outstanding character making them the obvious model after which their category had been crafted – a classical bias in category-making) in the biography of the real and often remarkable poets in the corpus (this remarkable character in all likelihood being for nothing in the global image from which these categories were created; the bias is classic). The "Ancien Régime" method opened all the inherent questions to a typology (from when to consider an individual to be similar to this type? What criteria are used to justify the aggregates that are produced to create these types?, etc.). To this was added an embarrassing question: what happens if the practice of scientific poetry cannot be reduced to the Bourdieusian category of the strategy and the distinction that massively founded the analysis in question? The digital approach, for its part, gave different results in large measures: it suggested that the practice of scientific poetry did not offer real specificity, the existence of scientific poems not actually creating scientific poets, such that the typization returned to ontologizing a phenomenon that was undoubtedly just a "practice", at a given moment, in the range of an individual's practices [LOU 12]. Yet the scientific subject was often just a particular case, a subsection of a wider literary movement that, for an individual, consisted of participating in a community built around an event (emotionally, politically, etc.) by means of poetic inscription. And that, be this event a sensational but punctual scientific experience or the collective awareness of transformations resulting from technological progress – while at other times, as a function of the current state of the world or the library, other poetic productions by the same authors covered national history or the political incidents that then gave reason for this participation. Another work in progress on the corpuses of poems sent to academic cooperations has shown that the forms and authors intersect considerably, whatever the subjects may be.

A "sociology of scientific poems", even for sociological reasons, could additionally have difficulty making sense on the century level. By processing the droves of scientific poems through visualization, the appearance could instead be seen of configurations that were specifically socio-historic: for example, the emergence of the medical poem brought by doctors in search of renown around the 1860s, or the abandonment of the subject by professional littérateurs in favor of non-specialized intellectuals, professors or lawyers starting in 1870, all while science was becoming a national debate. Another benefit, then, of visual data processing is freeing phenomena from a lecture based on prominent individuals who cry out to us or seduce us (for reasons that are often very far removed from their connection to the genre) and lead to the ontologization of a practice. By offering intellectual recovery disconnected from individual cases, the graph allows for the emergence of interpretations without a theoretical takeover. The digital approach is then a precious asset against the demon of theory, which is forced to wait, like in medicine, for the corpus to say what it could say concerning the practitioner's questions and investigations.

Yet it is not uncommon for classical literary analysis to be based on a mixture of theory and intuition, and researchers can have the feeling that the hermeneutical "proceduralization" of practices tied to digital processing cuts them out of that part appropriately considered creative. We also must not underestimate the strength of the protection reflex of individually produced data: to pool your reference column on Zotero is to allow others to benefit, even within a limited team, from your works, before the publication that marks your legitimate ownership and scientific recognition. The idea that each researcher will benefit from a wide opening up of research data, thereby saving human time and allowing us to focus on what makes our expertise real, i.e. personal training coupled with a singular vision, none of that is enough at this time to counterbalance these concerns. It is true that the rarity of these practices in literature condemns the early adopters to an unequal exchange at first, but it is indicative that in the Biolographes team, only the doctoral and postdoctoral students, regardless of whether they are under contract, have shared their data – they are nonetheless the ones with the most fragile institutional position, but also the ones who could benefit the most from an exchange and for whom collaboration is becoming a generational indicator. From that, a very sensitive resistance for insiders and the temptation to compartmentalize, if digital archives must exist, the project's different moments and actors. Against the threat of the process and the outside appropriation of personal work, computer science will gladly be made the researcher's servant, distrusted but kept at bay at the same time.

2.4.2. The digital "black box"?[24]

The digital exploitation of archives actually updates tensions between researcher identifications, the way that they represent themselves, and the functions that they assign to technology. Computer science produces not only data or visuals; it also solidifies representations. Thus, it seems that for the social science researcher, computer science is often a black box, managed by others, which researchers wish functioned autonomously and whose productions they wish to thoroughly comment and analyze, but which they do not know how to touch without risk, as they are entering a territory where they only have limited, if any, skills.

It also seems to us that the types of project management particular to computer science are very different, even quite opposed to those of researchers in the humanities, who privilege long design phases before moving to action (most often writing), and consider the iterative sequences familiar to quick methods, the rapid testing of unfinished production, which allows their rapid improvement, with suspicion. More broadly, it is not impossible for the suspicion in the social sciences of project management methods to largely join the difficulties of articulation between the different actors coming from different disciplines.

Faced with this limitation, it is essential to place the expression and sharing of researchers' intuition at the heart of equipping the digital humanities, for this is what distinguishes the human's lack of action from the machine's. It is thus good to conceive of collaboration, teamwork, that is disrupted by the demands of work on digital archives related to the articulation of skills, but also to the notion of expertise, which moves, as it is henceforth the archive that "knows" – and the researcher can be led to wonder where the space where he exercises his knowledge, the foundation of his authority, resides from then on.

---

24 We are borrowing the expression from [MIL 13].

2.4.3. *From individual expertise to group intelligence*

Interdisciplinarity, which becomes an often very formal demand for research financing, is the ideal framework for the redefinition of this area of expertise in group work. In a project involving the exploitation of vast corpuses in which no researcher can claim he has real competence, the insert point for each researcher's skill can only change. This is thus at stake in the example of Biolographes. It was not only asked of the science historian that he redefine certain concepts or trace the genealogy of an expression in scientific terminology, but also that he participate in the elaboration of the ontology that defines the categories structuring the data collection. Each specialist is summoned here: the specialist of literary social skills will validate or complete the list of salons or meeting places pertinent to the understanding of where scholars and the literati could have exchanges; the science historian will say what the medical categories are that make sense at the time and will thus be pertinent for organizing the data collected, etc. What the Biolographes project shows is that the digital archive is not a given that researchers use, but like all archives in the classical sense, it implies a structure that will be all the more efficient as it is supported by the researcher's knowledge and not delegated to the machine.

An anecdote relative to the same project illustrates the difficulty of gaining acceptance for a collaborative conception of research, beside the significant scholastic *disputatio* model dear to symposium fans. Faced with the breadth of work involved in studying digital archives, we have proposed the use of students to collect factual information on location, data and actor. Almost unanimously, the researchers and doctoral students reacted negatively, which shows how far collective intelligence practices are from research methods that do not see what the collective organization of computer work can bring to the fine exploration of a very large corpus. And inversely, what this sort of meticulous work on a corpus segment can lend to a student's reflections, the reverse of an entire editorial tradition that recognizes in the establishment of a text the height of closeness responsible for the understanding of a text. The underlying question is that of the collective and the disappearance of the expert: what we proposed was the observation of textual corpuses as is done by thousands of volunteers who take an inventory of the biodiversity of gardens, and just as was done in the 18th and 19th Centuries by hundreds of hobby scholars organized into scholarly societies, in the century the researchers are studying. Ironically, our researchers do not apply to themselves or their epistemological situation the task of nuancing and de-hierarchizing that they applied to the field of knowledge/discourse on biology when they showed the existence of a shared, co-elaborated space between scholars and non-scholars. In doing this, they renew disciplinary divisions whose historicity and variability they are familiar with.

The visualization of data conversely appears as a way to reproduce an interpretative space for researchers made to work with massive corpuses, with an historic dimension, and impossible to manipulate without technological artifacts. This, however, implies that the researchers accept to work as closely as possible to these instruments; that is to say, they are capable of manipulating the tools themselves, to bring them into play and have them available when an inspiring configuration shows up. In fact, the curious developer will also see these phenomena, but will not know if they make sense or not: it is subjectivity fed by a researcher's expertise that will allow the immediate classification of the phenomena observed, the detection of anything picturesque that appears, or of what only confirms known facts, and the identification of what, on the other hand, provides a new facet, an angle of approach opening promising paths.

Collective intelligence has resided at the heart of scientific practices for a very long time, but with the appearance of digital intellectual technologies, other methods of organizing the work must be invented, particularly for the exploration and mapping of large social science corpuses:

> "These work and function systems integrate reliable new standard system procedures of writing and representation. They imply the learning and adoption of norms, programs, routines, writing devices, and largely flexible interfaces. They imply that complex, distributed, cooperative methods of representation and space–time navigation be developed and appropriated." [JUA 10, p. 38]

2.5. Conclusion

The practices of exploiting digital archives are in a state of total expansion by virtue of the number of researchers and institutions that have recently become interested as well as the breadth of certain projects that are inconceivable without these powerful aids. The success that the digital humanities have seen today makes questions of using computer science in the humanities all the more crucial. More specifically, we have observed a lack of training in the domain of information epistemology, particularly with regard to the limits of its calculability and its overtaking by collective intelligence. Nevertheless, data visualization is a very productive instrument for the social science researcher if he accepts to get in touch with this technology, if he accepts to move off center, to no longer be the master of everything, by trusting the skills of others, while not forgetting that his own skill is that of making sense, of saying what makes sense and what is worth being explored. It is under this condition that he will avoid the dead-end of the positivism that is often waved before his face as a threat, but he will discover that the machine, contrary to what he believes, will open a new area of research.

2.6. Bibliography

[ANG 12] ANGJELI A., "ISNI: un identifiant passerelle", *Documentation et Bibliothèques*, vol. 58, no. 3, pp. 101–108, 2012.

[BER 99] BERTIN J., *Sémiologie graphique les diagrammes, les réseaux, les cartes*, Editions de l'EHESS, Paris, 1999.

[CHA 03] CHATEAURAYNAUD F., *Prospéro: Une technologie littéraire pour les sciences humaines*, CNRS Editions, Paris, 2003.

[CIT 08] CITTON Y., "Les lois de l'imitation des affects", in *Spinoza et les sciences sociales: de la puissance de la multitude à l'économie des affects*, Editions Amsterdam, Paris, 2008.

[DER 95] DERRIDA J., *L'avenir Mal d'Archive*, Editions Galilée, 1995.

[GAL 14] GALLANT K., LORANG E., RAMIREZ A., "*Tools for the Digital Humanities: A Librarian's Guide*". Seminar: Emerging Technologies in Libraries, 2014.

[GAM 14] GAMBETTE P., EGGERMONT H., LE ROUX X., "Mapping the biodiversity research landscape with the BiodivERA database: temporal and geographical trends in the type of biodiversity research funded on a competitive basis", *European Countries, BiodivERsA Report*, p. 33, 2014.

[JUA 10] JUANALS B., NOYER J.-M. (eds), "De l'émergence de nouvelles technologies intellectuelles", in *Technologies de l'information et intelligences collectives*, Hermes Science-Lavoisier, 2010.

[LAT 12] LATOUR B., *Enquêtes sur les modes d'existence: Une anthropologie des Modernes*, La Découverte, 2012.

[LEV 10] LÉVY P., "De l'émergence de nouvelles technologies intellectuelles", in *Technologies de l'information et intelligences collectives*, Hermes Science-Lavoisier, 2010.

[LOU 12] LOUÂPRE M. MARCHAL H., "La poésie scientifique, l'autopsie d'un genre", available at: http://www.epistemocritique.org/IMG/pdf/1_LOUAPRE.pdf, 2012.

[MIL 13] MILLIGAN I., "Illusionary order: online databases, optical character recognition, and Canadian history, 1997–2010", *Canadian Historical Review*, vol. 94, no. 4, pp. 540–569, 2013.

[MOR 08] MORETTI F., JEANPIERRE L., DOBENESQUE E., *Graphes, cartes et arbres: Modèles abstraits pour une autre histoire de la littérature*, Les Prairies Ordinaires, Paris, 2008.

[PAR 16] PARISI L., "La raison instrumentale, le capitalisme algorithmique et l'incomputable", *Multitudes*, no. 62, pp. 98–109, 2016.

[PEC 11] PECCATTE P., "L'interprétation des graphiques produits par Ngram Viewer", in *Read/write book 2. Une Introduction Aux Humanités Numériques*, available at: http://books.openedition.org/oep/284, OpenEdition Press, 2011.

[SCH 13] SCHENK D., "Aufheben, was nicht vergessen werden darf", *Archive vom alten Europa bis zur digitalen Welt*, Steiner, Stuttgart, 2013.

[SCH 14a] SCHENK D., "Pouvoir de l'archive et vérité historique", *Ecrire l'histoire*, no. 13–14, pp 35–53, 2014.

[SCH 14b] SCHENK D., *Kleine Theorie des Archivs*, Steiner, Stuttgart, 2014.

[VAI 06] VAILLANT A., *La crise de la littérature: romantisme et modernité*, Ellug, Grenoble, 2006.

From the Digital Archive to the Resource Enriched Via Semantic Web: Process of Editing a Cultural Heritage

3.1. Influencing the intelligibility of a heritage document

For years now, digital technology has been a major support for most content, particularly heritage material. With time, the digital document is subject to two major problems that alter its use: gaps of technological obsolescence and intelligibility [BAC 10a, p. 22]. The latter epitomizes the effect of the time that has gone by on the cultural legibility of archived content. Decontextualized, the archive loses its role as a receptacle for memory; it must therefore be interpreted to recover its intelligibility.

Fortified by the assessment of a sensitivity of the digital heritage document to the issue of the preservation of meaning, the question that stirs this research is oriented towards the possibilities for preserving the intelligibility of a digital document with heritage character. Joining the field of information science and communication, this research advances the hypothesis of the possibility to preserve the archive's intelligibility by means of management of the archive's content in a specific context: an architext.

Particular to the digital environment, content management is a "process consisting in the enlistment of resources to include them in a new publication" [BAC 07b, p. 21]. Parallel to its limited historical meaning, the term has recently taken on a wider meaning, henceforth designating "all the

Chapter written by Lénaïk Leyoudec.

dynamics that produce the digital space" [VIT 16, p. 1]. Facing increasing adoption [VAL 15], the notion is taken here in its historical sense considering the operational role of the notion in this research.

Experiments are done on the content management process, considered in this light, in a specific context: an architext, created *ex nihilo*. Originating from the Greek *arkhè*, origin and commandment, the architext designates "the tools that allow for the existence of the 'écrit à l'écran'[1] and that, not content with representing the text's structure, orders its execution and realization" [SOU 03, p. 23]. The exploratory framework of the content management process applied to the archive therefore resides in an architext co-created in the context of the CIFRE convention. The architext takes the form of a technological device [BAC 07a] intended to lend heritage value to the private individual's archive. The author joins a research process exuding editorial and ergonomic recommendations aimed at the architext, also becoming the object of a study with respect to its impact on the archive.

Within itself and experimentally, the planned content management process enlists the "data web", taken as a network of linked, open information [GAN 11] able to be repatriated at the heart of a third technological device.

3.2. Mobilizing differential semantics

Differential semantics, text interpretation methodology, is mobilized here according to the premise of this approach's compatibility with other cultural objects: "the issue of interpretation goes beyond texts and can spread to other cultural objects, like images" [RAS 09, p. VI]. This research also joins the program of cultural sciences developed around the linguist cited [RAS 02].

Concerning the document's intelligibility, we are drawing on the notion of "understanding" [RAS 01, p. 12]: "understanding [...] is an interpretation: it consists in stipulating [...] (i) what semantic traits are updated in a text, (ii) what the relationships are that structure them, and (iii) what indicators and/or prescriptions allow these traits to be updated and these relationships to be established, which are so many elementary paths for interpretive processes". Here, we are seeking to grasp the document's intelligibility through a constructed interpretive approach.

---

1 From the written text to the digital screen.

Our hypothesis is to draw on a specific interpretive approach towards the archive in order to discern the semantic traits particular to the memorial register: so many memory indicators pertinent during the interpretation of the heritage document. The combination of semantic elements provides part of the answer to the question, "What effects of meaning relative to the memorial register emerge during document consultation?"

The approach is available in three consecutive phases: the semiotic analysis of a corpus of documents by means of an interpretive methodology constructed using differential semantics [RAS 09], the aggregation of the memory indicators obtained using a method of document validation and, finally, the implementation of the chosen content management approach at the heart of an architext in order to verify the hypothesis of a possible reconstruction of the archive's intelligibility.

In the first experimental phase of this research, the created corpus is examined using a semiotic analysis methodology: here, the goal is to question the image to extract the memory indicators from it. The query of updated semantic traits − "stabilized moments in interpretive processes" [RAS 09, p. VI] − thus operates at three levels (micro-, meso- and macro-semantics) that must be compared in the scope of an interpretive process. We understand this as the result of cognitive operations allowing meaning to be assigned to a linguistic sequence.

Strengthened by this theoretical baggage, the objective of this experimental phase is to realize an interpretive process on the archive and to aggregate the memory indicators that emerge from the document.

3.3. Applying an interpretive process to the archive

The archive, as a research object, joins a corpus, created from several audiovisual heritage collections, which include the Cinémathèque de Bretagne, the Établissement de communication et de production audiovisuelle de la Défense (ECPAD), the Forum des images or the Institut national de l'audiovisuel (INA).

Among these collections are excerpts of the same kind of semiotic objects: films belonging to the register of "private cinema" [ALL 94] that the author also considers "ordinary esthetics" [ALL 02]. In differential semantics, the genre is defined by "(i) the cohesion of a body of criteria, as much at the level of the signified as that of the signifier, and by (ii) its repercussion on the textuality, on those two levels as well" [RAS 99, p. 89]. The interpretive process is encouraged by the homogeneity of the corpus concerning the question of the semiotic object's genre, a point also defined by the author: "the well thought-out characterization of genres remains a prerequisite for the constitution of corpuses that are fully utilizable for tasks of linguistic description. Whatever the chosen criteria, little can be extracted from a heterogeneous corpus, for the specificities of the genres cancel one another out, and the remaining contrasts cannot be interpreted to characterize the texts" [RAS 99, p. 92].

Concerning the actual corpus, from the four audiovisual collections is created the "archive": "all of the documents accessible for a task of description or an application" [RAS 11, p. 36], from which a reference corpus – a film from the collection – and different study corpuses – all the films from a single corpus realized by a single moviemaker-videographer.

Initiating the validation process for the archive created in this research, a document extracted from the reference corpus is here examined from the beginning to the end of the publishing process: *Fête de Jeanne d'Arc, 4ème centenaire du collège d'Ancenis* (1946–1947). The archive is made up of 182 shots in total, of varying lengths, for a total duration of 13'16". According to the metadata linked to the document, obtained from the Cinémathèque de Bretagne, the movie was filmed in 1946–1947 by Eugène Dupont, a resident of Nantes, France. It is part of a series of nine movies filmed between 1935 and 1949 by this hobby moviemaker.

In the scope of the interpretive process, we captured shot no. 48 (3'04" – 3'13") as an excerpt to examine at the micro-semantic level. The shot-by-shot analysis performed mentions a wide exterior shot where a woman can be observed walking along with a young girl in a white dress (Figure 3.1). The hypothesis raised is that we are dealing with a religious custom and, in fact, the recording of an out-of-the-ordinary event. Several questions arise: are we dealing with a woman and her daughter? A godmother and her goddaughter? Are we on the Dupont family's property? Finally, for what occasion is the young girl dressed in white?

TCR 01:11:50:19

Figure 3.1. *Frame from shot no. 48*

The convergence of the segment studied with the two collateral segments (meso-semantic level) allows the interpretive process to densify. The preceding segment (shot no. 47, 3′00″–3′04″) features a woman and her two children heading to a car parked on the side of the road. A noteworthy fact in this shot lies in the attitude of the boy in front, who turns and raises his head towards the camera (Figure 3.2). We are in the presence of a specific indicator that we are approaching the figure in the camera's eyes: one of the figures of the family film identified by Roger Odin [ODI 79, p. 348]; this indicator shows a connection between the person on screen and the moviemaker. Having viewed other films from the collection, we are able to recognize Mr. Dupont's wife and their children. This supplementary information opposes an interpretive process devoid of all prior knowledge of the film: here, the order in which one watches the films in the collection allows us to accelerate the interpretive process by a stage: the convergence of the segments with the film's metadata and the other documents from the corpus at hand allow us to arrive at the same conclusion. On the other hand, the following segment (shot no. 49, 3′13″–3′20″) presents a family scene where a man and two boys are playing with a dog in a private courtyard (Figure 3.3). In terms of interpretation, we can determine that none of the people reappear in any other section. The Dupont family appearing in the car during the first segment, it would seem that the house featured then is not their property; they are probably guests.

Figure 3.2. *Frame from shot no. 47*

Figure 3.3. *Frame from shot no. 49*

Finally, what the other film segments (macro-semantic level) bring to the process of interpreting the chosen segment is substantial: the moviemaker's close family appears in the preceding section; the young girl in a dress is also potentially a member of the Dupont family. The metadata indicate the "communion" event following a brief visit to the banks of the Sèvre. The segments just before the three segments studied containing a river, we can state that it is definitely the filming of a young girl during her first communion, one of the seven sacraments of the Catholic Church. The young girl's specific clothing – a communicant's outfit – is in fact consistent with the particular status of this day for her: she is taking communion for the first time at church. Contrary to the confirmation where the godfather and godmother have a role to play, the first communion does not necessarily require their presence. In fact, it is more likely the mother and the child and not her godmother in the segment examined.

As an assessment of the memory indicators identified during the interpretive process, different elements relative to the diegesis can be brought up: each person appearing in the first or second shot in the extracts, the architectural elements appearing in the background (they allow an understanding of the geographic framework of the extract), as well as the significant material elements that may be the object of a date approximation (car, clothing). Furthermore, certain details provide additional indications, like attention to the camera and movements (the image shakes at the beginning or end of the shot) that punctuate the three extracts. Finally, the joint between shots no. 48 and 49 presents two other figures from the family film [ODI 79]: a discontinuous temporality (it is unknown how much time went by between the two frames) and a lack of spatial differentiation: we go from a rural garden to a building's courtyard. Those identified elements are the results of the interpretive process of the film *Fête de Jeanne d'Arc, 4ème centenaire du collège d'Ancenis* focused on the corresponding passage in shot no. 48.

3.4. Assessment of the semiotic study

The case study in question allows us to draw preliminary conclusions vis-à-vis the project of a semiology of memory indicators associated with the archive. Two groups of memory indicators emerge from the interpretive process: the contextual indicators and the cinematographic indicators.

Non-exhaustive, these categories favor an increase in generality, necessary in the scope of the editorial construction that follows. The contextual indicators gather the perceptive saliences corresponding to the context elements: the people show up onscreen, the places and the moment where the action takes place, as well as the different props embodying as many parts of the answer to the question of context. On the other hand, another group of perceptive saliences emerge from the interpretive process: the cinematographic indicators.

In his *Essais sur la signification du cinema*, Christian Metz defended the hypothesis [MET 68, pp. 67–68] that "understanding and the integration of the entire message of a film implied the mastery on the spectator's part of at least five large categories of systems [...]: 1. visual and auditive perception [...]; 2. the recognition, identification, and enumeration of the visual or sound objects that appear onscreen [...]; 3. all the 'symbolisms' and connotations of various orders that are attached to the objects [...]; 4. all the large narrative structures [...]; 5. all the strictly cinematographic systems, that is, those particular to individual films and shared by all films, which organize the various elements provided to the spectator by the four preceding instances into a special kind of discourse" [MET 71, pp. 23–24]. It is this fifth category in particular that interests him, at the heart of which he places the codes – as significant configurations [AUM 12, p. 139] – specific to cinema, which he sets against non-specific codes. The exclusively cinematographic codes are connected to the movement of the image; the codes of camera movement and the codes of dynamic connections are rediscovered. At the heart of the film object, these codes are articulated with numerous non-specific codes such as the codes of visual analogy or the codes of photography, for example. Metz' systematic undertaking concerning the existence of codes that line cinematographic language has not been completed; it makes its popularization more difficult: "if it is not possible to give a precise list of the specifically cinematographic codes because their study is again insufficiently detailed, this attempt becomes absurd for the non-specific codes, which would require an encyclopedic dictionary" [AUM 12, p. 143]. Our hypothesis remains in the comparison of all the memory indicators identified with the category of codes particular to cinema created by Christian Metz. Movement or addressing the camera makes up as many semiotic indicators specific to the cinematographic image; in fact, an interpretive process applied to the specific document that is the family film cannot disregard those salient elements forming the essence of private cinema. Strengthened by their common origin, they integrate themselves at the heart of a category of specific indicators that coexists with the contextual indicators.

If the two categories of memory indicators do not constitute an exhaustive list of the indicators that can be extracted from an interpretive process applied to the archive, all the perceptive saliences form a whole, which we have attempted to deconstruct here, which Roger Odin qualifies as "memorial diegesis" [ODI 79, p. 373]. Defined as "what belongs, 'in the intelligibility', to the story told, to the world assumed or proposed by the fiction of the film" [SOU 52], the diegesis – central notion of fictional cinema – is tinted with a different color in the framework of private cinema: the world of the family film takes the shape of a world of memories, while the film becomes a memory object, witness to a "that was" [BAR 80] mediated by the projector. The cinematographic memory indicators also designate the film's belonging to the cinematographic genre of private cinema and integrate themselves in the associated communication space [ODI 11] – the family setting: "At the end of this research, the family film appears as a cinematographic genre in its own right, a genre strongly characterized by a remarkable harmony of its form with its function: without the figures of break and aggression that stimulate the fantastical activity of the Recipients and that contribute (with the organization of the entire projection device) to positioning them as 'participants' in the collective process of recreating the memorial diegesis, the family fiction could not blossom; without the diegetic scarcity of the images projected, without the weaknesses of their structure, this family fiction could not be accepted as a 'good object' by the family group" [ODI 79, p. 373]. If the contextual memory indicators can constitute a diegesis in the scope of fictional cinema in and of themselves, the specificity of private cinema implies the presence of additional indicators. In this way, they complete the diegesis, which is qualified as "memorial" at the heart of this communication space.

The different memory indicators identified constitute a solid foundation that should be transcribed to an archive editorialization approach.

3.5. Popularizing the data web in the editorialization approach

Semiotic study allows us to grasp various memory indicators associated with the archive. Our hypothesis is to editorialize the archive in order to preserve its intelligibility. In its limited sense, the principle of editorialization implies the association of new resources with a document, the whole thus constituting a new publication. Our editorialization approach consists in the annotation of the archive in the specific framework of the architext. Extracts of the archive, the results of the interpretive process, are as many pertinent annotation elements. From there, it is a matter of transcribing the identified memory indicators into annotations, but also the constructed categories into a typology of annotations.

The contextual indicators, forming the first category of indicators, are intuitively transcribed into a typology of annotations: the following typology is obtained from the indicators extracted from the interpretive process associated with the film *Fête de Jeanne d'Arc, 4ème centenaire du collège d'Ancenis*: "person", "place", "object", "date" and "activity", this last kind of tag allowing the documentation of the studied passage's subject: a first communion ceremony. The generic nature of the obtained annotation categories allows the editorialization to go further by drawing on the linked, open data. In fact, there is contextual information on the Web that can clarify the annotation made by associating it with an explanatory note: for example, by searching for information on the town of Ancenis, a contextual note including a certain number of properties is displayed to us (Figure 3.4). The convergence of contextual notes coming from the Web with the contextual annotation created by the user is thus foreseen. The constraint coming from this place rests in the technical possibility of using and repatriating the note in the digital environment (the architext) where the annotation is made. This issue of resource interoperability is grasped by the use of the linked, open resources on the Web (*Linked Open Data*).

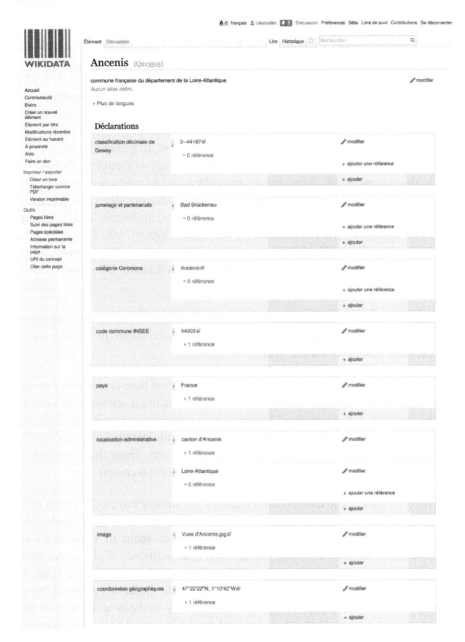

Figure 3.4. *Screenshot of the "Ancenis"
note in French on the website Wikidata.org*

The name *Linked Open Data* illustrates the convergence – at the data level – of a structure (linked data) and a status (open data). This specific context created an interoperability that was simultaneously technical (supported by the RDF format), juridical (absence of copyright), but also economical (freedom of access). The *Linked Open Data* initiative was launched in 2006 by Tim Berners-Lee, who published four principles [BER 06] focused on the notion of a *Uniform Resource Identifier*. The *Linking Open Data* project emerged in 2007; first, it gathered universities, then different institutions like the BBC or the Library of Congress [HEA 09]. From this moment on, these actors published linked and open data on the Web, thereby promoting the emergence of an interoperable encyclopedic ecosystem that is popularized by the editorialization approach. In 2014, more than 570 data silos were identified by the *Linked Open Data Cloud* project; in total, more than 900,000 documents describing more than eight million resources were released. Generalist silos (e.g. Wikidata, DBpedia) coexist with specific silos.

Strengthened by an audit of the available notes on the different data silos, the typology of contextual indicators finds an equivalent in categories of linked, open resources on the Web.

The part of the editorialization process showcased here corresponds to the possibility in the framework of the architext of realizing a semantic annotation on the archive. For example, "Ancenis" is a semantic entity in the location category, with different associated properties. By annotating "Ancenis" in the archive through the device, the linked, open resource from the data web is associated here with the archive, then repatriated to the architext.

Nevertheless, if the contextual indicators are mostly covered – given their generic nature – by the resources available on the data web, the cinematographic indicators, more specific, do not seem to be able to be exploited and enriched in the same way. Furthermore, if the contextual indicators correspond to elements of diegesis understanding on the level of time, location and action units, the cinematographic indicators respond better to a "plastic" relationship to the document. They embody a section of the understanding process that is less focused on the history than on the emotion, constituting another aspect of the memorial diegesis. Another section of the editorialization approach thus remains to be built in the device while its discussion will take place at a later stage due to the prospective character of this part of the research.

3.6. Archive editorialization in the Famille™ architext

The device, co-designed in the framework of a CIFRE convention with Perfect Memory, an editing software in knowledge engineering, shows up as a web editorialization application called "Famille", incorporating several views: connection window to the portal, gallery window for the documents uploaded, document consultation window, to which intermediate views are added like a profile administration window, an interaction view between resources in the form of a graph of entities, and an advanced interdisciplinary research view in the document gallery. In the scope of the presentation of the editorialization chain for the document *Fête de Jeanne d'Arc, 4ème centenaire du collège d'Ancenis*, several views are explained in detail here to decipher the semiotic polyphony present in this ecosystem of "écrits d'écrans". As a reminder, the écrit d'écran, as a "specific form that the writing takes on a digital support equipped with programs and provided with physical means of acting on it (peripheral devices)" [JEA 14, p. 11], joins a general framework theory: "the display of an écrit d'écran actually requires embedding a series of at least four successive frames": the material frame, the system frame, the software frame and the document frame [SOU 02, p. 102].

The first scenario to describe in the editorialization chain of the document *Fête de Jeanne d'Arc, 4ème centenaire du collège d'Ancenis* is the result of importing the document into the architext. The document follows a transcoding process with proxy creation; it is analyzed by a speech-to-text module while another module extracts the semantic entities of the document's associated metadata (the "Description" section). Finally, the archive, henceforth an enriched resource, is published on the consultation module (trivially named "player"), which can be seen in Figure 3.5. In this figure, we observe a stage of the archive consultation view where the user has scrolled down the drop-down list of properties associated with the archive to consult the semantic entities associated with it, shown here in the red box. Using the document's associated metadata – given in the "Description" section located further up on the drop-down list – the module automatically produced four annotations, three of which are categorized as "location", so many towns recognized in the metadata whose associated notices have been repatriated into the architext.

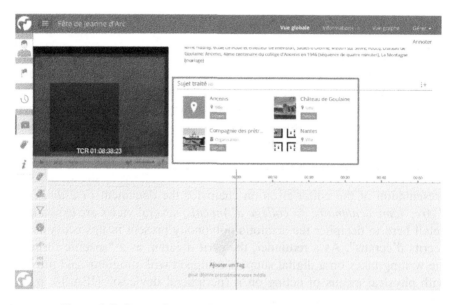

Figure 3.5. *Stage of semantically enriching the Famille architext*

Here, we should note the "small form" making up the icon for the "location" category of semantic annotation, allowing the visual association of the annotation with its role (the contextual information in the "geographic" category). We understand a "small form" as a "condensed, conventional media form (metaform) that is popularized, automatized, and disseminated in all sorts of contexts to support typical cultural or daily gestures" [JEA 14, p. 13]. The semiotic form of the geographic indicator is a recurring element in architexts destined to be used geographically, notably Google Maps or Open Street Map. The circulation of this "location pointer" icon particularly via smartphone GPS applications has confirmed its common meaning; the icon henceforth unilaterally designates the geographic content of the information associated with it, as in the architext studied. These four automatically produced annotations embody the first stage of editorialization (the automatic stage); it can be noted that it is largely incomplete: as a function of the popularized module's efficiency, other semantic entities could have been identified and added through the "town" semantic entity, e.g. "the mountain"; the high possibility of ambiguity connected to this location can also be noted. It should also be clarified that because the chosen movie did not have a soundtrack (it was filmed in 1946), the speech-to-text module was unable to produce additional metadata. In all other cases, these are recorded in a rubric beneath the rubric of semantic entities associated with the archive, which would have been increased in value itself.

The second photograph of the editorialization process is embodied by the result of a cycle of manual annotations. Figure 3.6 is a photo of the archive consultation view after a manual annotation phase. Two elements of interest can be observed: the timeline at the bottom of the page and, superimposed, a box corresponding to an annotation's detail.

At first, the choice to develop and implement a timeline gathering "time-coded" annotations responds to the issue of an ever-more advanced description of the document and particularly the temporal media. This timeline, destined to be filled with annotations, encourages a graphic experience of the document and pertains to the appropriation of the document by its user while being an inscription space. Inspired by the timelines of digital editors, the idea of a timeline as an annotation space initially joins the software of the same name developed in 2007 by the Institute for Research and Innovation [IRI 09].

Figure 3.6. *Manual annotation stage on the Famille architext*

The timeline responds here to the hypothesis of a chance for a document, its annotations and contextual information favoring the understanding of a document by the user to coexist in the same view of a document: all of this making a context emerge that is favorable to the construction of a document's intelligibility. This coexistence is an important editorial choice, as it pertains to the user's interpretation process: if the information allowing the film in question to be understood is found a few clicks further into the tool, doesn't the user risk missing the information? The timeline present here welcomes into its midst different annotations, realized manually during archive consultation. We also observe annotations in the "person" category, designating the members of the Dupont family presented in the passages studied. Furthermore, we observe different generalist annotations gathering the perceptive saliences appearing onscreen: objects like a bicycle or a car, but also different indications in the "location" category like a garden or a river. Identified using metadata, the river could be further qualified: it is the Sèvre Nantaise.

The second point of interest – the box detailing an annotation – is the in-depth study of this editorial choice to make several systems of écrits d'écran coexist. In the example, at the moment in the film where the Sèvre Nantaise, river in the Loire-Atlantique department of France, is seen, an annotation has been added allowing the data web resource "Sèvre Nantaise" to be associated with the archive. The semantic entity "location" "Sèvre Nantaise" is thus placed on the timeline at 2'57". The selection of the annotation on the timeline opens a box allowing the user not only to consult the contextual information on the location, but also to edit the annotation (e.g. move or delete it) or leave the annotation to find other semantic entities by browsing the graph of entities. This coexistence of écrits d'écran whose temporality and authority differ deserves to be questioned.

The third photo of the editorialization process consists in the presentation of the resource consultation interface via graph of entities (Figure 3.7). The editorial party taken in the conception of this representation of information is the chance offered to the user to enter the archive no longer through film consultation, but rather through enriched film metadata in the subject of semantic entities tied to the archive. In the archive consultation interface, the timeline welcomes the annotations covering the relationships "mentions (audio)" and "displays" while the annotations covering the relationship "subject dealt with" (among other relationships) are present in the drop-down column to the right of the video. In the interface of navigating via graph, the different semantic entities connected by a relationship with the archive are presented while the user can filter them by categories, but also click on one of the resources displayed. The graph is thus reassembled by putting the chosen resource in the center and so on.

This interface being based on the heuristic character of ferrying signs embodied by the icons associated with the resources is a view leading to the emergence of a use that comes closer to serendipity, or the fact of making a chance insightful discovery while looking for something else. As a reminder, the ferrying sign is understood as a "type of sign particular to écrits d'écran that depends on a triple meaning-production process – integrating a sign particular to the text available onscreen, the indicator subject to being activated, to anticipate through it the text destined to be posted" [JEA 14, p. 15]. The icon introduced in this type of view initially presents a mystery for the user, who at first does not know what he will find by clicking on it: a detailed view? Contextual information? The learning process of browsing via graph is quick, while the user's question progressively becomes: if I click on this icon, what shape is the new graph going to take on?

Figure 3.7. *Navigation window of the Famille architext via graph. For a color version of the figure, see www.iste.co.uk/szoniecky/collective.zip*

The fourth photograph of the editorialization process consists in the presentation of the advanced research interface (Figure 3.8). Once the annotation process has been realized, in the case of studying the importation of an entire collection, the chance to find an extract displaying a specific element is championed. The research interface therefore includes several filters: the chance to classify by archive type (audio, video, text, photograph), then the chance to search for a specific entity and the relationship that joins it to the archive. In our case, we looked for a document displaying the semantic entity "location" named "Sèvre Nantaise". Only one document responds to the criteria, which is the archive *Fête de Jeanne d'Arc, 4ème centenaire du collège d'Ancenis*. Finally, the user can also disregard the semantic search to obtain the results of a text search.

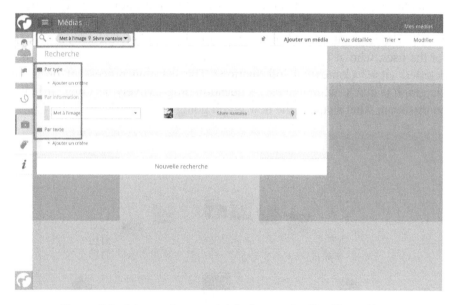

Figure 3.8. *Advanced research interface on the Famille architext*

The fifth photograph of the editorialization process is interested in the possibility of creating a semantic entity that does not exist in the open knowledge databases (Figure 3.9). In the context of the archive studied, manual annotation consists in the association of the archive with resources existing on the Web. Yet in the precise case of the entity "First communion", no result was present among the generalist *Linked Open Data*; only the entity "communion" was represented. The possibility offered to the user to create a subject is thus implemented. In this way, at the moment when the little girl in the communion robe appears, the user can associate the semantic entity "First communion" with the archive. This entity can remain devoid of information or be enriched locally (the resource will not enrich the open knowledge databases) at the user's discretion. This new annotation can thus be the subject of an advanced search while a graph can be created from it, rich with later links tied to other resources.

Figure 3.9. *Subject creation interface on the Famille architext*

The thusly described editorialization chain is made up of several steps: the importation of the archive, its semantic enrichment, manual annotation and, finally, consultation in different forms: detailed view or navigation via graphs of entities. The co-created architext allows this migration of the digital archive to the enriched resource. We observed the way in which it allowed the existence of écrits d'écran, more the architext than the constraints appends to the use below the device: the mediation of the family memory.

3.7. Assessment of the archive's recontextualization

The data web seems like an efficient source concerning the recontextualization function requiring the restoration of the heritage document's intelligibility. The data's open, linked characteristics promote their reuse in the scope of third-party devices like the one co-constructed in this study. It is original in its identity given the coexistence of different semiotic objects (audiovisual documents, annotations and contextual notes from *Linked Open Data*) on the same graphic level.

If the problem – the loss of intelligibility associated with the archive – the semiotic approach, the resources – the data web – and the device – and architext dedicated to editorialization – seem coherent, several questions remain salient. The evolution of the heritage document's status through the prism of editorialization poses a question. By annotating the archive, we re-documentize it, which is to say: "documentize a document or a collection again by allowing a beneficiary to rearticulate the semiotic contents according to its interpretation and uses" [ZAC 07]; yet during the stage of importing the archive to the web application, we delete its materiality, which is associated with it by the file's name, its size, its properties and its extension. All of this information disappears during import into the cloud and thus its documentary status, only the name of which survives, transcribed in writing.

Similarly, does the archive, rich in associated annotations, preserve its documentary integrity? If it is possible to consult the archive associated with its contextual resources via architext, it is only itself with the architext, for by rematerializing the archive with the help of a potential upload or by burning the document onto a CD-ROM, the archive finds itself cut off from the resources that were associated with it. Yet if "editorialization is the logical conclusion of the content digitization process [...] it has a tendency to break the link existing between the resource and its document of origin, introducing a break between the new production and the documents on which it is founded" [BAC 07b, p. 21].

If the architext allows the patrimonial enhancement of the archive, it also monitors the methods of its existence. By going further, by taking back up the premise that all technology is the result of a calculation [BAC 10b], the digital heritage document is actually reconstructed by the architext each time it is consulted. In fact, the heritage status associated with the archive can only be preserved if the document's integrity is preserved: the stakes of patrimonial enhancement become more complex as *ex nihilo* resources are associated with digital documents. The system of historicity of écrits d'écran coexisting in the archive also questions the understanding of the archive's heritage status. In Figure 3.6, we observed that three types of écrits d'écran coexist with the mother resource: the metadata automatically produced by the enrichment modules, the manual annotations and the contextual notes. Considering the context of architext use – the framework of cultural and patrimonial mediation – two questions arise from this semiotic polyphony: the historicity and the authority of écrits d'écran. If the designation and moderation of automatically produced annotations are implemented, the user remains confronted with an architext combining écrits d'écran from different temporalities and multiple authors, this analysis being able to harm the user's experiment. Fortunately, Annette Beguin-Verbrugge's conclusions concerning the printed page [BEG 06] lead us to put this analysis into perspective: in the presence of disparate elements in a single setting, the user-reader intuitively seeks to create meaning among these elements.

In the same way that everyone is questioning the archive armed with its own "encyclopedia", to cite Eco, each user of the device develops a unique experience with it, by redirecting it: thus poaching [DEC 90] the behaviors and uses previously defined by the creators. In fact, what behavior should be displayed: accepting the future controlling dimension of the device or neutralizing it by implementing neutral functionalities? Can the architext, thusly created, resist its experimentation? The semiotic prism does not allow this dimension to be fully disregarded: a study of the uses can fill this gap and fuel new ergonomic and editorial recommendations aiming to enrich the architext.

3.8. Bibliography

[ALL 94] ALLARD L., L'espace public esthétique et les amateurs: l'exemple du cinéma privé, PhD Thesis, University of Paris III, 1994.

[ALL 02] ALLARD L., ODIN R., Esthétiques ordinaires du cinéma et de l'audiovisuel, rapport de recherche rédigé dans le cadre du contrat de recherche "Ethnologie de la relation esthétique", Mission du Patrimoine Ethnologique, 2002.

[AUM 12] AUMONT J., BERGALA A., VERNET M., Esthétique du film, 3rd ed., Armand Colin, 2012.

[BAC 07a] BACHIMONT B., Ingénierie des connaissances et des contenus: le numérique entre ontologies et documents, Hermes Science-Lavoisier, Paris, 2007.

[BAC 07b] BACHIMONT B., "Nouvelles tendances applicatives : de l'indexation à l'éditorialisation", in GROS P. (ed.), L'indexation multimédia, Hermes Science-Lavoisier, Paris, 2007.

[BAC 10a] BACHIMONT B., "La présence de l'archive : réinventer et justifier", *Intellectica*, vols 53–54, pp. 281–309, 2010.

[BAC 10b] BACHIMONT B., *Le sens de la technique : le numérique et le calcul*, Les Belles Lettres, Paris, 2010.

[BAR 80] BARTHES R., *La chambre claire : Notes sur la photographie*, Gallimard, Paris, 1980.

[BEG 06] BEGUIN-VERBRUGGE A., *Images en texte, Images du texte. Dispositifs graphiques et communication écrite*, Presses universitaires du Septentrion, Villeneuve d'Ascq, 2006.

[BER 06] BERNERS-LEE T., "Linked Data", *W3C*, available at: http://www.w3.org/DesignIssues/LinkedData.html, 2006.

[DEC 90] DE CERTEAU M., *L'invention du quotidien*, Le Seuil, Paris, 1990.

[GAN 11] GANDON F., FARON-ZUCKER C., CORBY O. (eds), *Le Web sémantique: comment lier les données et les schémas sur le Web?*, Dunod, Paris, 2011.

[HEA 09] HEATH T., HEPP M., BIZER C. (eds), "Special Issue on Linked Data", *International Journal on Semantic Web and Information Systems*, 2009.

[INS 09] INSTITUT DE RECHERCHE ET D'INNOVATION, "Lignes de temps", available at: http://www.iri.centrepompidou.fr/outils/lignes-de-temps/, 2009.

[JEA 14] JEANNERET Y., *Critique de la trivialité : les médiations de la communication, enjeu de pouvoir*, Editions Non Standard, Paris, 2014.

[MET 68] METZ C., *Essais sur la signification du cinéma*, Klincksieck, Paris, 1968.

[MET 71] METZ C., *Langage et Cinéma*, Larousse, Paris, 1971.

[ODI 79] ODIN R., "Rhétorique du film de famille, Rhétorique sémiotique", *Revue d'Esthétique*, vols. 1–2, pp. 340–373, 1979.

[ODI 11] ODIN R, *Les Espaces de la communication : Introduction à la sémio-pragmatique*, PUG, Paris, 2011.

[RAS 99] RASTIER F., PINCEMIN B., "Des genres à l'intertexte", *Cahiers de Praxématique*, vol. 33, pp. 83–111, 1999.

[RAS 01] RASTIER F., CAVAZZA M, ABEILLÉ A. (eds), *Sémantique pour l'analyse. De la linguistique à l'informatique*, Masson, Paris, 2001.

[RAS 02] RASTIER F., BOUQUET S. (eds), *Une introduction aux sciences de la culture*, PUF, Paris, 2002.

[RAS 09] RASTIER F., *Sémantique interprétative*, 3rd ed., PUF, Paris, 2009.

[RAS 11] Rastier F., *La mesure et le grain. Sémantique de corpus*, Honoré Champion, Paris, 2011.

[SOU 52] Souriau E. (ed.), *L'univers filmique*, Flammarion, Paris, 1952.

[SOU 02] Souchier E., Jeanneret Y., "Écriture numérique ou médias informatisés?", *Dossier pour la science*, no. 33, pp. 100–105, 2002.

[SOU 03] Souchier E., Jeanneret Y., Le Marec J. (eds), *Lire, écrire, récrire. Objets, signes et pratiques des médias informatisés*, Bibliothèque publique d'information, Paris, 2003.

[VAL 15] Valluy J., "Éditorialisation" (recherche bibliographique, avril 2015), *TERRA-HN*, available at: http://www.reseau-terra.eu/article1333.html, 2015.

[VIT 16] Vitali Rosati M., "What is Editorialization?", *Sens critique*, available at: http://sens-public.org/article1059.html, 2016.

[ZAC 07] Zacklad M., "Réseaux et communautés d'imaginaire documédiatisées", Skare R., Lund W. L., Varheim A. (eds), *A Document (Re)turn*, Peter Lang, Frankfurt am Main, 2007.

Studio Campus AAR: A Semantic Platform for Analyzing and Publishing Audiovisual Corpuses

4.1. Introduction

This chapter discusses the scientific and technological issues of a digital platform called *Studio Campus AAR*. Studio Campus AAR is intended for subjective appropriative activities of existing audiovisual data with a view to transform them into *objects* with *symbolic value* (i.e. a particular *"meaning"*) for a given community.

For example, in the "academic world", a growing number of individual (i.e. researchers, educators, doctoral researchers, even students) and collective (research teams and laboratories, educational facilities, associations, and other scientific or educational organizations, etc.) actors more and more frequently use *digital audiovisual* resources. Whether this be to document concrete field research activities and knowledge domains, or to collect, process, analyze, publish, exploit and conserve scientific heritages or, more broadly, cultural heritages in the form of *sites* or *portals* of *audiovisual archives*, online video libraries, etc. This is a typical but also very recent situation forming part of the *culture* of the *"digital humanities"* and constitutes a powerful driving force for a dynamic and innovative economy of knowledge where the "academic world" (i.e. the world of research and higher education), plays a central role as a *strategic market* for knowledge: the "academic world" is its

Chapter written by Abdelkrim Beloued, Peter Stockinger and Steffen Lalande.

main producer and it is also one of its most important "consumers" (for its needs in terms of research and development, education and training, service provision, etc.). But *for lack of an appropriate work environment*, this process is having a hard time becoming widespread.

Studio Campus AAR[1] is an attempt to bring the concerned actors a solution based on a semiotic approach to digital archives, the theory of conceptual graphs and the technologies of the semantic web.

Divided into seven sections, this chapter first proposes a succinct presentation of the general context that the conception and development of Studio Campus AAR and the functional architecture of this platform fit into (section 4.2). Then, the main points to consider during the conception and development of such a platform will be discussed in greater depth (sections 4.3 to 4.8).

4.2. Context and issues

The general socio-economic and cultural context today is characterized unquestionably by a growing interest in the issue of cultural heritage, its constitution in the form of an archive *sensu lato*, its exploitation, and its concrete use. Archive "*sensu lato*" means: all projects (institutional or personal, professional or amateur, imposed by the law or freely undertaken by the parties concerned, following or not following archival standards, etc.) constituting a textual and audiovisual database provided with a set of data storage, classification, conservation and exploitation criteria.

A sign of this general tendency is that of Web 2.0 platforms like *YouTube*, *Flickr*, *Scribd*, etc. But clearly, the will to maintain cultural heritages on a large scale has long existed, for example, with the existence of institutions specialized in this domain, such as libraries, archives (in the classical sense of the term), or even museums. This is also the case for institutions and

---

1 Campus AAR is an R&D project financed for three years (from 2014 to 2017) by the ANR (French National Research Agency). It is made up of four partner institutions: ESCoM-AAR – Equipe Sémiotique Cognitive et nouveaux Médias – Archives Audiovisuelles de la Recherche (program housed by the FMSH in Paris until the end of 2015); INA (National Audiovisual Institute); the Armadillo society; the CNRS's Center for Direct Scientific Communication. For more information on the project, see http://campusaar.hypotheses.org/?lang=en_GB. To access the experimental Campus AAR portal, log in to https://hal.campus-aar.fr/

professions that depend more crucially on access to knowledge, for example, for scientific research, law or diplomacy.

There are various stakes at play in the constitution, conservation, transmission and exploitation of a heritage. Let us mention more specifically that which attributes to *sensu lato* digital archives the status of a *hub*, a *point of reference* for entire "communities" ("ethnic", professional, informal, "virtual", etc.). A typical example is provided by the various channels on *YouTube*: each channel is made up of an open and more or less sizable collection of videos that serve as a reference for a *community* made up of producers, directors, anonymous spectators, critical commentators, etc. There is very great diversity in such communities – communities of *taste* (for fashion, cuisine, extreme sports, etc.), *brands, opinion, practices*, communities organized around a *medium* (a newspaper, a magazine, a television channel, etc.), *an institution* (a political party, an association, a university, etc.), *a territory, a personality* or a *star*, etc. These communities can vary in size; they can be gathered geographically in a certain location or, the opposite, be spread across the entire world; they can enjoy a longer or shorter presence in time and even be renewed in the form of successive generations of members in a community. They can function "self-sufficiently", as sorts of closed clubs, or exchange and interact with other communities, using and reusing *audiovisual data themselves*, or *reeditorialized versions* of these data, just as well as the *comments* (and the comments on comments) on these data in the most diverse social settings, all thanks to the technological potentialities of social networks.

In fact, these communities form *communication ecosystems*, an essential element of which is a *common* or *shared data* ("content") *collection*. The data collection offers what could be called *the discourse universe* of a communication ecosystem composed notably of a system of *utterances* and *maxims* (i.e. of a system of *topoi*) that constitute the *epistemic framework* (of evidence, certainties, *a priori*, etc.) *in reference* to which a "discourse community" identifies and processes the *reference objects* (the domain or domains of interest).

By considering the central role of digital archives in a communication ecosystem, we can easily convince ourselves of the importance of the research and development activities devoted to them. A particularly important issue here is that of *understanding* a part of the data themselves, of their *affordance* as signifying objects (i.e. as entities possessing a meaning for an agent, an actor) and, on the other hand, of *activities around* and *initiated by* these data. It is this aspect that we, in other publications, have called the *semiotic turn* in research on digital archives in particular and (digital) data in general (see [STO 12, STO 15a, STO 15b, BEL 15]).

Let us take, for example, audiovisual data, an unrefined registry, or an author montage. Such data possess a *particular*, *internal* structure that manifests itself in the form of *affordances*, constraints and freedoms of interaction between itself and an agent. As with all textual data, they possess two levels (the *content* level and the content *expression* level). Each level can itself be broken down – like a *puff pastry*, to cite the image proposed by Algirdas Julien Greimas to understand the structure of a text – into *more specific strata*. The *content level* is typically broken down in this way into a thematic stratum, a rhetorical stratum and a discursive stratum. The *expression level* can be grasped through a series of strata dedicated to audio and visual staging, the perspective, spatial, and temporal organization of the textual surface of audiovisual data.

Furthermore, audiovisual data belong to a *genre* (a genre being an historic model – a *tradition* – that imposes a certain organization, or configuration, on the different strata making up the data). In this way, a distinction can be made between, for example, fictional films, documentaries, "simple" recordings of pro-filmic events, amateur and ephemeral films, etc. Each genre not only imposes a certain order on the different strata making up audiovisual data (see [STO 03]), but also restrains the interactions between the audiovisual data, their environment and the actors that form their ecosystem. We can thus observe systematic variations in the reception, interpretation, and reutilization of author films, ephemeral films like ads or even amateur films.

Finally, audiovisual data can be broken up into smaller entities (e.g. sequences, visual outlines, arbitrary time segments, etc.) and form larger entities (e.g. collections, corpuses, intertextual networks, even whole archives, etc.). In other words, the audiovisual data are signs or rather systems of signs that form texts or, as we prefer to say using the analogy of a *landscape*, signify textscapes developed and used by the actors in a communication ecosystem to produce a universe of values (of meanings), put on a performance, circulate and share messages, and transmit and teach traditions.

These three aspects – the *stratification of audiovisual data,* their *belonging to a genre* and their *compositional nature* – form a general theoretical framework of structural semiotic inspiration for the construction of *metalanguage* and *description models,* either to analyze audiovisual corpuses or to publish, or rather republish, corpuses of such data.

At the same time, this metalanguage and its description models also serve to impose a "*policy*", even a *style of analysis* and *publication/republication,* and to coordinate, to manage the *concrete activities* of analysis and publication/republication performed by individual or collective actors forming a "discourse" community around a taste, a brand, an opinion, a star, etc. and depending on a shared collection of audiovisual data.

4.2.1. Archiving and appropriation of audiovisual data

Typical activities are organized around audiovisual data, in the form of concrete actions or interactions generally expressing *practices* (professional, personal, etc.), more or less formalized (i.e. being performed in reference to a model or an underlying script). Among these various activities, we can particularly distinguish between:

– the *construction activities of the "(audiovisual) data" object.* This includes activities like those of conception, elaboration, publication, diffusion or even the conservation of audiovisual data (or a corpus of data);

– the *appropriation activities of the "(audiovisual) data" object.* For example, the (selective) reception of audiovisual data, their interpretation, modification, adaptation and exploitation in specific situations, etc.

The first category of activities combines all those that fall more specifically under the category of "authoring" audiovisual data like, for example, the writing of a synopsis or a scenario, filming preparation activities, filming, rough assembly, assembly, postproduction, etc. also A part of this first category of activities also includes all activities that intersperse – through a textual genetics perspective – the different life stages of audiovisual data, from their "birth" to their "death" by going through the different phases of updating, editing and distributing them.

More specifically, concerning the sector of audiovisual research archives, this first category is made up of those that are part of the reference model for the *constitution of an audiovisual archive*. In [STO 11a], this process is described in greater detail in five stages:

– *Stage 1: Preparation activities* before the recording of a *setting sensu lato*, i.e. including the recordings of scientific settings strictly speaking in ethnology, sociology, linguistics, etc. as well as those of a scientific event (colloquium, seminar, etc.) or a cultural one (concert, exposition, etc.).

– *Stage 2*: *Setting recording activities* and *data collection activities* with an eye to constitute a *site documentation corpus* (*sensu lato*, see above).

– *Stage 3*: *Processing and analysis of a corpus (work)* documenting a setting (*sensu lato*, see above).

– Stage 4: Prepublication and publication/republication of previously processed and analyzed audiovisual corpuses.

– Stage 5: *Activities finalizing* the process of working on the corpus.

Each of these stages is distinguished by a *series of more specialized activities*, has *explicit procedures* that govern these activities, *is instrumented* (i.e. is supported by an environment of tools necessary for the realization of an activity), *is explicitly documented* (i.e. is the object of practical guides) and *produces a corpus* of data and metadata documenting a heritage.

Concerning the second category of activities introduced above, they fall under the active and subjective appropriation of audiovisual data (or a corpus of audiovisual data) by an individual or collective actor. In fact, here we find the phenomena debated today, such as those of (re)mediatizing audiovisual data, (re)editorializing it, enriching it, rewriting it or even reassembling it (see [STO 11a, STO 11b, STO 12]). We also find here the issue of the *creation of value* of or through textual and audiovisual data – a central issue in the emerging reflections on new economy shapes based on meaning (value) and experience.

In fact, there are few digital data (audiovisual or otherwise) that constitute, in and of themselves, a true resource in the framework, for example, of teaching, university research or even for a communication/promotion campaign for a scientific heritage. In general, the user of audiovisual data (such as a teacher, a student, a trainer, a researcher, an editor, a "communicator", etc.) must make more or less significant additions, modifications, etc. in order to adapt them to his usage needs. In other words, the user of the audiovisual resource (the teacher, the student, the researcher, etc.) becomes, in turn, the author of the audiovisual resource – author in the traditional sense or the more broad, figurative sense. Here, we are faced with the problem, so widely discussed in the knowledge industry, of the *auctorial function* underlying the (more or less definitive) questioning of its classic and traditional definition (the author as an easily identifiable person or group of people).

Let's quickly consider some scenarios to demonstrate the reeditorialization (resegmentation, reanalysis, republication, etc.) process for audiovisual data or a corpus of audiovisual data. It is a matter of adapting the cultural profile of audiovisual data or even a corpus of audiovisual data to the cultural profile of potential users, that is, to their expectations, their knowledge and, finally, their needs and interests. This adaptation can concern the different semiotic strata identified above, it can be applied to specific segments of audiovisual data, and it can lead to more or less significant modifications such that the original corpus or part of the original corpus "changes skins" to acquire all the characteristics of a new text.

In this way, existing audiovisual data can be rewritten at the *thematic level* by deleting certain themes, adding other themes and specializing an already existing theme in order to modify the selection of appropriate information. For example, an already published interview dedicated to presenting a social group's culture can be gradually completed with new information on this group, more detailed information or even modified, updated, etc. information. This is a rewriting that targets the *subjects* of a corpus of audiovisual data, in particular. It is an essential form of rewriting insofar as specific contexts of using an already existing audiovisual corpus necessarily require the consideration of all subjects that can but do not have to be present in the said corpus. This vital conformation of the subjects or topics available in a given corpus in relation to the thematic attempts of a community of users is, moreover, one of the main driving forces of activities such as localization and the update of information (thematically pertinent, it must be understood). Also, this form of rewriting – alone or in unison with other forms of rewriting – serves to "update" information previously relevant to a field of knowledge and to the management of the lasting quality of this information.

Audiovisual data can be rewritten at the *narrative level*, for example, as a change in a subject's position in a given *reading process*. In this way, the linear series of sequences making up the interview with a researcher dedicated to the culture of a social group can be modified and reassembled such that the themes filtering the information relevant to a certain aspect of the group in question are gathered at the start of the series of sequences. However, modifications concerning the reading process, the process of appropriating the content of an audiovisual datum, can be numerous and take on subtle and complex forms; it all depends on the structure of the narrative pattern underlying a given process. A field of central application, here, is that of learning, and acquiring knowledge relative to a given field.

The *discursive and rhetorical rewriting* of audiovisual data can concern, for example, the framing of specific information, that is, focusing on a given piece of information and its hierarchization in relation to others. In this way, a specific aspect of the social group dealt with in an interview with a researcher can be – *a posteriori* – emphasized in the form of specific *discursive expansion processing* using comments, explanations, critiques, even aids for understanding, etc. Such "processing" only shows that a particular aspect dealt with *a priori* in an already published interview takes on particular importance in the scope of a *new* communication such that the discursive and rhetorical rewriting of this part of the document disseminating the information in question becomes a condition *sine qua non* for its *new* appropriated and efficient use. This specific form of rewriting "serves" again to conform existing audiovisual data, *a posteriori*, to pedagogic usage contexts, but it also serves for all sorts of professional communication where it is a matter of clarifying, debating and commenting on a given piece of information in order to acquire a more complete vision, also more in depth, of a domain, a question or a problem.

Finally, the *rewriting* of data or a corpus of audiovisual data at the *level of expression* of a piece of information covers different forms of translation in the semiotic sense of the information concerned: translation from a source language to a target language, translation in the sense of oral transcription (for information expressed in written form), etc. In this way, information produced in French during an interview with a researcher dedicated to the culture of a social group can be *subtitled, literally translated, dubbed,* but also *recapped, summarized,* even reinterpreted and adapted in Russian, German or any other natural language. Published in spoken form, it can be transcribed into a printable text and *vice versa*. But this is also the visual staging (*sensu lato*) of given information that can be rewritten so as to be better adapted to a new use, to the habits and attempts of a "new" community. In this way, information on a certain aspect of a social group can be published in the form of a fixed visual frame exposing an "American shot" showing the researcher as he speaks at the camera. This staging, very unsophisticated, can be perfectly rewritten in various forms: the researcher filmed by two, even many cameras, allowing a montage of a certain variety of camera angles and frames, the exposition of the information developed by the researcher in the form of a montage completing the researcher's discourse with sequences of static images, even audiovisual recordings from "on site", etc.

Let us not forget that the analysis and reanalysis just as well as the writing and rewriting of a corpus of audiovisual data are complex cognitive operations aiming to "pass on" a message to a potential recipient. These are operations that are necessarily placed in a defined *intercultural* context, on the one hand, by the cultural profile making up the identity, the specificity of the corpus, and, on the other hand, by the cultural profile of the potential recipient of this corpus. Let us remember that the operations of writing/rewriting an audiovisual corpus or a part of it are cognitive operations that are part of *cultural mediation* at the support of one or several media (hence the significant *change in terminology* from cultural *mediation* or *remediation* to *remediatization*). These cognitive operations appear, in fact, as "solutions" (more or less successful, more or less effective) in the face of large questions concerning all communication.

In order that a digital archive may fully occupy the aforementioned function and status of a *reference model* in the communication ecosystem of a community of actors, particular interest must be shown in the modeling and instrumentation of these different activities that we have just discussed briefly. This is one of the central objectives of the research and development project Campus AAR ("AAR" for "Archives Audiovisuelles de la Recherche", Audiovisual Research Archives), which is the result of some 20 years of research on archives and digital libraries, of which 15 years were dedicated more precisely to the issue of the constitution and exploitation of audiovisual corpuses documenting research in the social sciences and humanities.

4.2.2. *General presentation of the Campus AAR environment*

The principal objective of the Campus AAR project is to develop a deployable software infrastructure and a collection of terminological resources allowing an archive owner to analyze, display, republish, research and render audiovisual resources interoperable according to a semiotic approach for a varied public including actors in the world of research as well as those from the world of preservation and promotion of cultural heritages. By adopting a resolutely *cognitive and semiotic* [STO 12] approach of audiovisual archives, the Campus AAR project prioritizes the analysis of the structural specificities (thematic, narrative, discursive, pragmatic, visual and sound, etc.) particular to all audiovisual media. The base hypothesis is that this approach can satisfy the multiple attempts and needs of all actors – all participating parties – who hope to *actively* get involved with an audiovisual medium to *transform* it into an *intellectual resource in the strictest sense* or into a *resource adapted* to specific usage contexts: education, research, promotion and cultural mediation, strictly speaking.

From the scientific and technological point of view, the specificity of this project depends on the development of a solution constructed entirely on "semantic web" technologies being articulated around the development of an RDF triplestore adapted to the description of audiovisual content to ensure the persistence of the metadata produced, but also to construct innovative description, content research and multimedia publication services adapted to the use of expert communities from the SSH domain. The heart of the project is thus made up of a Campus AAR work environment namely made up of a "back office" and a tool for the analysis, publication and modeling of an archive's discourse universe entitled Studio Campus AAR (Figure 4.1). In Figure 4.2, the different functionalities offered by Studio Campus AAR can be seen. Of particular note are:

– the *uploading* of audiovisual data stored in an OAI repository and its (virtual) (re)segmentation;

– the *analysis* of audiovisual data (of media, in the project's terminology) with the help of a *domain ontology*, i.e. representing an archive's *discourse universe* (particular among them, the topoi or "large themes");

– the constitution and analysis of *corpuses of audiovisual data* with the help of a domain ontology;

– the *management of the individuals* (named entities, terms, etc.) making up a domain ontology (or several ontologies) and that are used or created by the analyst to perform a description of audiovisual data;

– the *publication/republication* of data or a corpus of audiovisual data with the help of a publication ontology specifying different publication formats or genres such as video-lexicons, thematic folders or even narrative paths;

– the semantic search through audiovisual data;

– the modeling of an archive's discourse universe in the form of a domain ontology and appropriate description models.

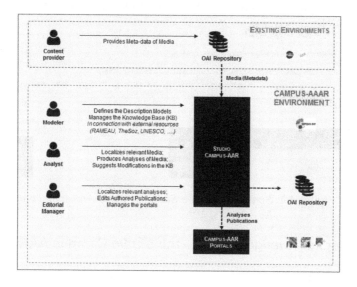

Figure 4.1. *The Campus AAR environment with its Studio; graphic created by F. Lemaitre*

Figure 4.1 more precisely identifies the *three main roles* that interact with the Studio Campus AAR:

– the modeler is the person or the group of people who develop, test and validate the domain's ontology and the audiovisual data's description models;

– the analyst is the person or the group of people whose principal tasks are the identification (localization) of audiovisual data (of media, in the project's terminology) accessible in one or several OAI repositories, the uploading and analysis of data one by one or in the form of a corpus and, finally, the management of the individuals (terms, lexicons, named entities, non-verbal signs, etc.);

– the editorial manager is the person or group of people who, depending on a publication scenario, searches for and localizes the previously analyzed audiovisual data (media) to perform a new publication with the help of a publication ontology.

The analyses and publications realized with Studio Campus AAR can either be distributed to specialized portals (see Figure 4.1) or integrated into websites. The analyses can be exported into OAI repositories by harvesters like ISIDORE[2].

Figure 4.2. *Screenshot of the Studio Campus AAR menu bar*

4.3. Editing knowledge graphs – the Studio Campus AAR example

Studio Campus AAR is a client-server platform dedicated to the description, search and reeditorialization (republication) of audiovisual content. As mentioned above, it is based on semantic web languages and technologies to offer expressivity, extensibility and interoperability along the whole information processing and valorization chain.

This platform targets expert communities in particular by allowing them, on the one hand, to develop or reuse ontological resources relevant to their domain for the description of audiovisual content and, on the other hand, to

2 See http://www.rechercheisidore.fr/

emphasize this content through website creation assistance. In a fully integrated way, the platform manages the content descriptions and (re) publications, and the named entities (people, organizations, locations, etc.) as RDF knowledge graphs controlled by ontological resources formalized in RDFS/OWL.

The editing of these two types of resources, ontologies and instance graphs, by modelers and analysts, who are not specialists in knowledge engineering, constitutes the most important element of this work. One efficient solution consists of using the language OWL2 to guide the realization of well-formed graphs through various adaptive interfaces. These capabilities are accompanied by great flexibility in data management thanks to the use of triplestore RDF databases for their persistence and querying through the use of the language SPARQL.

4.3.1. Context

In recent years, more and more operators (industrial and institutional) are abandoning the eternal relational model in favor of alternate solutions exploiting knowledge graphs to represent their data. Among these systems, "triplestores" represent a particular category exploiting the languages of the W3C such as RDF, RDFS, OWL or even SPARQL.

The notion of formal ontology lies at the heart of these new data management systems. It describes real-world interactions in the form of abstract classes and relationships between the individuals (instances) of these classes. The Instanciation of these ontological elements produces a graph that links the knowledge available at a given moment. The ability to reason with this knowledge represents a centerpiece of these new systems. It allows new facts to be deduced from existing facts; let us cite, for example, the works of the BBC [KIR 10] and Red Bull [KUR 12], which propose solutions for the management and enrichment of sport content.

The shape of the knowledge graph must respect the abstract definition of the ontology's elements. For example, to establish a particular relationship between two individual instances of two ontological classes, these two classes must belong to the set of authorized classes as declared in the formal definition of the relationship. We are referring to all of the domains (in the RDFS formalism) and all of the ranges. The W3C's norms and recommendations define the modalities of data representation, reasoning and control. The RDF standard establishes the general framework of data representation in the form of triples (subject, predicate, object). RDFS defines the data representation schema and establishes a first control level based on the signature of the properties, which ensures the coherence of the data. OWL2 expands this schema by including the possibility of describing complex classes in the form of class intersections, for example, and also allows restrictions and cardinalities to be defined for the properties.

The editing of knowledge graphs is potentially a complex task, especially when the genericity constraint excludes the realization of a "tailor-made" interface totally adapted to a fixed model. This problem has been addressed by [CHE 09] and [LAL 09] where the graphical editing of knowledge graphs is guided by the provision of a collection of template graphs defined in the ontology. These templates are developed by the modeler to guide the user and ensure coherence to all the descriptions. This approach has been instrumented in the CoGui[3] software. The work described here uses the OWL2 axiomatic used to define complex editing templates. For example, if the writers of a literary work are restrained, in the ontology, to only French writers of the 20th Century, the graph editor must analyze this expression and only propose the writers with French nationality and a date of birth situated in the 20th Century.

The axiomatic OWL2 can also be used *a posteriori* to classify individuals. In this case, the individuals are created freely without any previous control of the restrictions defined in the ontology. The reasoners (see Hermit [GLI 10], Pellet [SIR 05], etc.) applied to the data *a posteriori* allow the logical descriptions to be interpreted and the individuals to be typed by the named and anonymous classes.

In the case of high dynamicity of the ontology, where the anonymous class identifiers are often changing, we propose a hybrid approach that combines an OWL2-based guidance of the editing process while only storing in the knowledge base a simplified version of the edited graph in conformance with RDFS. The following paragraphs present the solutions proposed for editing knowledge graphs in more detail.

---

3 See http://www.lirmm.fr/cogui/

4.3.2. *Representations of OWL2 restrictions*

The signature of a property is always represented by its *domain* and its *range*. The domain is the set of instances on which this property can be applied. For example, the domain of the property "writer" is the class of literary works. The range represents the span of possible values for this property. For example, the range of the property "writer" is the physical people. An OWL2 restriction is always set on a property and allows its range to be restricted by defining:

– the exact values, as an enumeration of values. For example, the genre of a literary work must be one of the following values: history, science-fiction, crime, biography or story;

– the complex (anonymous) classes which combine several named classes with the help of set theory operators like intersection, union, complement, etc. For example, the opera singer must be an Italian or French performer.

A restriction is defined with the help of logical, first-order formulas. Logical connectors as well as universal and existential quantifiers are the main logical operators used to describe a restriction. Two types of restrictions can be distinguished:

– A simple restriction, which is applied to one depth of properties by specializing their ranges. Figure 4.3, taken from Stanford's Protégé software, shows an example of a simple restriction placed on the two properties "performer" and "work" of a musical performance restricted to physical people and musical works, respectively. This type of restriction is easy to implement and interpret by a reasoner. However, in certain cases, it requires the creation of "anonymous" intermediate classes that are only used in the particular context of the restriction;

Figure 4.3. *Simple restriction on Stanford's Protégé*

– A recursive restriction, which is applied to a chain of properties. First of all, it specifies the range of the first property of the chain, the range itself possessing properties that undergo this restriction, etc. Figure 4.4 shows an example of a recursive restriction that limits the property "work" to only musical works composed by French women. The advantage of this restriction is that it allows the description of intermediate complex classes (anonymous classes) without explicitly creating new named classes. In this example, the two classes "musical work composed by a French woman" and "French woman" are implicitly created by the restriction formula. The drawback lies in the difficulty of implementing and interpreting the formula.

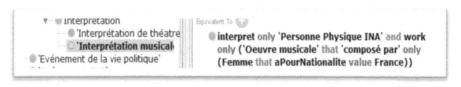

Figure 4.4. *Recursive restriction on Stanford's Protégé*

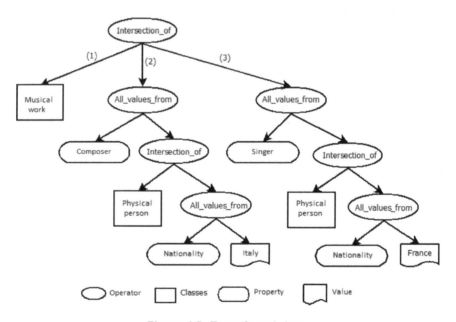

Figure 4.5. *Tree of restrictions*

An OWL2 restriction is interpreted by the reasoner in order to identify and suggest the classes and individuals that are compatible with the context. It is implemented in the form of a tree whose nodes are the logical operators (intersection, union, complement, universal and existential quantifiers) and the leaves are the classes, properties and property values. The reasoner goes through this tree and suggests the most appropriate basic ontological elements (classes, individuals) for each level of interpretation. For example, the restriction "musical work composed by an Italian composer and performed by a French singer" is represented by the following tree (Figure 4.5):

4.3.3. Resolution of OWL2 restrictions

Several strategies from the literature for processing the tree can be applied to the tree of restrictions: the depth first approach, and the breadth first one, etc. Each of these has advantages and disadvantages. In certain cases, this process can be realized in parallel, which would improve the resolution time. For example, in the previous figure, the two large branches of the tree (2 and 3) concern two completely independent properties (composer and singer of a work). It is thus possible to apply the corresponding filters to each musical work at the same time.

In this article, we are interested in a depth-first processing approach to illustrate our solution. The reasoner starts by analyzing the first branch of the tree (1) and retrieves all the instances from the "musical work" category. He then applies the filter defined in the second branch of the tree to each of these. This concerns the composers of the work who must be "physical people" of Italian nationality. If the work responds to this constraint, it will undergo the filter in the third branch, which only keeps those works whose performers are physical people of French nationality. If the work is kept, it will then be suggested to the user.

The reasoner adopts the same tree-processing approach for the suggestion of classes that are compatible with the restriction. The analysis of the first branch allows all the sub-classes and classes equivalent to the "musical work" class to be retrieved. The filter from the second branch only keeps, among all those classes, those whose "composer" property or one of its super-properties undergoes a category constraint ("physical person") and a nationality constraint ("Italian"). In the same way, the third filter only keeps those whose "singer" property or one of its super-properties undergoes category constraints ("physical person") and nationality constraints ("French"). The classes which fit will then be suggested to the user.

In a client/server configuration where the client only has a partial view of the knowledge base, it is mandatory to generate SPARQL queries from the tree of restrictions in order to propose to the user the individuals who are not present in the memory. The reasoner goes along the tree of restrictions and transforms the logical operators (*intersection_of*, *union_of*, *complement_of*) into SPARQL operators (AND, UNION, NOT). Each elementary restriction (the restriction on the composer, the singer and the nationality) is transformed into a SPARQL goal. The query constructed in this way allows us to find the entities compatible with the restriction in a remote knowledge base. The following outline (Figure 4.6) shows the SPARQL query generated from the tree presented in Figure 4.5.

```
Select ?work where {
    ?work rdf:type <Musical work>.
    ?work ontology:composer ?composer.
    ?work ontology:singer? singer.
    ?composer rdf:type <Physical person>.
    ?composer ontology:nationality <Italy>.
    ? singer rdf:type <Physical person>.
    ? singer ontology:nationality <France>.
}
```

Figure 4.6. *SPARQL query generated from the tree represented in Figure 4.5*

4.3.4. *Relaxing constraints*

Our issue of interpreting formulas to control knowledge editing is distinguished from the classification approach of existing reasoners like Hermit [GLI 10], Pellet [SIR 05] or Racer [HAA 04] by considering problems of information incompleteness during the editing phase and thus through a more flexible interpretation of the notion of *Open World Assumption* of OWL2.

In fact, the universal ($\forall$) and existential ($\exists$) quantifiers can make a restriction strong or weak. The universal quantifier tolerates the presence of properties without values. The existential quantifier, on the other hand, requires the existence of at least one value per property. However, the named entities, which are created independently of all restrictions, do not necessarily respond to the particular conditions requested by a given object; as a result, there is a certain incompleteness of the data due to ignorance of information to seize or due to the time given to do this. The graph editor must therefore be able to loosen certain constraints to allow the user to find the sought-after entities.

Let us take the example of the following restriction placed on the property "writer" of a literary work and that must take the value of all Francophone writers having won the Prix Goncourt. The restriction is represented here by the constraints placed on the author's writing language, which must be "French", and the prize won by this writer, which must be the "Prix Goncourt". However, an author's writing language is not necessarily mentioned in its authority record. The relaxing of the constraint on the language thus allows finding Francophone writers whose writing language was not given.

The constraints relaxation consists of ignoring certain branches of the tree of restrictions while going along it. This can be partial or total. In a partial relaxation, the branches concerned are all of those that define a constraint on the property values. Consequently, the new tree (after loosening) will be made up only of constraints on the properties' range. For example, after relaxing the constraints in the example of Figure 4.7, we obtain the following tree:

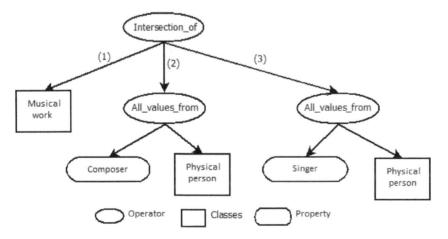

Figure 4.7. *Constraints relaxation*

This relaxation allows the structure of the initial restriction to be respected and the suggestion of irrelevant individuals to be limited. However, it can miss certain pertinent individuals that do not perfectly fit into this framework.

In a complete constraints relaxation, the only branches maintained are the root classes, that is, the constraint on the range of the property concerned by the initial restriction. This relaxation widens the field of values for this property, but can include irrelevant individuals. In the previous example, the total relaxation of constraints leads to a tree including the single node "Musical Work".

Constraints relaxation is presented in the graph editor as a supplementary option to the classical selection of individuals. It promotes the reuse of existing individuals, thus the creation of fewer repetitions. It also highlights the individuals whose properties are not entirely filled to be able to complete them later. Failing that, this relaxation can render the knowledge base incoherent owing to a possible lack of respect for the restrictions expressed in the ontology.

4.3.5. *Classification of individuals*

The classification of individuals is the mechanism that allows an instance to be associated with named or anonymous classes. In addition to its "*rdf:type*" identifying its direct named class(es), this mechanism depends on other RDFS/OWL characteristics. Among these characteristics:

– the transitivity of "*subClassOf*" allows an instance to be typed by the super-classes of its direct named classes;

– the transitivity and symmetry of "*equivalentClass*" allows an instance to be typed by the classes equivalent to its direct named classes;

– an instance can also be typed by the range of a property of which it is the value.

In OWL2, an anonymous class is a class stemming from an axiomatic definition that restricts the use of another class. For example, "Francophone writers", defined as a logical formula, is an anonymous class that restrains the "writer" category. Contrary to named classes, an anonymous class does not have a lasting URI between two editions of the ontology. An instance from an anonymous class is locally typed by that class's URI and will thus be submitted to its restrictions. This type can evolve during the graph editing process and is recalculated each time an operation is performed on the corresponding instance, which can therefore be reused in another model graph. Let us consider the example of two restrictions:

– R1: the literary work (O1) must have writers typed as "Francophone writers" (S1);

– R2: the literary work (O2) must have writers typed as "20th Century French writers" (S2).

In this way, an instance of S1 (a Francophone writer) cannot be used to edit O2. However, if his nationality (French) is listed as well as his date of birth (20th Century), this instance will then be typed by S2 and can thus be used in O2.

When a graph is stored in the triplestore, the reasoning engine exchanges all the anonymous types for the most highly represented named classes in each of them. In order to do this, the engine must go along the tree of restrictions with total relaxation of constraints in order to determine the named classes that will replace the anonymous classes.

Then, during a new graph editing session, a classification engine reestablishes these anonymous types by going along the tree of restrictions and partially relaxing the constraints to consider the incomplete data. For each instance, it verifies the partial respect of the different constraints expressed by the tree's branches. If the check is conclusive, the instance will be typed by the anonymous class that corresponds to this tree. This process can be seen as a projection of the model graphs (defined by restrictions) onto instance graphs and consequently as instance classification, in the manner of existing OWL2 reasoners like Pellet and Hermit.

In the previous example, an instance from the anonymous class "20th Century French writers" will be stored in the knowledge base in the "writer" category. When loading the graph containing this instance, its anonymous types will be recalculated as a function of its properties and the context of its use.

4.3.6. *Opening and interoperability with the web of data*

The adoption of the W3C semantic web standards (rdf/rdfs, OWL, SPARQL) facilitates the interoperability between the data produced locally by the graph editor with external knowledge bases and particularly those that are open on the Web, such as DBpedia, Geonames, VIAF and MusicBrainz. This interoperability allows:

– the identification of the individuals created locally by identifiers accepted around the world, such as the ISWC (*International Standard Work Code*), which is a unique identification code attributed to works;

– the assurance of a certain quality of the knowledge base by comparing the local entities with entities identified on the Web and highlighting potential incompatibilities with them;

– the completion of the semantic search performed on the local knowledge base by requests directed to the web of data in order to resolve data incompleteness;

– the enrichment of the local entities by external information, information currently used for data publication;

– the annotation of the audiovisual content by individuals or concepts available on the web of data;

– the support for the annotator in his documentation task by proposing rich, trustworthy information from web knowledge bases.

Access to these bases can be achieved via:

– SPARQL queries, if the knowledge base exhibits a *"SPARQL Endpoint"* on the Web;

– HTTP queries, if the knowledge base is reachable through a REST API;

– access to a local implementation of the knowledge base if a dump of that base is available on the Web and is installed on a server connected to the company's Intranet or on the Cloud.

Entities coming from different sources can designate a single entity in the real world. Their similarities are detected by recursively comparing their key properties. These properties or combination of properties allows a given entity to almost certainly be identified. For example, it is accepted that the combination of first name, last name, date of birth and date of death form a certain key for identifying a physical person. Similar entities can have similar, complementary or even contradictory properties. A data fusion task allows these properties of a single entity to be regrouped recursively. Various regrouping criteria can be imagined: the precision of property values (complete data with month/date/year vs. year alone), the number of occurrences of each value (voting system), the quality of the knowledge bases concerned (reliability of data), etc. This allows a compact and simplified view of the data to be presented to the user.

4.3.7. *Graphical interfaces*

A knowledge graph generally presents rather complex data connections for direct exploitation by a lambda user. The graphical interfaces developed over this type of graph must reduce the complexity of editing it and respond to certain criteria:

– simplicity: the graphic interface must present a simple data display by grouping it according to various perspectives. This grouping allows the user to be guided during data exploration by presenting him, at each stage, with a partial view of the knowledge graph. Several grouping criteria can be imagined, the first of these being the exploitation of the data hierarchy that allows the display to be marked off at a single level for a given node on the graph. Groupings according to precise properties or classes can also be performed, in which case access to the data is granted following those criteria;

– adaptability: the graphical interface must be automatically adapted to the ontology currently used to edit a knowledge graph and to all changes made on its classes and/or properties;

– dynamism: the interface must be dynamically adapted to all changes occurring during the editing of a knowledge graph. This includes: changing the editing ontology and the selection of a new object to edit;

– reusability: the interface must be reusable to edit different types of semantic graphs in the scope of any activity: media analysis, management of individuals, semantic search, management of corpuses, author publication.

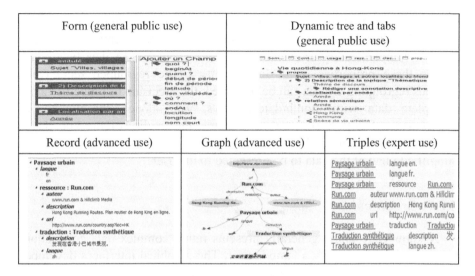

Figure 4.8. *Knowledge graph editing interfaces*

The interfaces that we have developed to edit knowledge graphs respect these criteria and exploit all the completion functionalities presented in the previous parts of this work. They are each dedicated to a precise use, as presented in the table above (Figure 4.8).

4.4. Application to media analysis

The semiotic analysis of a medium consists, among other things, of describing the subjects evoked by the medium from different points of view (thematic, visual, sound, rhetorical, etc.). Formal knowledge representation languages allow descriptions to be produced in the form of a graph that compares these subjects by combining knowledge, concepts and objects from the real world. Figure 4.9 shows the thematic and rhetorical analysis of a medium, performed in two distinct strata. The segments from the thematic stratum evoke the following subjects: "archaeology", "the history of ancient Egypt" and "Mayan civilization". Each of these promotes a certain number of concepts, objects and individuals. The subject "archaeology", for example, concerns an archaeological excavation site and the material remains discovered there, all explained by an archaeologist. The segments from the rhetorical stratum, on the other hand, present rhetorical relationships between these objects and individuals. The first segment, for example, describes a discussion between the archaeologist, who explains the excavation operation, and the historian, who talks about ancient Egyptian constructions.

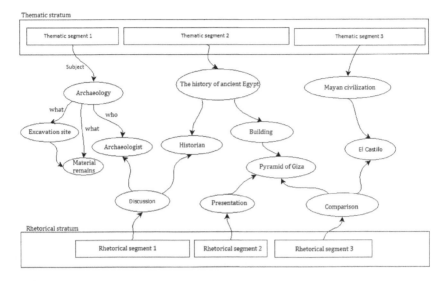

Figure 4.9. *Example of a knowledge graph for medium analysis*

The application of our graph editing solution (presented in the previous section) to the domain of medium analysis produces a system of semiotic description of audiovisual content that allows graphs like the one presented in the previous figure to be produced. The characteristics of this system are presented in detail in the following paragraphs.

4.4.1. *Model of audiovisual description*

The thematic, rhetorical, visual and sound aspects of an analysis of an audiovisual document are represented, in the annotation tool, in the form of description strata, as shown in Figure 4.10, and displayed on a timeline synchronized with a video player. A stratum is made up of several segments that temporally describe the subjects covered in a medium. The user can create/delete as many of these as desired. He can also adjust a segment's time codes to position it correctly on the timeline. These two objects (stratum, segment) can also be created automatically by an annotation tool if the corresponding restrictions demand no user choice.

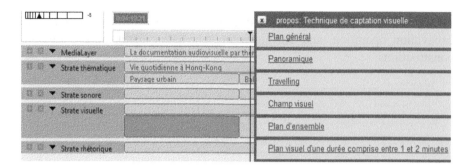

Figure 4.10. *Example of a generated visual segment map and the associated metadata*

4.4.2. *Reference works and description models*

4.4.2.1. *Modularity of the ontologies*

A semantic graph must be created under the control of an ontology describing a given domain's annotation objects and their interactions. Our annotation system is capable of managing several domain ontologies simultaneously; each of these completes and/or specializes the system's core ontology according to the specificities of the domain it describes. As such, a medium can be analyzed differently according to different domain ontologies.

From an archaeological standpoint, for example, the analysis of a medium must highlight the material remnants discovered and the scenarios envisioned around this discovery. From an academic research standpoint, however, the analysis of this same medium must emphasize the tools used and the methods adopted to successfully complete the archaeological excavation. In the scope of the Campus AAR project, several domain ontologies were tested in this system, among them:

– the description ontology from the INA archives;

– the description ontology from the *Archives de l'histoire des mathématiques* (AHM[4]);

---

4 To access the AHM portal through the HAL – CAMPUS AAR site, log in to https://hal-campusaar.archives-ouvertes.fr/

– the description ontology from the *Archives rencontre des cultures* (ARC[5]);

– the description ontology from the *Patrimoine audiovisuel de la recherche en SHS* (AGORA[6]).

4.4.2.2. Use of SKOS vocabularies

The semiotic analysis of a medium also consists of associating thesaurus terms with it to thematize and classify it. This also allows it to be searched for or even accessed (in a publication in the form of a website) by properties like the genre and the classification. In the RDF world, a thesaurus is generally represented by using the SKOS (*Simple Knowledge Organization System*) norm as being a collection of principles connected to one another by generalization (*broader*) and specialization (*narrower*) relationships. This pattern where the thesaurus terms are represented by SKOS concepts is perfectly integrated into our description system, which provides the mechanisms necessary for the search and allocation of these concepts to the media analyzed. Proprietary thesauruses like the INA's thesaurus of common nouns or even the BNF's Rameau (*Répertoire d'Autorité-Matière Encyclopédique et Alphabétique Unifié*) have been tested in this system.

Web reference works are also integrated into the description system thanks to mapping put between local ontological elements and their web matches. These links allow existing data in external databases to be exploited for the annotation of a medium. These data can be different types of named entities (person, location, work, etc.) or thesaurus terms like the Wiki categories available on the DBpedia database in the form of SKOS thesauruses.

4.4.3. Description pattern

A description pattern is a guide allowing the user to follow an annotation process. This pattern completes the description model and defines restrictions on certain elements of it. The restrictions allow the specification of the fields that

---

5 To access the ARC portal through the HAL – CAMPUS AAR site, log in to https://hal-campusaar.archives-ouvertes.fr/

6 To access the AGORA portal through the HAL – CAMPUS AAR site, log in to https://hal-campusaar.archives-ouvertes.fr/ http://www.agora.msh-paris.fr/agorafr.aspx

must be filled in by the user, as well as the specification of the range of values for each of these fields. At each step of the annotation process, the system must be able to provide the user with the right classes and individuals that are compatible with the corresponding restrictions.

In our annotation system, a description pattern is modeled in the form of an OWL2 formula where the constraints set on the properties allow the values of the fields to be restrained in the note. The annotation process can be specified with the support of recursive restrictions, e.g. "a thematic medium analysis must contain a thematic stratum, which is solely made up of thematic segments. These must describe some subjects that contain annotation objects". This pattern will be represented in the system by a tree of restrictions as explained above in section 4.3.2. The reasoning engine goes along this tree and suggests compatible instances and classes to the user at each step of the process. It is also possible to instantiate this whole annotation chain and to compare all of its elements.

The disadvantage of this representation of the model graph lies in the inability to express links between elements belonging to two distinct branches of the tree. In other words, we cannot enforce cycles in graphs defined purely in OWL2 (adding a system of rules would allow this restriction to be resolved). The creation of new classes, on the other hand, allows this obstacle to be bypassed.

4.4.4. *The management of contexts*

Descriptions in Campus AAR are articulated around two kinds of objects: *analysis procedure* and *named entity*. An analysis procedure is, for example, a thematic, rhetorical, visual and sound description performed on a medium. Each of these procedures is represented by a stratum that can itself be broken up into several time segments (for the description of the ontology, see section 4.4.2.1). A named entity, also called an individual, is a lexical entry that describes a real-world object (physical person, legal entity, location, etc.). It can be used by one or several analyses under certain conditions (restrictions). A restriction is all of the conditions of a "content" object's use (entity, stratum, segment, etc.) by a "containing" object.

In a semantic annotation system, the description of a medium is always represented by an RDF graph that compares the individuals describing this medium. An individual is an instance of a given class and is characterized by a group of properties. For example, Jacques Chirac (instance of a physical person) is identified by his first name, last name, date of birth and profession.

The notion of context is important to define the range of assertions made in a knowledge graph because, in the model presented, the different graphs are strongly interwoven due to the presence of shared nodes: the named entities. The notion of a named RDF/SPARQL graph, completely distinct from the notion of a knowledge graph, allows a knowledge graph to be very finely partitioned by specifying for each triple a fourth component taking the form of a simple URI. The triple (subject, predicate, object) becomes a quad (subject, predicate, object, graph).

An individual is always created in a named graph in which its "rdf:type" (belonging to a class) is inserted. We call this graph the individual's initial context. This can also be referenced in another graph where other properties of the individual are inserted. This graph is called context of use. For example, in a segment discussing Jacques Chirac as president, the "profession" property will have the value "President of the French Republic". In a segment where Chirac appears as mayor, on the other hand, his profession will be "Mayor of Paris". Three types of contexts are used in Campus AAR:

– the context of a segment where all information relative to this segment is inserted, e.g. the subjects dealt with in this segment;

– the context of an analysis that regroups information describing this analysis (author, date last modified, etc.);

– an individual can also have his own graph, in which case we speak of a shared named entity (see the following section).

4.4.5. *Suggestion of properties*

The graphical interface is organized in the form of a dynamic form that is automatically adapted to the entity in the course of editing. The form's fields represent the editable properties of this entity. The controls and suggestions made on each field are the result of the transformation of the axiomatic defined in this field. Figure 4.11 shows the form of an instance of the subject "Global cuisine" defined in the ARC ontology. All the properties of the instance that were already described are presented on the left; on the right, those available. The user can select certain ones to complete his form.

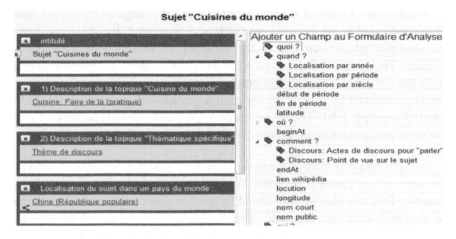

Figure 4.11. *Dynamic formula*

Editing is done hierarchically (hypertextually) where the fields that point out complex objects give access to new form sheets describing these objects. Figure 4.11 shows the form for the subject "Global cuisine". This includes a heading, the description of the topic "global cuisine", the description of the topic "specific theme" and the localization of this subject in a country of the world, which is "China". This last point is itself a complex object that gives access to a new form sheet in the "Country of the world" category.

4.4.6. *Suggestion of property values*

The objective of a model graph is to guide the user in his annotation task. This includes precise suggestions of the most appropriate ontological elements. The OWL2 restrictions are transformed into Prolog and SPARQL queries in order to find the classes of the ontology, the individuals already created in local contexts and the shared entities in the triplestore.

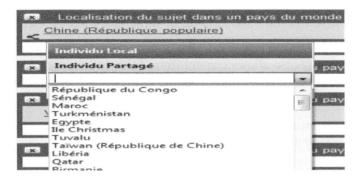

Figure 4.12. *Suggestions of named entities*

In this way, for each property of an editable entity (note, named entity, etc.), the annotation system suggests the compatible classes and individuals. In Figure 4.12, a list of countries has been suggested by the tool, as the restriction set on the property "localization" of a "subject" stipulates that the values of this property must be countries of the world.

4.4.7. *Opening on the web of data*

Manual annotation is the more reliable method to guarantee high quality data and is often adapted by businesses/institutions that worry about this quality. However, the human annotator is naturally subject to error and slightly less trivial annotations generally require expertise and familiarity with very diverse domains, otherwise the annotator can spend a considerable amount of time searching for the relevant, reliable information he needs. Historically, the annotator has searched for this information in encyclopedic books and manually completed his analysis.

With the appearance of the Web, this practice has evolved towards online research where the annotator can consult encyclopedic websites like Wikipedia. In recent years, the Web has seen significant progress in the representation and accessibility of data where information searches are done more often on better-structured knowledge bases that offer new data processing capabilities. For example:

– the interconnection and binding of these bases allows the problem of data incompleteness to be overcome;

– this binding also allows content from different origins to be connected among themselves, thereby improving the visibility and accessibility of these contents;

– the structuring and formalization in the form of semantic graphs promotes reasoning of the data.

The idea is thus to take advantage of these abilities to find and collect the data the annotator needs online; this allows him to accomplish his documentation task quickly and efficiently. The semantic annotation system that we propose here exploits the same mechanisms provided by the graph editor (presented in section 4.3.6) to access certain knowledge bases (DBpedia, Geonames, Viaf and MusicBrainz) with the goal of:

– helping the annotator in his documentation task by offering him rich, reliable information from web knowledge bases;

– annotating the audiovisual content with individuals or concepts available on the web of data to ensure the interoperability of the local knowledge base with external bases;

– connecting the local audiovisual content to external media available on the Web to improve its visibility and accessibility.

4.5. Application to the management of individuals

4.5.1. *Multi-ontology description*

An individual is an instance of a given class and is characterized by a set of properties. For example, Charles de Gaulle is an individual in the "physical person" category and is characterized by properties like his first name, last name and date of birth. An individual can have different descriptions according to the domain in which they are performed. From a political standpoint, for example, Charles de Gaulle can be presented as the person who established the Fifth Republic and was its first president, as well as the person who instituted election by universal suffrage in France. From an historic standpoint of 20th-Century military conflicts, however, he would instead be presented as a resistance fighter from the onset, the liberator of France and the person who put an end to the Algerian conflict. The system that we propose for managing individuals allows a multi-ontology description of the individuals. In this way, an individual has a minimal description common to all the domains of description performed by using the system's core ontology. However, this same individual can have different properties (and/or property values) according to different domain ontologies. All of these properties are stored in the same individual graph with no reference made to the ontologies in which they are declared. When they are displayed, however, they are filtered by the annotation system as a function of the ontology selected by the user.

4.5.2. *Faceted browsing*

The faceted browsing of individuals is the operation that aims to establish groups of individuals according to certain criteria. For example, the facet "20th Century German writers" is a group of individuals from the "physical person" category who have "writer" as their profession and who were born in the 20th Century. This type of grouping can be expressed with the support of OWL2 expressions and implemented in the system in the form of a tree of restrictions. The reasoning engine goes along this tree to extract the individuals who respond to the different constraints expressed in the restriction.

A facet is always stored in the triplestore in the form of a logical expression and has no permanent attachment to the individuals that it contains. These individuals are dynamically added and deleted as a function of the conformity of their properties to the conditions required by this facet.

4.5.3. *An individual's range*

A local individual is an instance that is created locally, at the heart of an analysis, in a given context (e.g. the context of a segment). It can be reused and enriched in other local contexts belonging to the same analysis. Different properties can thus be associated with it according to its different contexts of use.

A media individual is an instance that is created in its own graph (initial context) and can be reused in the different analyses of this medium. The initial context includes information that will be valuable for any possible use of this individual. The reuse of the individual consists of defining or adding certain properties that will only be useful in the new context of use. This individual can be searched and found by the reasoner with the help of SPARQL queries and can be deleted if it is not a reference in any other context.

The third category of individuals is that of shared entities. Like for media individuals, a shared entity has its own graph where the information able to be shared by several documents is inserted. It can be found with the help of SPARQL queries and reused (contextualized) several times to describe the different media stored in the database.

An individual can be promoted from one category to another. For example, the user can start by creating a local individual within a given segment. This individual is reused several times within the same analysis, in different segments. In the course of his documentation work, the user realizes that this individual is starting to play a central role in the medium analyzed. He then decides to promote it as a media individual so as to be able to reuse it in other analyses of the same medium. Then, by working on other documents, he realizes that this same individual from the real world is referenced in the form of doubles in other media. He then transforms his media individual into a shared entity and can thus use a single reference in the description of new documents or by recovering descriptions containing doubles.

4.6. Application to information searches

4.6.1. Semantic searches

The information retrieval solution that we propose is a semantic search that allows the sought objects to be structured, this structure to be projected onto the knowledge base and sub-graphs that match it to be produced, as shown in Figure 4.13. This structure is established with the support of the graph editor (section 4.3) in the form of an RDF graph.

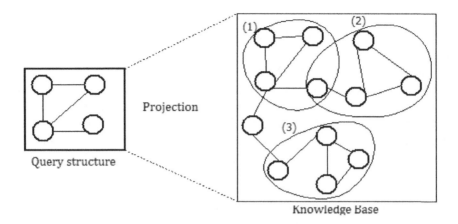

Figure 4.13. *Representation of semantic queries*

Semantic searches are always performed according to domain ontology. It allows the exploitation of RDFS/OWL2 reasoning capabilities to find objects whose descriptions do not exactly follow the precise outline of the query. Let us take the example of the following query, "Where is the Eiffel Tower?" knowing that geographic locations are connected among themselves by a single relationship: "is in". In this way, a classic information search results in the single individual that is directly tied to "the Eiffel Tower", namely, "the 7th arrondissement". A semantic search engine, on the other hand, exploits the transitivity of this relationship and deduces the entire corresponding geographic hierarchy, namely, "the 7th arrondissement", "Paris", "Île-de-France", "France" and "Europe".

In the framework of audiovisual content analysis and publication, semantic searches allow us to find:

– media, media extracts and segments to which a precise description graph has been attached;

– structuring objects like the analyses and description strata that respect a given annotation outline;

– individuals and named entities whose description responds to different constraints expressed by the semantic query graph.

4.6.2. *Transformation of SPARQL query graphs*

The semantic query graph must be transformed into a SPARQL query so as to be able to question the knowledge base. For this, each trip of this graph is transformed into a SPARQL endpoint. It is impossible, however, to express set theory operations (intersection, union, complement) on the triples of an RDF graph. To overcome this problem, the triples must be stored in three different graphs depending on the operator that ties them: the first for the intersection, the second for the complement and the third for the union of the triples. Each of these will then be transformed into a SPARQL operator (AND, UNION, NOT).

The SPARQL operations of number comparison ($>$, $>=$, $<$, $<=$) or chains of characters (regex) are implemented in the form of an ontological extension where each of these operations is represented by a new property in the ontology. This will then be transformed into a corresponding SPARQL operator.

The semantic query is stored in the triplestore in the form of an RDF graph. It can be reproduced, completed and re-executed as many times as possible. Contrary to a representation using OWL2 axioms (see section 4.6.3), an RDF representation of a semantic query allows cycles to be specified. The SPARQL operators, on the other hand, are not natively representable in RDF.

4.6.3. *Transformation of OWL2 axioms into SPARQL*

Semantic queries can also be defined in the ontology with the help of the OWL2 axiomatic. They can be:

– mandatory queries for the proper function of certain system operations like the search for a certain type of medium that responds to certain criteria;

– search operations that are often requested by the user as for instance the search for an analysis containing a certain type of stratum that itself contains a certain type of segment;

– queries responding to the description patterns allowing the objects/individuals that were defined according to these patterns to be found.

As described in section 4.3.2, an OWL2 axiomatic defines complex anonymous classes whose properties are recursively subject to several property/value restrictions. The OWL2 resolution method presented in section 4.3.3 allows the corresponding SPARQL queries to be generated. Contrary to RDF structuring, the axiomatic representation of a semantic query offers more expressivity. In fact, the different SPARQL operators are natively implemented in an OWL2 expression. However, this representation does not allow cycles to be specified.

4.6.4. Interface

The knowledge graph editing interfaces presented in section 4.3.7 are reused to edit the semantic queries. Figure 4.14 shows the graph that corresponds to the search for "all time segments in which there is a musical rendition of a song".

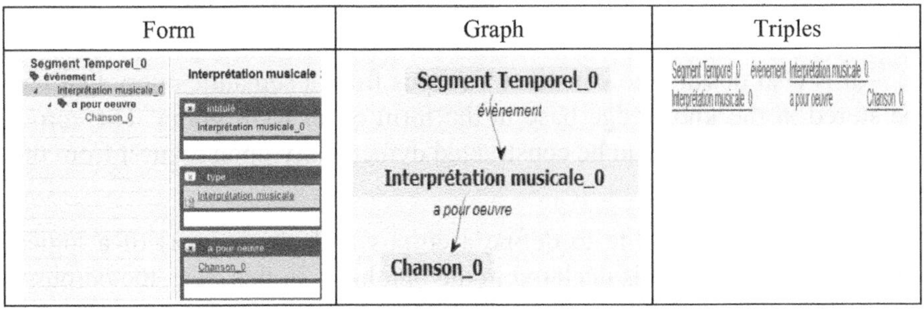

Figure 4.14. *Graph of a semantic query*

This graph is transformed into a SPARQL query and executed by the semantic search engine. Figure 4.15 shows all possible combinations (in the knowledge base) of segment, rendition and song that reproduce the query structure.

◆ Segment Temporel_0	Interprétation musicale_0	Chanson_0
Alain Barrière "Elle va chanter"	Elle va chanter	Elle va chanter
Catherine Sauvage "C'est l'ho...	C'est l'homme	C'est l'homme
Chantal Goya et Thierry Le Lu...	Une fille de Provence	Une fille de Provence
Claude François "Belles ! Bell...	Belles ! Belles ! Belles !	Belles ! Belles ! Belles !
Claude François "Chanson po...	Chanson populaire	Chanson populaire
Claude François "Comme d'h...	Comme d'habitude	Comme d'habitude
Claude François "Il fait beau, il...	Il fait beau, il fait bon	Il fait beau, il fait bon
Claude François "J'ai joué et p...	J'ai joué et puis j'ai perdu	J'ai joué et puis j'ai perdu

Figure 4.15. *Results of a semantic query*

4.7. Application to corpus management

A corpus is a mandatory object in an audiovisual content description/publication system. It allows all elements sharing certain common characteristics to be grouped. These elements can be media, media extracts, segments, individuals, etc. In a classic corpus management system, a corpus is always defined with the support of one or several queries and is stored entirely in the database. In our system, we propose several corpus construction and storage approaches:

– the basic approach consists of establishing a corpus from a semantic query and storing the corpus entirely in the triplestore as a graph;

– it is also possible to construct a corpus from a semantic query that will be stored in the knowledge base in the form of an RDF graph. The corpus will not be stored and can be constructed dynamically upon request from this query;

– finally, it is possible to define a corpus with the support of a logical OWL2 expression that is declared in the ontology. In this case, the corpus is reconstituted dynamically from this expression.

A corpus can itself be an annotation and analysis object. The properties to be informed can concern the objects that it contains or even its own relationships with other corpuses. Let us take the example of the corpus of the "best French singers of the 90s". The definition of this corpus can be made with the support of OWL2 expressions in the following way: "All musical works whose composer is of French nationality, the release date is included between 1990 and 2000, and the number of albums sold is above 1 million". Consequently, the four properties, "type of work", "composer's nationality", "song's release date" and "number of albums sold" constitute this corpus's annotation properties. It can also be connected to another corpus, e.g. through the relationship of belonging to the corpus of "songs from the 1990s". This allows, for example, the response and hierarchization of the responses to questions like, "what are the corpuses that gather songs from the last 30 years?"

A corpus can also be a publication object where its content is reused in another context to support a given thesis, explain an historic event, etc. (see section 4.7). For example, the previous corpus can be used to generate the website of the best French songs of the 90s.

Enrichment operations can also be performed on a corpus of named entities. They allow the web knowledge bases to be queried, information concerning these entities to be retrieved and these entities to be inserted into their authority notices. The enrichment approach presented in section 4.3.6 is applied to the corpuses to accomplish this task.

Statistics can also be established on a given corpus in order to help make certain annotation and/or publication decisions. For example, if the previous corpus includes a significant number of singers, then there must be access to the songs published on the website generated from this corpus.

4.8. Application to author publication

The analysis of audiovisual archives and the creation of the corresponding knowledge base aims primarily to facilitate the search of and access to this content. Once access is ensured, the content must be showcased to make it available to a large audience. The publication of this content in the form of a web portal fed by the knowledge base guarantees a rather wide diffusion. However, this content must be permanently given a new value from different angles: historic, cultural, academic, etc. There are many examples of use, of which we will cite a few:

– using the audiovisual content as a testimonial element to support a given thesis. For example, a publication about political affairs can emphasize possible relationships between certain political events by using certain video extracts to support the hypotheses set forth;

– providing academic support focused on precise issues. For example, a narrative process about World War II guiding the reader/viewer through a series of events that took place during the period of this military conflict, all illustrated by video extracts and images;

– assuring coverage of certain cultural elements. For example, the reuse of certain video extracts about the Chinese New Year to present the different facets of this event: festivity, attire, family, gastronomy, etc.

These examples demonstrate the fundamental concept allowing an institution's audiovisual archives to be given permanent life: *recontextualization*. Recontextualization (or editorialization, more commonly known as author publication) is the operation that aims to reuse audiovisual content in a context other than the one in which it was created in order to support a discourse made on a precise editorial line, called publication genre. The new content created in this way can have varying natures:

– a new video that is the result of assembling several extracts and/or images/texts;

– a website with several pages bringing together diverse annotation and editorialization resources (video, image, text);

– an article or presentation in the form of a PDF/PowerPoint file, etc.

In this article, we are interested in a single publication support: the website. The publication genre designates the general framework guiding: (1) the author in his editorialization work and (2) the process of creating a new website that must conform to the specificities of this genre. It first describes the basic elements that must be created by an author to make a new publication and later the definitive form that the assembly of these elements must take (see Figure 4.11). Between the two ends of the chain, a process of assembling and arranging the base elements of the publication takes place, which we will refer to here as the transformation engine.

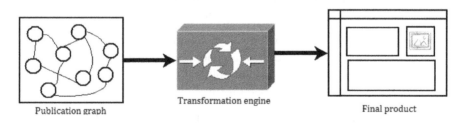

Publication graph   Transformation engine   Final product

Figure 4.16. *Simplified architecture of the transformation engine*

Dozens of publication genres are used to come up with websites. Among these are, for example:

– the lexical video (multimedia dictionary) that groups thematic base elements in the form of rubrics and articles and for each of these provides textual descriptions illustrated by video extracts and images;

– the narrative process that traces a reading path in a set of elements made up of texts, videos and images, all while assuring a narrative progression of these elements;

– the thematic file that is a multidisciplinary file organized around numerous pedagogical resources in text, image, video and sound form.

The processes earlier and later in the publication chain vary as a function of the publication genre adopted. These processes are modeled as publication ontologies that are presented in the following paragraph.

4.8.1. *Publication ontologies*

In the same manner as solutions proposed for annotating and searching for information, the publication system is also founded on concepts drawn from the semantic web. The data manipulated by the transformation engine are made up solely of knowledge. First, it receives knowledge relative to the base elements of a publication, applies behaviors to them and generates knowledge relevant to the final product (website). The specification of source and target elements for this chain is performed as:

1) a *publication ontology stricto sensu* and

2) a final product ontology.

4.8.1.1. *The publication ontology*

The publication ontology is based on the core ontology that defines the main principles of an author publication, namely:

– The topic: a generic concept that designates the central element of a publication to which audiovisual contents are added. It can be stated differently as a function of the chosen publication genre. For example, it is given as a rubric and article in the lexical video, as a sequence in the narrative process, etc.;

– The audiovisual document (content): a concept taken from the description ontology that designates all audiovisual resources able to contribute to the illustration of the topics. These can be different types of resources: text, image (whole image, part of an image), video (whole video, video extract, segment) and sound (whole, sound segment);

– The corpus: a concept also taken from the description ontology that designates all possible groupings of audiovisual documents (see the previous section);

– The rhetorical relationships that can be used in any publication genre to propose a rhetorical exploration of the topics.

The publication ontology always depends on the publication genre and extends the underlying core ontology by defining elements that are particular to it. For example, the lexical video's ontology extends the class "topic" to define two subclasses: "rubric" and "article". The knowledge graph editor presented in section 4.3 is used by the author to create publication graphs in accordance with this ontology. These define and compare the base elements (topics, resources, corpuses, rhetorical relationships) of a given publication.

4.8.1.2. *The hypermedia product's ontology*

In the same line of thinking, a final product ontology (or website ontology) always depends on a publication genre and a core ontology that defines the structure of a web page and the graphical components able to be used in creating it. A web page is recursively divided, into several display areas, each of which contains a graphical component. This can be a standard HTML5 component like the video player, a freely accessible online widget like Google Maps, or even a simple textbox. The final product ontology extends the core ontology by defining a structuration of the page particular to the corresponding publication genre.

This structuration can be considered as the web page's model graph and defined in two different ways:

– as a partially instanced graph that designates and positions the display areas before composing the web page. For example, the banner area must be located at the top of the page, followed vertically by the main menu area. The area below this menu must be horizontally composed of two areas: to the left, the vertical menu; to the right, the player.

– with the help of OWL2 expressions, which defines restrictions on the areas constituting a web page.

The transformation engine analyzes the publication graph, applies behaviors to its elements and generates the website's graph in accordance with the final product ontology. This graph formalizes the structure of each page to be created and the graphic components to be displayed.

4.8.1.3. *The publication's configuration*

In order to personalize the use of rules and give the author a chance to define the website structure that he desires, we have made it possible to configure these rules. The author can thus personalize the different components of the web page by activating and deactivating certain properties. These components may be: the main menu for access functionality, the left menu for contextual access, the links to the named entities, etc. These configuration options are defined as an ontological extension of the publication ontologies that allow certain properties to be annotated. Figure 4.17 shows the detailed architecture of the publication system that we propose.

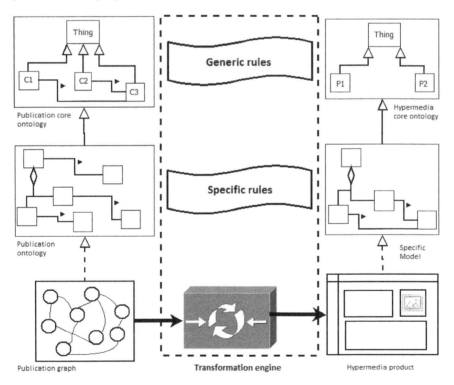

Figure 4.17. *General architecture of the publication system*

4.8.2. *Transformation engine*

The transformation engine is the process allowing the publication graph to be transformed. It transforms the elements of a publication into the form of a final product graph specifying the graphic components of a web page as well as their spatial–temporal arrangement. The Campus AAR engine is implemented as a forward-chaining RDF inference rule engine that explores the solution space and proceeds, for each rule, in the following way:

– identifying the publication elements likely to be concerned by these rules by verifying their conformity to the rule's premises;

– once identified, applying the behaviors defined in this rule to them.

The premises of a rule define the conditions it requires for a publication element to be concerned by the behavior(s) it defines. These conditions generally concern certain properties of publication elements. In order to ensure the generic nature of these rules, their premises must target the properties declared in the core publication ontology or one of its configuration extensions.

The behaviors applied to the publication elements presenting properties that conform to the premises of a rule can be:

– the creation of a virtual page according to the web page model defined in the ontology;

– the creation of a virtual graphic component (textbox, image, player, timeline, map, menu) for each of these elements;

– the grouping of these elements to create a new entity, called publication block. This formalizes the content of a complex graphic component like, for example, the assembly of several video extracts along with a descriptive text;

– inter-block behavior that formalizes the interactions between the elements in the same block. For example, in the case of video assembly, it must determine the order in which the concerned video extracts will appear;

– intra-block behavior that specifies the spatial–temporal placement of each block in relation to the others (line and column number on the page) as well as the links between them (following, preceding, see also, etc.).

All of the construction decisions for the resulting website are made at this stage, which benefits from the abstraction and inference capabilities of the languages used.

4.8.3. *Final product*

The final product graph generated by the transformation engine undergoes one last XSLT transformation to generate the true HTML5 pages with Javascript code and corresponding style sheets.

A web page is represented as an HTML5 table where each box represents a display area and can contain:

– either an HTML5 component (player, list, etc.) or a graphical widget available online (Google Maps, Timeline, etc.);

– or another HTML5 table if this area must contain several components/ graphical widgets.

This organization in the form of HTML5 tables allows the graphic components to be positioned spatially by indicating their line and column numbers in the table. The temporal positioning is ensured either by the player in the case of an arrangement of several videos/images or by the specific components implemented in HTML5/Javascript in the case of more complex display elements.

Components available online have also been integrated in this platform. Among these are: Google Maps, Timeline.js and Dynatable.js. It is also possible to connect the publication to other components by adapting the XSLT transformation's output format.

4.8.4. *Opening on the web of data*

The publication of audiovisual content essentially depends on the annotation metadata created during the analysis (description) phase. These metadata can be incomplete or not necessarily respond to the needs of an author in terms of the data type that he would like to put online. The exploitation of data available on the knowledge bases of the LOD (Linked Open Data) can lead to a response pertaining to this need. The publication system that we propose is capable of:

– searching for named entities on external knowledge bases like DBpedia, Geonames, VIAF and MusicBrainz. The same procedure presented in section 4.6 is used to accomplish this task;

– recovering the properties an author needs from a named entity, e.g. the first name, last name, date of birth and date of death for a physical person. These properties are declared in a pivot ontology that compares the classes and properties of the local ontology with their matches in the distant ontology;

– enriching the publication graph with information retrieved from the web of data;

– integrating this information in the transformation process to generate enriched web pages.

4.8.5. Graphical Interface

The knowledge graph editing interfaces presented in section 4.3.7 are reused to edit the publication graph, as shown in Figure 4.18.

The first column of this table shows an audiovisual corpus publication graph from the INA's archives. The publication engine applies transformation rules to this corpus and generates the corresponding website. The table's second column shows the web page of the segment in which Julio Iglesias and Sheila sing the song "Vaya con Dios mi vida". This page is made up of the extract of the performance, its summary and links to the entities present in this extract (rendition, singer, director/producer).

Publication graph editing form	A web page generated by the publication motor
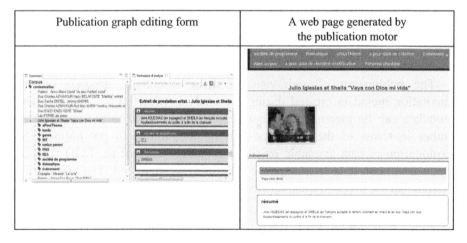	

Figure 4.18. *Publication graph and web page*

4.9. Conclusion

In this article, we have presented a solution for the creation of RDF knowledge graphs subject to the OWL2 axiomatic. This solution is oriented towards documenting and publishing audiovisual documents where the incompleteness of data is a central problem. Different algorithms have been presented to respond to the underlying problem of creating well-formed, incomplete graphs, the storage of these graphs in their simplified form and their reclassification with regards to editing.

The Campus AAR platform promotes this notion of knowledge graphs in the set of resources it manipulates: content descriptions, knowledge bases, queries and author publication. It proposes a complementary set of editing interfaces taking advantage of property and property value suggestion algorithms to guide the annotator/author's work.

Ontology construction also represents a promising application for the solution proposed in this article. In fact, an ontology can itself be considered a knowledge graph that follows the RDFS/OWL pattern and whose editing concerns two levels of description. The first level concerns the abstraction of real-world objects and their representation as classes and properties that are instances of certain RDFS/OWL resources (*Class*, *Property*, *subClassOf*, *subPropertyOf*, etc.). The second level concerns the OWL2 expressions for representing model graphs.

The information retrieval solution that we propose in this article is based on the transformation of an RDF graph and/or an OWL2 expression into a SPARQL query. We also foresee the instrumentation of facets (section 4.5.2) for data exploration. In fact, the combination of several facets allows the data to be grouped differently according to various criteria. These groupings allow the solution space to be explored efficiently and the user to be guided towards relevant solutions.

In the world of Web data (*Linked Open Data*), a search engine must be able to query several knowledge bases to overcome the problem of data incompleteness. Two approaches can be foreseen to accomplish this task. The first was implemented in our platform for searching for named entities on online knowledge bases (section 4.3.6). It consists of sending the same semantic query to several knowledge bases. The results sent back will then be fused and presented to the user. The second approach consists of distributing the same semantic query to several knowledge bases. This distribution can be performed following criteria relative to data incompleteness. It allows a local search for weakly informed data to be completed through the search for lacking information on external bases.

4.10. Bibliography

[BEL 15] BELOUED A., LALANDE S., STOCKINGER P., "Modélisation et formalisation RDFS/OWL d'une ontologie de description audiovisuelle", *Les Cahiers du Numérique*, vol. 11/3, pp. 39–70, 2015.

[CHE 09] CHEIN M., MUGNIER M.L., *Graph-based Knowledge Representation and Reasoning: Computational Foundations of Conceptual Graphs*, Springer, 2009.

[GLI 10] GLIMM B., HORROCKS I., MOTIK B., "Optimising ontology classification", in PATEL-SCHNEIDER P.F, PAN Y., HITZLER P. *et al.* (eds), *Proceedings of the 9th International Semantic Web Conf. (ISWC 2010)*, pp. 225–240, Shanghai, China, 7–11 November 2010.

[HAA 04] HAARSLEV V., MÖLLER R., WESSEL M., "Querying the semantic web with Racer + nRQL", *Proceedings of the KI-2004 International Workshop on Applications of Description Logics (ADL 04)*, 2004.

[KIR 10] KIRYAKOV A., BISHOP B., OGNYANOFF D. *et al.*, "The features of bigowlim that enabled the BBC's world cup website", in KRUMMENACHER R., ABERER K., KIRYAKOV A. (eds), *Proceedings of Workshop of Semantic Data Management (SemData@VLDB2010, Singapore)*, 2010.

[KUR 12] KURZ T., SCHAFFERT S., GÜNTNER G. *et al.*, "Adding wings to red bull media: search and display semantically enhanced video fragments", *Proceedings of the 21st International Conference Companion on World Wide Web*, Lyon, France, pp. 373–376, 2012.

[LAL 09] LALANDE S., STAYKOVA K., CHEIN M. *et al.*, "Using domain knowledge to speed up the annotation of digital content with Conceptual Graphs", *Bulgarian Academy of Sciences, Cybernetics and Information Technologies*, vol. 9, no. 3, Sofia 2009.

[SIR 05] SIRIN E., PARSIA B., GRAU B. *et al.*, "Pellet: a practical OWL-DL reasoner", *Tech. Rep. CS 4766*, University of Maryland, College Park, 2005.

[STO 03] STOCKINGER P. *Le document audiovisuel*, Paris, Hermes Science-Lavoisier, 2003.

[STO 11a] STOCKINGER P. (ed.), *Digital Audiovisual Archives*, ISTE, London and John Wiley & Sons, New York, 2011.

[STO 11b] STOCKINGER P. (ed.), *Introduction to Audiovisual Archives*, ISTE, London and John Wiley & Sons, New York, 2011.

[STO 12] STOCKINGER, P., *Audiovisual Archives*, ISTE, London and John Wiley & Sons, New York, 2012.

[STO 15a] STOCKINGER P., LALANDE S., BELOUED A., "Le tournant sémiotique dans les archives audiovisuelles: Vision globale et éléments conceptuels de mise en œuvre", *Les Cahiers du Numérique*, vol. 11/3, pp. 11–37, 2015.

[STO 15b] STOCKINGER P., "The semiotic turn in digital archives and libraries", *Les Cahiers du Numérique,* no. 1, p. 4, 2015.

5

Digital Libraries and Crowdsourcing: A Review

Cataloguing, indexing and correcting the OCR of digitized documents, libraries have often externalized certain activities to service providers with recourse to a low-price workforce in developing countries like Madagascar, India, or Vietnam. From now on, though, they could instead call on the masses of Internet users, that is, crowdsourcing, to realize tasks their own staff cannot handle.

The development of crowdsourcing in libraries is particularly important in the domain of OCR correction. In fact, character recognition software that converts photos of digitized book pages into texts do not provide 100% reliable results and, depending on the quality of the original document, its digitization, its typography and the possible presence of handwritten notes, it may be necessary to correct the texts produced with the help of dictionaries. OCR correction is necessary to enable more efficient whole-text searches of the digitized texts, better referencing of the contents by search engines, the production of eBook in EPUB or MOBI formats so they can be read on eReaders, data extraction through text mining technologies, or even scientific exploitations related to culturomics[1].

Chapter written by Mathieu ANDRO and Imad SALEH.
1 Culturomics could be defined as the quantitative analysis of culture through large volumes of digitized texts.

This question of recourse to crowdsourcing is being asked more and more today of libraries, from the very largest of them to the very smallest. In order to bring them part of the solution and bring about an original conceptual contribution to crowdsourcing in libraries, we have written this state of the art, which comes from thesis work.

It will offer conceptual elements to understand this phenomenon, a taxonomy and panorama of the initiatives, and analyses from library and information science points of view.

5.1. The concept of crowdsourcing in libraries

5.1.1. *Definition of crowdsourcing*

Crowdsourcing literally means outsourcing to Internet users, according to Jeff Howe's expression proposed in Wired Magazine in June 2006 [HOW 06]. According to an authoritative definition:

> "Crowdsourcing is a type of participative online activity in which an individual, organization or company with enough means proposes to a group of individuals of varying knowledge, heterogeneity, and number, via a flexible open call, the voluntary undertaking of a task. The undertaking of the task, of variable complexity and modularity, entails mutual benefit. The user will receive the satisfaction of a given type of need, be it economic, social recognition, self-esteem, or the development of individual skills, while the crowdsourcer will obtain and utilize to their advantage that what the user has brought to the venture, whose form will depend on the type of activity undertaken." [EST 12]

Contrary to these authors, we think crowdsourcing can also exist as participation that is not necessarily and strictly voluntary, as is the case with projects where Internet users contribute by playing games, which are qualified as gamification. We even think crowdsourcing can also call on the involuntary or unconscious participation of Internet users, as is the case, for example, with the reCAPTCHA project. The millions of books digitized by Google Books are OCRized. Words not occurring in dictionaries are then sent to Internet users who, for security reasons, are forced to reassemble jumbled words to prove that they are not robots. In doing this, by creating their accounts on websites, they involuntarily contribute to OCR correction for Google Books and Google Maps. We qualify this involuntary participation of Internet users as implicit crowdsourcing.

Having defined crowdsourcing, all that remains is to explain what it is not. Crowdsourcing must not be confused with outsourcing, for there is indeed a sort of call for bids in the form of a call for contributions; the relationship with the contributor, however, is not contractual. It also must not be confused with "user innovation", as the undertaking remains at the project's initiative, not with the open source since the contribution method is not necessarily collaborative, but can, quite the opposite, appeal to competition.

5.1.2. *Historic origins of crowdsourcing*

This economic model finds its source in:

– government appeals to the people to solve scientific problems for recompense starting in the 18th Century;

– competitions and public offerings;

– free service and free access that allowed the consumer to take over part of the producer's work, then the "on-demand" model that allowed him to take over the production decision itself.

Below, we propose a chronology of the historic origins of crowdsourcing and citizen science. This chronology is the result of analyses done on the literature on this subject. It was created using a collection of the most important events at the core of crowdsourcing (call for participation, recompense, collective work, microtasks, outsourcing, wisdom of crowds). The events assembled here are also the most representative of the taxonomy that we propose later in the chapter.

1714	The English government launches a call for scientists to find a solution to determine maritime longitude from a boat. John Harrison, a carpenter and clockmaker, wins the 20,000 pound reward over more than 100 competitors, including Cassini, Huygens, Halley and Newton
1726	A ruling by the King of France, Louis XV, requests that ship captains bring plants and seeds back from foreign countries that they visit
1750	British astronomer Nevil Maskelyne calculates the position of the moon for navigation at sea, thanks to the calculations of two astronomers who made their calculations twice each, and then were verified by a third
1758	Mathematician Alexis Clairaut manages to calculate the orbit of Halley's comet by dividing the calculation tasks among three astronomers
1794	French engineer Gaspard de Prony organizes addition and subtraction microtasks for 24 unemployed barbers in order to develop detailed logarithmic and trigonometric tables
1810	With his new methods of food preservation that will lead to canned food, Nicolas Appert receives 12,000 francs from the French government after a call for contributions
1852	The store *"Le Bon Marché"* is the first self-service store. From then on, consumers directly access merchandise without going through the intermediary of a merchant and thus take on part of the producer's work
1857	After a call for volunteer contributions, the Oxford English Dictionary benefits from more than 6 million documents containing word proposals and citations of use
1884	The Statue of Liberty is financed by public donations
1893	During a competition on the livestock market to guess the weight of the cow, Francis Galton notices that the average of a crowd's estimates is closer to the truth than experts' estimates, implying the existence of the "wisdom of crowds"
1900	The National Audubon Society (USA and Canada) organizes a "Christmas bird count"
1895	Librarian James Duff Brown invents free access in libraries. Readers of the Clerkenwell Public Library from then on have direct access to part of the collections
Early 19th Century	In the field of editing, public offerings multiply to finance the publication of books
1936	Toyota gathers 27,000 people and chooses the best proposed design for its brand logo
1938	In the United States, the Mathematical Tables Project employs 450 out-of-work victims of the economic depression, led by a group of mathematicians and physicists, to tabulate mathematical functions, long before the invention of the computer

In the 1950s	A Toyota industrial engineer, Taiichi Ōno, invents the "just-in-time" model, predecessor of the "on-demand" model, which would allow production without reserves or unsold articles, just-in-time manufacturing as a function of demand. In a way, it is a matter of outsourcing the production decision itself to the consumer. This model is at the root of on-demand digitization through crowdfunding and on-demand printing
1954	The first telethon in the United States allows fundraising to fight cerebral palsy
1955	The Sydney Opera House is designed and built after a public competition that encouraged ordinary people from 32 countries to contribute to this design project
1979	The Zagat survey (restaurant guide) bases its ratings on a large number of testers. The project was purchased by Google in September 2011
1981	The 3rd edition of the Lonely Planet travel guide is written through the participation of independent travelers
1996	Birth of the Internet Archive
1997	*Le livre à la carte*: facsimile reproduction of books kept in libraries (on-demand digitization and printing)
1997	Rock band Marillion finances its US tour, thanks to fan donations amounting to $60,000
1998	The Dmoz directory offers content generated by its users. Web 2.0 is born
2000	Philanthropic crowdfunding platform justgiving.com and the participatory artist financing platform artistshare.com see the light of day. They are followed by multiple initiatives until today
2000	Distributed Proofreader: first participatory book transcription project
2001	Birth of Wikipedia
2003	ESP Game: a game for image indexing
2005	Amazon launches the crowdsourcing platform Amazon Mechanical Turk Marketplace for its own needs and also allows coordination of research societies and institutions and workers on the Web for microtasks
2006	Espresso Book Machine for *in situ* on-demand printing
2006	Jeff Howe proposes the term "crowdsourcing" in Wired Magazine in June 2006
2007	Google Books uses reCAPTACHA to have its untreated OCR corrected by Internet users
2008	The gamification project Fold.it allows advances to be made in the knowledge of proteins, thanks to puzzle games
2011	The Good Judgement Project makes use of Internet users' wisdom of crowds through their geopolitical expectations, which rival those of intelligence experts
2011	Digitalkoot for OCR correction in the form of arcade games
2013	The video game Star Citizen raises $30,044,586

Table 5.1. *Chronology of crowdsourcing in libraries*

5.1.3. *Conceptual origins of crowdsourcing*

Crowdsourcing finds its conceptual origin in diametrically opposed ideologies such as socialism, libertarianism, humanism or liberalism [AND 14a], where the Californian Ideology would accomplish the most propitious synthesis for the development of crowdsourcing.

Socialist and Marxist ideologies	"From each according to his ability, to each according to his needs" production and abolition of the law of value, money is no longer the main motive, free products, spirit of sacrifice, work to serve humanity, socialist emulation, abolition of the fundamental separation of necessary labor and surplus labor, reconsideration of wage labor and social classes, each person able to be employer or employee in turn, overcoming private property through shared use, "collaborative communities", participatory, peer-to-peer contribution economy
Libertarian and anarchist ideologies	Critical of the authority of the dominating classes and totalitarianism, direct democracy, equal contribution from the hobbyist and the expert, disappearance of the boundary between producers and consumers, work becomes leisure, weisure (work + leisure) or playbor (play + labor)
Humanism	Digital humanities, Internet rehumanization and restitution of humans from a central place on the Web as origin and end, trust in man's abilities superior to those of algorithms, altruism and love of neighbor, concern for the weaker in the face of the strong
Liberalism	Outsourcing, integration of the consumer in production, meritocracy, increase in individual freedoms, defense of the freedom of expression, spirit of initiative and enterprise, "fun at work", universalism, internationalism, democracy, invisible hand, spontaneous order (Friedrich Hayek) of Wikipedia, which works through the autonomous action of individuals with no planning, trust in the market, self-employment, reconsideration of monopolies, "uberization"
Californian Ideology: Libertarian liberal philosophy, libertarian philosophy of hippie meritocratic entrepreneurs and philosophy of "digerati" (digital literati)	

Table 5.2. *The conceptual origins of crowdsourcing*

5.1.4. *Critiques of crowdsourcing. Towards the uberization of libraries?*

Crowdsourcing applied to libraries could also be considered a form of library uberization. Uberization could be defined as challenging established societies and professions through the emergence of web platforms allowing non-professionals to offer competing services. In the library domain, it could take the form of replacing the professional, authoritative data producer with a volunteer working for free or even an underpaid worker producing low-quality data outside any legal framework [FOR 11]. This exploitation of the invisible work of the Web's proletariat is sometimes considered "servuction". It is accused of unfair competition by traditional service providers. It would bring about disengagement on the part of workers, like those who employ this interchangeable workforce. It would create impersonal relations and fraud.

As a result, some thinkers, like Bernard Stiegler, talk about creating a "contributory revenue" [STI 15]; others speak of taxing data to return to citizens part of the value that they have created through their invisible data production work; and others discuss making data produced by the common goods.

As for libraries, they sometimes remain too focused on the constitution of collections as a means in and of itself rather than on satisfying the needs of readers. Before mass digitization, they enjoyed a sort of monopoly on access to information, and their administration, forming a corporation with a relative ideological homogeneity, benefited from prestigious titles of curators. Under these conditions, outsourcing expert work to hobbyists, opening up to the private as a renewed public/private partnership, risks being seen as questioning, losing control, disloyal competition, an attack against social benefits and, finally, an uberization of libraries.

The question of the quality of contributions, the costs connected with monitoring the quality, the individual appropriation of the collective heritage by uneducated laypeople, and the possible malevolence of Internet users will thus be pointed out against crowdsourcing projects that will not be able to develop without significant change initiatives.

5.2. Taxonomy and panorama of crowdsourcing in libraries

Most of the actors establish a typology of crowdsourcing projects as a function of the public's degree of engagement. In this way, with participatory or contributory crowdsourcing, Internet users are happy to produce data for institutions that come up with projects, pilot their development and frame the public's participation, which remains limited to microtasks only requiring a small individual investment. With collaborative crowdsourcing, Internet users can also interact with one another. Through co-creation, this individual investment is even stronger, as Internet users can actively weigh in on the policy and definition of projects' goals and premises, and sometimes even be the source of the projects themselves.

Beyond this quantitative distinction, we were led to propose a more qualitative taxonomy of crowdsourcing projects in libraries. We distinguish among the following large types (Table 5.3).

Explicit crowdsourcing	Definition	Identified projects
Volunteer crowdsourcing	Recourse to voluntary work from voluntary Internet users	*Participatory uploading and curation*: Oxford's great war archive, Europeana 1914–1918, Internet Archive, Commons Wikimedia, Wir waren so frei, Open Call – Brooklyn Museum, Pin-a-tale, Make history, Click! A Crowd-Curated Exhibition, The Changing Faces of Brooklyn, ExtravaSCANza. *Participatory OCR correction*: TROVE, Distributed Proofreader, Wikisource, California Digital Newspaper Collection, Correct, Franscriptor. *Participatory manuscript transcription*: Transcribe Bentham, What's on the Menu?, Ancient lives, ArcHIVE, What's the score, Transkribus, les Herbonautes, Do it yourself History, Monasterium Collaborative Archive, Citizen Archivist Dashboard, National Archives Transcription Pilot Project, Field Notes of Laurence M. Klauber, Notes from Nature, Transcribe Bushman, Smithsonian Digital Volunteers Transcription Center. *Folksonomy*: Flickr, The Commons, steve.museum, GLAM Wikimedia, Glashelder!, VeleHanden, 1001 Stories Denmark, Historical Maps Pilot, Mtagger, PennTags, Social OAC, Describe me, Tag! You're It!, Freeze tag!, Your Paintings Tagger, Operation war diary.
Paid crowdsourcing	Recourse to the work of paid Internet users	*All kinds of work*: Amazon Mechanical Turk Marketplace, 99design, CloudCrowd, Cloud-Flower, CrowdFlower, Upwork, Foule Factory, Freelancer, Guru, Innocentive, ManPower, Mob4hire, MobileWorks, oDesk, Postmates, quora.com, Samacource, sparked.com, TaskRabbit, Topcoder, Trada, Turkit, uTest.

Implicit crowdsourcing and gamification	Definition	Identified projects
Implicit crowdsourcing	Recourse to involuntary work by Internet users	*OCR correction*: reCAPTCHA.
Gamification "human computation" "games with a purpose"	Recourse to Internet users' work in game form	*OCT correction*: Digitalkoot, COoperative eNgine for Correction of ExtRacted Text, TypeAttack, Word Soup Game, Smorball, Beabstalk. *Indexing*: Art Collector, Google Image Labeler, ESP Game, GWAP, Peekaboom, KissKissBan, PexAce, museumgam.es, Metadata Games, SaveMyHeritage, Picaguess, Wasida.
Crowdfunding	Recourse to Internet users' financial contributions	*On-demand digitization*: eBook on demand (EOD), books à la carte, Éditions du Phoenix, Chapitre.com, les amis de la BnF, Numalire, revealdigital, Lyrasis, FeniXX, unglue.it, Maine Shared Collections Strategy, International Amateur Scanning League, "Sauvez nos reliures". *On-demand printing*: Espresso Book Machine, Electronic Library, Higher Education Resources ON Demand, Amazon Book Surge, CreateSpace, Jouve, lulu.com, Lightning source, Virtual Bookworm, Wingspan press, iUniverse, Xlibris.

Table 5.3. *Taxonomy of crowdsourcing and panorama of the projects for digital libraries*

All of these forms of crowdsourcing shown synthetically and introductorily in the above tables are the object of an analysis developed in the section that follows and returns to this taxonomy's structuration.

5.2.1. *Explicit crowdsourcing*

5.2.1.1. *Volunteer crowdsourcing*

This is the most obvious and classic form of crowdsourcing, but recourse to volunteers could quickly reach its limits faced with the proliferation of projects. Furthermore, nothing indicates that future generations of pensioners, who are sometimes a significant portion of contributors, will have the same interests.

Modification de Page:Faulon - De la névrotomie plantaire.djvu/21

Figure 5.1. *Page from an old thesis saved at the National Veterinary School of Toulouse for which OCR correction is proposed (via Wikisource)*

5.2.1.2. *Paid crowdsourcing*

The primary users of the largest paid crowdsourcing platform, Amazon Mechanical Turk Marketplace, are American research laboratories. This platform brings together those offering and those seeking online work, generally in the form of microtasks. With it, crowds of workers worthy of the largest multinationals, with diverse profiles, among more than 500,000 Internet users permanently available in nearly 200 countries, particularly the USA and India, are to be recruited in a few minutes time, without administrative procedures, at costs freely determined by supply and demand [IPE 10]. It thus allows the realization of jobs that would have required years of thankless work before, done by "burn outs", in half a day. As for the workers on the platform, they are free to work where they want, when they want, as much as they want, for whom they want, based on their own interests, to be employer and employee in turn, and to work for a client rather than a boss.

The name "Amazon Mechanical Turk Marketplace" is cleverly inspired by an automatic chess player thought up in the 18th Century that was supposedly gifted with artificial intelligence when, in fact, a human was hidden behind it. In the same way, behind the results that are believed to be done by powerful algorithms, there may, in fact, be crowds of hidden humans, particularly through paid crowdsourcing.

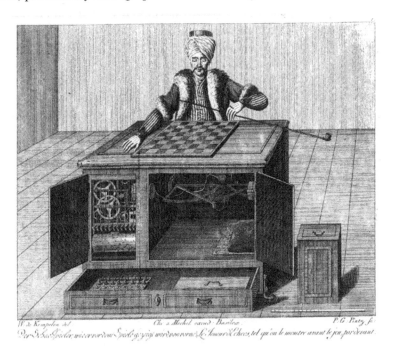

Figure 5.2. *"Türkischer Schachspieler" by Karl Gottlieb von Windisch. 1783. Public domain via Wikimedia Commons*

5.2.2. Gamification and implicit crowdsourcing

The contributor's will is not necessarily the primary goal for participants in these forms of crowdsourcing. They call on Internet users' desire to play to receive work from them (gamification) or make them work without their knowing it (implicit crowdsourcing).

5.2.2.1. Gamification

Gamification consists of making Internet users work through games with a useful and productive end ("games with a purpose"). It could be defined as the act of applying design, psychology and videogame elements in other contexts [DET 11].

The simple act of giving points for Internet users' participation therefore must not be confused with gamification, but rather results in a sort of "pointification". Gamification is also different from "serious games" because it does not aim to educate for personal development, but rather to achieve goals outside oneself like correcting OCR or indexing digitized photographs [AND 15b].

Unlike explicit crowdsourcing, doing randomly performed, out-of-context microtasks in a game is generally less favorable to personal development and the acquisition of knowledge, but it could allow work that is sometimes rather thankless to be done more easily.

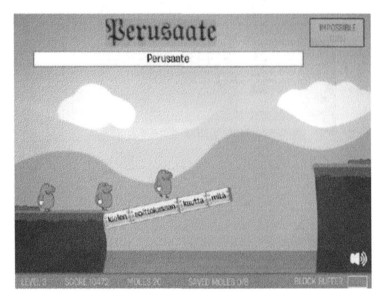

Figure 5.3. *Screenshot of the Digitalkoot OCR correction game [CHR 11]*

5.2.2.2. *Implicit crowdsourcing*

The notion of implicit crowdsourcing was conceptualized by [HAR 13], but the term is still not very widespread in the literature. The Internet users who participate do it involuntarily or unconsciously. Implicit crowdsourcing could thus be considered less ethical than explicit, voluntary crowdsourcing by unpaid workers on the Web, an intrusion of eCommerce seeking to instrumentalize Internet users.

The most emblematic project of this kind of crowdsourcing in the domain of digital libraries is reCAPTCHA. In order to create an account on a website and avoid any attack by robots, the websites require Internet users to reassemble jumbled words, thereby proving that they are not malicious bots. The programs Google Books and Google Maps have thus cleverly used this system to have untreated OCR from their campaigns of digitization by masses of Internet users corrected by comparing their input. Thus, 200 million words would be compared each day, 12,000 h of volunteer work collected and, according to our calculations, 146 million euros per year saved by Google through text correction services [AND 15a].

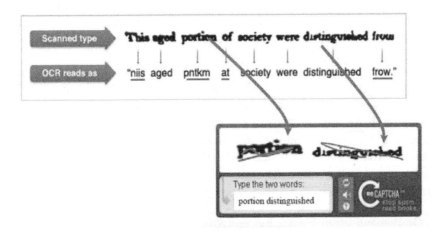

Figure 5.4. *Diagram explaining how reCAPTCHA works according to https://www.google.com/recaptcha*

5.2.3. *Crowdfunding*

Sometimes considered institutional begging [AYR 13], crowdfunding is indeed a form of crowdsourcing that calls not on the work of Internet users, but on their financial resources. In libraries, it can be used to acquire documents or to finance digitization.

5.2.3.1. *On-demand digitization*

On-demand digitization allows libraries to offer digital reproduction services by having Internet users support the costs, outsourcing part of the costly, thankless task of selecting documents that still deserve to be digitized and obviously completing their digitization programs. The user thus finds himself placed at the center of library policy [GST 11], whereas in the past, libraries sometimes tended to neglect them by principally focusing on their collections. The documentary policy of the digital library thereby becomes a co-construction between the librarians and the general public since the acquisition policy is from then on shared. For Internet users, on-demand digitization gives them access to a digital reproduction service. For potential patrons and investors, on-demand digitization could be the chance to finance the digitization of books that may interest such and such audience, and eventually to collect a return on investments through web traffic created by these books on the advertisement model Google Adwords.

This economic model could allow public funds, which have become more rare, to be concentrated on the digitization of documents with patrimonial, historic and scientific interest but not interesting private sector and allow private funds from individuals or patrons to finance the digitization of works interesting the general public or communities of scholars. In doing this, libraries would have a chance to better refocus on their own areas of expertise and better value the skills of curators in the patrimonial, historic and scientific domain.

On-demand digitization by crowdfunding is a new form of public subscription allowing new life to be given to a work. It is particularly well adapted to the current situation, where only leftovers still need to be digitized after large mass-digitization programs pass through.

The main difficulty of on-demand digitization projects consists of automatically evaluating the costs of document digitization. In fact, it is claimed that for these projects, a cost estimate is necessary for each demand. This estimate serves to evaluate the cost of digitization. Producing this estimate requires verifying the presence of the document, its state, its actual page count, its format and how wide it opens, all of which will determine how many pages must be digitized and the type of scanner to be used, thus the cost of digitization. Unfortunately, after the Internet user receives the estimate, he only very rarely proceeds with his demand through an order, as his desire to purchase has been surpassed and he may be surprised by the cost to be paid. At the end of the day, the time spent producing estimates costs as much as the money collected from Internet users, and in the absence of an automatic calculation for digitization costs or a subsidy through public funds, on-demand digitization projects are hardly ever viable [AND 14b].

5.2.3.2. On-demand printing and libraries

Although it is not a matter of crowdsourcing, the economic model is identical to that of on-demand digitization, from which is it often indistinguishable. Here we are dealing with the revival of a print through the digitized document. This model, more and more often used in publishing to produce just in time, without reserves or unsold articles, has been applied to library digitization programs [AND 15c].

As we have seen with on-demand digitization, the documentary policy of digital libraries and the constitution of digital collections are henceforth more of a co-construction; furthermore, they are henceforth partly the work of Internet users. With on-demand printing, we could even go so far as to imagine a physical library directly made up of prints demanded by its readers, printed in a few minutes through an Espresso Book Machine and, after being returned by the reader, constituting a collection built by the user and made up of works having all been consulted at least once [LEW 10]. This way of functioning would be radically different from the acquisition of libraries, which currently depends essentially on the anticipation of needs and the purchase of books in case they one day interest a reader, a policy that is thus not exclusively focused on the user. In this way, it extends the possibility already offered by libraries to their readers to suggest acquisitions.

Espresso Book Machine®
A Xerox® Solution
Overview

Figure 5.5. *The Espresso Book Machine*
according to http://ondemandbooks.com

Beyond this taxonomy, there are forms of crowdsourcing that have probably not yet been invented, such as gamification paid according to the results obtained through playing, the resource to citizens, possibly paid, for themselves digitizing documents within libraries, or even the application of a reCAPTCHA benefitting public libraries or a reCAPTCHA charging for the OCR corrected and sharing its profits with the sites that accepted to implement it.

5.3. Analyses of crowdsourcing in libraries from an information and communication perspective

5.3.1. *Why do libraries have recourse to crowdsourcing and what are the necessary conditions?*

Clay Shirky thought that if Americans spent their time on projects like Wikipedia instead of watching television, they could create 2,000 projects on the same scale as the famous participatory encyclopedia [SHI 08]. As for

Luis Von Ahn, he claimed that the 425 million images on Google Images could have been indexed in just 31 days by 5,000 Internet users playing the ESP Game [VON 08]. Whatever it is, there would be a significant reserve of good will that libraries could benefit from, especially as they already have experience in motivating communities, the setting of these good wills; they have a good image with the public to whom they seem worthy of trust and they seem to serve general interests and whom they could, consequently, more easily recruit.

They could therefore have recourse to crowdsourcing, that is to outsourcing microtasks to masses of Internet users to reduce their costs or to multiply their human resources and realize a painstaking, tedious task that they do not have the means to take on, or even to complete, undertake, or make possible projects that until now were unachievable, impossible or even unimaginable [HOL 10]. By taking advantage of the collaboration of Internet users, libraries could benefit from limitless knowledge and skills, far beyond that of their limited teams, even despite the excellent general education of their directors. Crowdsourcing therefore challenges the borders of the organization, as it allows value to be created beyond its borders [REN 14]. Libraries could thus tap into the greater strength lying beyond their organizations and recruit such and such scholar or specialist to identify a location or person in a photograph, recognize a book cover, date an object in a curio cabinet, etc. Libraries could thus get engaged in a participatory redocumentarization process and see their collections revisited and reinvented. Beyond these incentives, libraries could also seek to deeply engage the user in their collections, to democratize heritage conservation in the form of an "empowerment", an emancipation, and a change in relations between heritage and society in the name of a right to information and participation, to improve their image, to seek to innovate or, unfortunately, also to start institutional communication around a trendy subject.

Although it is absolutely possible to talk about an authentic use of data produced by users, there seem to be two different conceptions in libraries. One thinks that libraries need Internet users, while the other thinks that Internet users need libraries. The first is utilitarian and economical. It humbly recognizes its need for reinforcements and is truly seeking to produce a result, thanks to collaboration between heritage and society. The second is more strongly tied to democratic considerations and seeks instead to practice crowdsourcing for the sake of practicing crowdsourcing, publicizing the process and increasing public participation as an end in itself.

While this second conception holds sway, the work produced by Internet users is barely valued or used and the metadata that they seize will only rarely be integrated into library information systems, which may discourage and be seen as a betrayal by volunteers, as we will see in a later chapter.

Whatever the case may be, libraries will only be able to get engaged in the crowdsourcing path under the condition that the tasks concerned can be performed online as microtasks, that they do not involve confidential data, that they can be undertaken independently and requiring little interaction, education and communication, and, finally, that they can be accomplished by non-specialized amateurs.

There is a growing interest for crowdsourcing in libraries in the world literature, as illustrated in Figure 5.6.

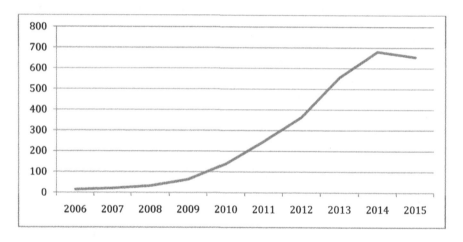

Figure 5.6. *Number of publications indexed in Google Scholar as a function of their years of publication and responding to the search "crowdsourcing AND library AND digitization"*

Despite this growing interest in the literature, a relatively weak interest in the subject has been seen in France, such that the bibliography of 216 publications created as part of a thesis on the subject by authors in this field contains only seven articles with at least one French author, as shown in Figure 5.7.

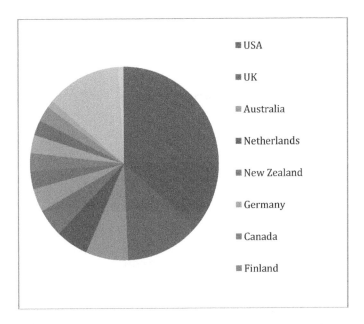

Figure 5.7. *Relative influence of different countries in the thesis bibliography (216 publications). For a color version of the figure, see www.iste.co.uk/szoniecky/collective.zip*

Moreover, a state-of-the-art from the OCLC forming a definitive work on the subject and indexing the crowdsourcing projects in libraries [SMI 11a, SMI 11b] never mentions France in 350 pages, and we would have to wait until February 2013 for the first study on the subject to be published in France [MOI 13], in the scope of a project by the National Library of France.

5.3.2. *Why do Internet users contribute? Taxonomy of Internet users' motivations*

Among the many motivations that lead Internet users to contribute to crowdsourcing projects in libraries are mainly seen as intrinsic motivations pushing the individual to act selflessly and for the pure joy that the work brings him and the extrinsic motivations pushing him to work for the effects and results obtained, thanks to this work, like recognition, recompense or remuneration. We have identified and organized the motivations shown in Figure 5.8 from the literature.

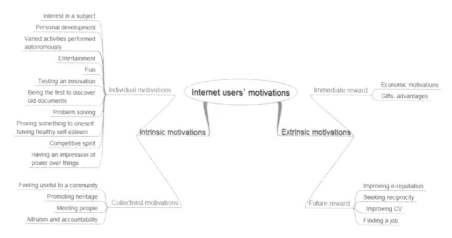

Figure 5.8. *Taxonomy of the motivations of Internet users*
who participate in crowdsourcing projects in libraries

The kinds of motivations can be very diverse as a function of the types of crowdsourcing types of individuals and cultures, so if volunteer crowdsourcing encourages Internet users to seek personal development, gamification is rather appealing to the need for useful entertainment. The emergence of extrinsic motivations and particularly symbolic recompense, real or virtual, can sometimes take place to the detriment of the quality of data produced and of intrinsic values, that is, those that lead them to act out of pure interest in the job itself. Starting in 1975, an experiment by Edward L. Deci showed that if people were remunerated for doing puzzles, they lost all interest in these activities if they no longer saw rewards for doing it.

5.3.3. *From symbolic recompense to concrete remuneration*

As the preceding concept map of motivations shows, crowdsourcing projects are necessarily carried out for the mutual benefit of the institution and the Internet user. In addition to the intrinsic movements, the rewards can range from symbolic rewards (ranking, grades, medals) to very real rewards, from gifts even to remuneration. As such, volunteers with the Foldit project were publicly thanked in an article in the celebrated academic journal *Natural Structural & Molecular Biology* (vol. 18, 2011) for having made the discovery of a very important enzyme's structure possible. Other volunteers with other projects were mentioned in newsletters and invited to talk about their work at conferences, and they were rewarded training courses, subscriptions, books, t-shirts, MP3 players, gift certificates, tours or trips.

5.3.4. *Communication for recruiting contributors*

Cultural institutions benefit from a good public image and seem worthy of trust and to serve public interests. As a result, they have solid advantages for recruiting volunteers. Among the communication means used for crowdsourcing projects, we could mention campaigns in the associative, local, national and trade press, the publication of articles and posters, the distribution of leaflets, putting up stickers and posters particularly for conferences and symposia, the organization of public meetings or specific events, and radio and television presence, but also the production of videos, the use of social networks, forums, mailing lists, direct mail campaigns, institutional websites, and, finally, the purchase of specific words in the Google Adwords campaign.

A crowdsourcing site must always have a homepage that describes the project simply and clearly explains its end goal and progress, and immediately invites volunteer participation by showing them how their participation will be useful and how they will be guided and recognized [MCK 15].

5.3.5. *Community management for keeping contributors*

The majority of the data produced in the framework of crowdsourcing projects has been produced by a well-determined minority of participants and not by anonymous masses.

As seen in the previous diagram where each square corresponds to the contributions of a single person and where the size of each square is proportionate to quantity of contributions, all volunteer crowdsourcing projects also show us that the largest part of contributions is the result of a minority and that it is thus not really a matter of anonymous crowds, but rather of a well-defined community of volunteers [OWE 13]. Under these conditions, it would therefore be more judicious to speak of communitysourcing [CAU 12] or even nichesourcing and to seek to recruit well-targeted people rather than addressing faceless crowds.

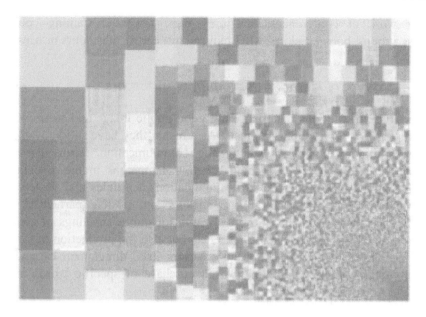

Figure 5.9. *A few Internet users produce the largest part of contributions (according to Brumfield's blog manuscripttranscription.blogspot.fr in 2013)*

If the standard profile of a volunteer is a college-educated man with a high level of studies, in an elevated socio-professional category and having just finished his studies or who is retired, the communities of contributors also include more diverse profiles and form communities of pairs having similarities and common goals whose dynamism must be maintained by community management. In fact, the volunteers will have to be recruited by communication acts, supervised, managed, supported by hotlines, helpdesks, forums, educated with manuals, tutorials, motivated, regularly updated, their contributions moderated, their quality controlled, the participation statistics followed, and, finally, the produced data reintegrated.

5.3.6. *The quality and reintegration of produced data*

The issue of quality and vandalism is a central argument of opponents of outsourcing data production to amateur Internet users. There are, however, many proven ways to guarantee one and prevent the other using robots, self-regulation, inspection by professionals or volunteers, evaluations, votes, aptitude tests, or even double-keying.

Whatever the case may be, there are numerous studies that show that data produced by those who consult a digitized document online can be of the highest quality, as the person consulting the document is generally someone who knows the subject covered in the consulted document well. Furthermore, as expected by followers of the "wisdom of crowds", the diversity of profiles constituted by a crowd of Internet users and the "law of large numbers" would have the effect of neutralizing individual errors in the mass of accurate data [BOE 12] and sometimes even providing better results than those obtained by experts. This seems to be confirmed by several comparative studies [ROR 10, OOM 11].

However, the data produced by Internet users are not always reintegrated by institutions sometimes aiming more towards democratization of heritage or even institutional communication on a trendy subject than real Internet user participation. When they are reused, these data born of free, volunteer contributions should always be distributed under legal conditions authorizing the largest possible reuse.

5.3.7. *The evaluation of crowdsourcing projects*

Although it has proven difficult to collect figures in the literature except for [CAU 12], it seems that crowdsourcing projects are far from all being profitable in the sense that the profits in harvested data are not always on the level of the costs for project management, platform development, administration, maintenance, hosting, communication, community management and reintegration of produced data.

In a previous study [AND 15a], we had estimated that the California Digital Newspaper Collection project gathered more than 1,500 € of OCR correction work per month, the Digitalkoot project more than 2,000 € per month, the TROVE project nearly 35,000 € per month and the reCAPTCHA more than 12 million euros per month.

The projects that seem to work the best are those that have clear end goals, lead an efficient communication campaign, and have managed and motivated communities at their disposal. Those that fail generally call on overly complex tasks, overly specialized knowledge requiring too great an investment in training, do not communicate sufficiently with the volunteers [RID 13], and sometimes neglected internal change management.

5.4. Conclusions on collective intelligence and the wisdom of crowds

If we average the individual estimates of a crowd concerning the weight of a cow, the number of marbles in a jar, the temperature in a room or the response to a general culture question on a game show like "Who Wants To Be A Millionaire?", it will become clear that this average is closer to the truth. This phenomenon was identified long ago as "*vox populi vox dei*" and was well-understood by Machiavelli, who wrote:

> "I say that the people are more prudent and stable, and have better judgment than a prince; and it is not without good reason that it is said 'the voice of the people is the voice of God'; for we see popular opinion prognosticate events in such a wonderful manner that it would almost seem as if the people had some occult virtue, which enables them to foresee the good and the evil. As to the people's capacity of judging things, it is exceedingly rare that, when they hear two orators of equal talents advocate different measures, they do not decide in favor of the best of the two, which proves their ability to discern the truth of what they hear." [MAC 37]

Today, this phenomenon is known as the "wisdom of crowds" [SUR 04]. Many crowdsourcing projects rely on this phenomenon to obtain quality data or sometimes even true expertise. As such, an American intelligence agency, the "Good Judgment Project", relies on the geopolitical forecasts of crowds of Internet users quantitatively estimating the probability or improbability of such and such event. In the same way, big data and the analysis of geographic locations occurring alongside the name "Bin Laden" in the international press using text-mining technologies has shown that those locations were near where he was hiding. When data form crowds, they could therefore also form science, and thanks to crowdsourcing, human brains could be connected like high-powered processors contributing to a calculation much more massive than that of algorithms. We could thus speak of "human computation" [VON 06].

However, in history, crowds are not always distinguished by their wisdom, but sometimes rather by the criminal irresponsibility of the individuals making up the masses, as Gustave Le Bon brought up in his *The Crowd: A Study of the Popular Mind*, particularly in light of the events tied to terror in the French Revolution, and this long before the totalitarian experiences of the 20th Century. On the Web today, while the madness of the masses does not have the same breadth, the rumors, conspiracy theories and collective paranoia sometimes also seem to disprove the existence of any wisdom of the crowds.

But beyond the simple production of data, recourse to crowds of amateurs with diverse profiles not seeking to reproduce the established models with which professionals have been educated can also be a source of happy coincidences (serendipity), "unexpected readers", accidental discoveries or even innovative breakthroughs. In any case, it encourages the development of an ecosystem of innovation. Thus, according to Eric Von Hippel, the "user innovation" theorist, 46% of American companies in innovating sectors find their origins in a simple do-it-yourself consumer [VON 05].

5.5. Bibliography

[AND 14a] ANDRO M., SALEH I., "Bibliothèques numériques et crowdsourcing: une synthèse de la littérature académique et professionnelle internationale sur le sujet", in ZREIK D.K., AZEMARD G., CHAUDIRON S. *et al.* (eds), *Livre post-numérique: historique, mutations et perspectives. Actes du 17e colloque international sur le document électronique (CiDE.17)*, Fès, Morocco, p, 152, 2014.

[AND 14b] ANDRO M., RIVIÈRE P., DUPUY-OLIVIER A. *et al.*, "Numalire, une expérimentation de numérisation à la demande du patrimoine conservé par les bibliothèques sous la forme de financements participatifs (crowdfunding)", *Bulletin des Bibliothèques de France*, 2014.

[AND 15a] ANDRO M., SALEH I., "La correction participative de l'OCR par crowdsourcing au profit des bibliothèques numériques", *Bulletin des Bibliothèques de France*, 2015.

[AND 15b] ANDRO M., SALEH I., "Bibliothèques numériques et gamification: panorama et état de l'art", *I2D – Information, données & documents*, vol. 52, no.4, pp. 70–79, 2015.

[AND 15c] ANDRO M., KLOPP S., "L'impression à la demande et les bibliothèques", *Bulletin des Bibliothèques de France*, 2015.

[AYR 13] AYRES, M.-L., "Singing for their supper: Trove, Australian newspapers, and the crowd", *IFLA World Library and Information Congress*, Singapore, 2013.

[BOE 12] BŒUF G., ALLAIN Y.-M., BOUVIER M., "L'apport des sciences participatives dans la connaissance de la bioviversité", Report, French Ministry of Ecology, 2012.

[CAU 12] CAUSER T., WALLACE V., "Building a volunteer community: results and findings from transcribe bentham", *Digital Humanities Quarterly*, vol. 6, no. 2, 26 p., 2012.

[CHR 11] CHRONS O., SUNDELL S., "Digitalkoot: making old archives accessible using crowdsourcing", *HCOMP 2011: 3rd Human Computation Workshop*, San Francisco, 2011.

[DET 11] DETERDING S., DIXON D., KHALED R. *et al.*, "Gamification: toward a definition", *ACM CHI Gamification Workshop*, New York, 2011.

[EST 12] ESTELLÉS-AROLAS E., GONZALEZ-LADRON-DE-GUEVARA F., "Towards an integrated crowdsourcing definition", *Journal of Information Science*, vol. 38, no. 2, 2012.

[FOR 11] FORT K., ADDA G., COHEN K.B., "Amazon mechanical Turk: gold mine or coal mine? ", *Computational Linguistics*, vol. 37, no. 2, pp. 413–420, 2011.

[GST 11] GSTREIN S., MÜHLBERGER G., "Producing eBooks on demand: a European library network", *IFLA Journal*, vol. 35, pp. 35–43, 2011.

[HAR 13] HARRIS C.G., Applying human computation methods to information science, PhD dissertation, University of Iowa, 2013.

[HOL 10] HOLLEY R., "Crowdsourcing: how and why should libraries do it?", *D-Lib Magazine*, vol. 16, nos 3–4, available at: http://www.dlib.org/dlib/march10/holley/03holley.html, 2010.

[HOW 06] HOWE J., "The rise of crowdsourcing", *Wired*, available at: www.wired.com/2006/06/crowds/, 6 January, 2006.

[IPE 10] IPEIROTIS P.G., "Demographics of mechanical Turk", NYU Working Paper, 2010.

[LEW 10] LEWIS D.W., "The user-driven purchase giveaway library", *Educause Review*, vol. 45, no. 5, pp. 10–11, 2010.

[MAC 37] MACHIAVEL N., *Œuvres complètes*, vol. 1, Auguste Desrez, Paris, 1837.

[MCK 15] MCKINLEY D., Heuristics to support the design and evaluation of websites for crowdsourcing the processing of cultural heritage assets, PhD Report, 2015.

[MOI 13] MOIREZ P., MOREUX J.P., JOSSE I., "Etat de l'art en matière de crowdsourcing dans les bibliothèques numériques", Livrable L-4.3.1 du projet de R&D du FUI 12 pour la conception d'une plateforme collaborative de correction et d'enrichissement des documents numérisés, 2013.

[OOM 11] OOMEN J., AROYO L., "Crowdsourcing in the cultural heritage domain: opportunities and challenges", *5th International Conference on Communities & Technologies*, Brisbane, Australia, pp. 138–149, June–July 2011.

[OWE 13] OWENS T., "Digital cultural heritage and the crowd", *Curator: The Museum Journal*, vol. 56, pp. 121–130, 2013.

[REN 14] RENAULT S., "Crowdsourcing : La nébuleuse des frontières de l'organisation et du travail", *RIMHE: Revue Interdisciplinaire Management, Homme(s) & Entreprise*, no. 11, pp. 23–40, 2014.

[RID 13] RIDGE M., "From tagging to theorizing: deepening engagement with cultural heritage through crowdsourcing", *Curator: The Museum Journal*, vol. 56, no. 4, pp. 435–450, 2013.

[ROR 10] RORISSA A., "A comparative study of Flickr tags and index terms in a general image collection", *Journal of the American Society for Information Science and Technology*, vol. 61, no. 11, pp. 2230–2242, 2010.

[SHI 08] SHIRKY C., *Here Comes Everybody: The Power of Organizing without Organizations*, Penguin Books, London, 2008.

[SMI 11a] SMITH-YOSHIMURA K., SHEIN C., Social Metadata for Libraries, Archives and Museums Part 1: Site Reviews, *OCLC Research*, 2011.

[SMI 11b] SMITH-YOSHIMURA K., GODBY C.J., HOFFLER H. *et al.*, "Social metadata for libraries, archives, and museums: survey analysis", *OCLC Research*, 2011.

[SMI 12a] SMITH-YOSHIMURA K., "Social metadata for libraries, archives, and museums: executive summary", *OCLC Research*, p. 20, 2012.

[SMI 12b] SMITH-YOSHIMURA K. HOLLEY R., "Social metadata for libraries, archives, and museums: recommendations and readings", *OCLC Research*, p. 78, 2012.

[STI 15] STIEGLER B., *La société automatique. 1, l'avenir du travail*, Fayard, Paris, 2015.

[SUR 04] SUROWIECKI J., *La sagesse des foules*, J.-C. Lattès, Paris, 2004.

[VON 06] VON AHN L., "Games with a purpose", *IEEE Computer Magazine*, vol. 39, no. 6, pp. 96–98, 2006.

[VON 08] VON AHN L., DABBISH L., "Designing games with a purpose", *Communications of the ACM*, vol. 51, no. 8, pp. 58–67, 2008.

[VON 05] VON HIPPEL E., *Democratizing Innovation*, MIT Press, Cambridge, 2005.

6

Conservation and Promotion of Cultural Heritage in the Context of the Semantic Web

6.1. Introduction

Cultural heritage can be defined as the expression of the ways of life developed by a community and passed down from generation to generation, including traditions, practices, places, objects, artistic expressions and values [ICO 05]. Cultural heritage is characterized by two categories: the first is material cultural heritage, including movable cultural heritage (paintings, sculptures, coins, manuscripts, etc.), immovable cultural heritage (monuments, archaeological sites, etc.) and submarine cultural heritage (shipwrecks, underwater ruins and cities, etc.). The second category refers to immaterial cultural heritage (oral traditions, performing arts, rituals, etc.) [UNE 15].

Modeling knowledge in a cultural heritage domain is multidisciplinary and requires recourse to experts from both the computer domain and the domain in question [BOU 10]. Furthermore, there are several knowledge resources and models that should be considered to guarantee a high level of interoperability with other information systems in the domain.

Chapter written by Ashraf AMAD and Nasreddine BOUHAÏ.

In this chapter, we will present several knowledge resources, common difficulties and the possible solutions that we have studied in the literature, or propose in the scope of our research.

These solutions can be considered by cultural heritage documentation and promotion projects in the context of the semantic web. Several elements will be used to illustrate the ideas presented. To start with, we will present necessary theoretical elements before going into the problems and possible solutions.

6.2. The knowledge resources and models relative to cultural heritage

In this section, we present the different knowledge resources to consider when developing a solution of cultural heritage documentation and promotion.

6.2.1. *Metadata norms*

A metadata norm is a metadata schema made up of a set of properties and vocabularies developed by specific communities (libraries, archives, museums, editors, etc.) and used to describe the data in order to resolve specific problems like the structuring and exchange of data [DOE 06].

Metadata norms, however, are generally thought up for general descriptions; they are not intended to describe the semantic richness of the domain. The use of these metadata elements is useful for indexing and to achieve better interoperability between systems [ZAB 12].

6.2.1.1. *Dublin Core*

Dublin Core is a metadata schema based on 15 essential properties to describe online and physical resources [WEL 10]. The 15 elements are *contributor, coverage, creator, date, description, format, identifier, language, publisher, relation, rights, source, subject, title* and *type*.

The use of these elements can be combined with the DMCI Type vocabulary to designate the possible type of a resource, such as text, sound and image. Other vocabularies can be used as well, like DDC[1], LCC[2], LCSH[3], MESH[4], TGN[5], and UDC[6].

There are also qualified elements of Dublin Core that refine the 15 base elements, like *hasPart* and *hasVersion*, which refine the *relation* property. In the same way, the *created* and *modified* properties refine the *date* property.

Furthermore, the Dublin Core schema defines a certain number of classes that are used with the Dublin Core properties. For example, the property *medium* (material) associates the class *PhysicalResource* with the class *PhysicalMedium* to document the material observed in a physical resource.

In the following example (Figure 6.1), Dublin Core is used to add metadata on the Mona Lisa. As we can see, Dublin Core elements do not give rich, precise semantics. For example, the *<dc.title>* element is used to add the titles, but without any additional information on these titles. Moreover, the *<dc:creator>* element does not distinguish between the creator of the physical painting and the creator of the digital resources that represent the painting.

With dates, too, we cannot know the real meaning of the *<dc:date>* element, because we can imagine several dates, such as:

– the production date;

– the completion date;

– the date of acquisition by a museum.

Even when we use Dublin Core's qualified elements, we still need richer semantics, particularly for a domain as complex as cultural heritage.

---

1 Dewey Decimal Classification.
2 Library of Congress Classification.
3 Library of Congress Subject Headings.
4 Medical Subject Headings.
5 Thesaurus of Geographic Names.
6 Universal Decimal Classification.

```
<dc:title> Mona Lisa </dc:title>
<dc:title> Joconde </dc:title>
<dc:creator> Leonardo da Vinci </dc:creator>
<dc:creator> Portail des Collections des Musées de Franc </dc:creator>
<dc:creator> Louvre Museum </dc:creator>
<dc:subject> Mona Lisa, woman, half-length, seated, etc. </dc:subject>
<dc:description> Portrait of Lisa Gheradini </dc:description>
<dc:description> Wife of Francesco del Giocondo </dc:description>
<dc:publisher> Portail des Collections des Musées de France </dc:publisher>
<dc:contributor> Portail des Collections des Musées de France </dc:contributor>
<dc:date> 1503 </dc:date>
<dc:date> 1517 </dc:date>
<dc:date> 1797 </dc:date>
```

Figure 6.1. *An example of Dublin Core elements*

6.2.1.2. *LIDO*

In the museum domain, LIDO[7] is a metadata norm based on XML[8] and used to facilitate the harvesting of data on museum objects. LIDO is optimized for metadata exchange between museum institutions and data aggregators [MER 12].

The data providers who use LIDO as an exchange format and who conform to the OAI-PMH[9] protocol are compatible with the metadata aggregator Europeana, as the metadata model used by Europeana, called EDM[10], is compatible with LIDO [EUR 13].

For example, by using LIDO, we can describe the Mona Lisa with a type compatible with Europeana, as illustrated in Figure 6.2.

```
▼<lido:classification lido:type="europeana:type">
    <lido:term>IMAGE</lido:term>
  </lido:classification>
```

Figure 6.2. *LIDO use with Europeana elements*

---

7 Lightweight Information Describing Objects.
8 Extensible Markup Language.
9 Open Archives Initiative – Protocol for Metadata Harvesting.
10 Europeana Data Model.

LIDO is capable of providing descriptive metadata on several aspects of a museum object, including its classification, identification, measurements, history, condition, documentation, digital representations, etc. Moreover, LIDO provides administrative metadata on the objects and collections in a museum. Different types of museums can use LIDO, including museums of art, architecture, natural history, etc. Figure 6.3 presents an example of using LIDO to describe the painter of the Mona Lisa.

```
▼<lido:actor lido:type="person">
    <lido:actorID lido:source="Bildindex-KUE-Datei"
  ▶<lido:nameActorSet>...</lido:nameActorSet>
  ▼<lido:nationalityActor>
      <lido:term>Italy</lido:term>
    </lido:nationalityActor>
  ▶<lido:vitalDatesActor>...</lido:vitalDatesActor>
    <lido:genderActor>male</lido:genderActor>
  </lido:actor>
```

Figure 6.3. *An example of LIDO use*

6.2.1.3. *MODS*

In the domain of libraries, MODS[11] is an XML metadata schema developed by the Library of Congress and used to describe the data in libraries. MODS provides metadata descriptions richer than the Dublin Core norm and less complicated than the old MARC 21[12] format from the library domain since the use of XML markers makes it readable for humans and machines [BIZ 09]. MODS is, however, highly compatible with MARC 21. Moreover, MODS is more compatible for library use than the ONIX[13] schema used by institutions in the book industry, like Amazon.

6.2.1.4. *EAD*

In the archive domain, EAD[14] is a metadata norm based on XML and developed by the Society of American Archivists, and which is maintained by the Library of Congress in the United States. The main goal of this schema is to improve accessibility to archive documents by improving the

---

11 Metadata Object Description Schema.
12 MAchine Readable Cataloguing.
13 ONline Information eXchange.
14 Encoded Archival Description.

indexing and organization of these documents. This is very useful for the standardization of the archive description process [ZER 11].

This schema's elements are capable of describing collections and the documents they contain. At the collection level, we can document the title, the main subject, the documents included, etc. At the individual archive level, we can document the content, property rights, location on the shelves, etc.

6.2.1.5. EDM

EDM[15] is a schema used by Europeana for metadata harvesting. Its primary objective is to unify descriptions originating from various metadata providers to make data accessible on the Europeana website independently of the metadata schema used by the provider. The metadata sources for Europeana are essentially museums, libraries and archives [AKK 11]. EDM, a generic schema with a high level of abstraction, can be used by several users to deposit their data on Europeana. EDM is compatible with multilingual and intercultural metadata.

Certain conception principles of EDM [EUR 13]:

– a distinction must always be made between the real object (painting, book, movie) and its digital representation;

– an object can have several documentations, including contradictory declarations (which is important for documenting the different historic perspectives and arguments on the same object);

– the schema is generic to allow the specialization of the semantics;

– controlled vocabulary terms can be used, which is important for the enrichment of the data and the improvement of the contextual information.

Europeana is capable of describing metadata using two different approaches. These approaches are:

– the object-oriented approach: it focuses on the described object by creating a direct link to its characteristics. For example, Dublin Core uses this approach to create direct links between the object and its metadata. Europeana allows contextual information to be added for an object by using this approach combined with certain classes like *edm:Place, edm:Agent, edm:TimeSpan*;

---

15 Europeana Data Model.

– the event-oriented approach: it focuses on the events in which the object was implied and generates richer semantics than the object-oriented approach because it focuses on the history of the object and not on the object itself. Europeana uses the class *edm:Event* for this task. There are other models that use this approach, such as the CIDOC CRM[16] ontology that we will present below.

The choice between the two approaches depends on various factors, such as the nature of the data, the domain, the expected use, the relative semantic aspects and the level of detail in the semantic representation. Whichever approach is used, there are three main classes used by Europeana

Class	Description
ProvidedCHO	The heritage object itself (painting, manuscript, etc.) and not its representation
WebResource	A digital resource that represents the object
Aggregation	An aggregation that represents the provider's activity

Table 6.1. *The three main classes used by Europeana*

Furthermore, in the following table, we present some important relationships defined by the EDM schema.

Element	Use
edm:aggregatedCHO	To designate the heritage object with a unique URL
edm:hasView	To connect a physical object with its representation on the Web, such as a photo
edm:dataProvider	To designate the metadata provider
edm:hasType	To designate a resource's type using a classification system
edm:proxy	To accept different views on the same resource. Each edm:proxy can contain different metadata provided by a specific provider
edm:isRelatedTo	To connect two resources that are related in a certain way

Table 6.2. *Some important relationships defined by the EDM schema*

---

16 *Comité International pour la DOCumentation*/Conceptual Reference Model.

With the previous example of the Mona Lisa, it is possible to use the EDM model for harvesting metadata on the Mona Lisa, as illustrated in the following figure [EUR 13].

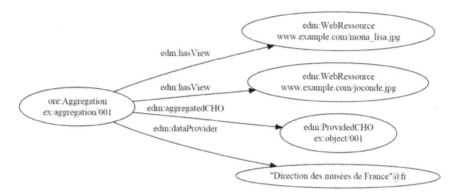

Figure 6.4. *An example of using the EDM model*

We can observe that Europeana provides general properties and classes in order to contain the semantics issued from different schemata used by the metadata providers. Moreover, Europeana enriches the data by using certain thesauri to include more information on the metadata harvested and the concepts used. The terms in these thesauri are themselves connected to other resources like Wikipedia articles, which creates a rich semantic network. It is recommended that metadata users employ the most precise classes and properties to provide refined semantics. It is necessary, however, for the providers to create semantics between their schemata and Europeana's. For example, a provider identified by the namespace "ex" could add the following triplet to connect to Europeana's EDM model.

Figure 6.5. *The creation of semantic links between the local schema and Europeana*

6.2.2. *Controlled vocabularies*

The domain vocabulary includes the terms that are representative of the domain. These terms can be structured in a knowledge organization system like a thesaurus. Knowledge organization systems (KOS) are mechanisms used to organize the terminological knowledge in a certain field in a structured way by using certain relationships like hierarchy and equivalence (synonymy) [ISE 14]. These systems are used to control the various identities of a resource like the preferred name and alternative names to improve information accessibility and management. Another utility is the improvement of searching and navigation in the system, even when the user has no preliminary knowledge of the field. It is impossible for a single KOS to contain all terms in the field. Consequently, several systems are generally used.

SKOS[17] is a model recommended by the W3C[18] intended to organize knowledge by using certain elements like *skos:Concept* to describe a concept, *skos:broader* to confirm that one concept is more general than another, and *skos:narrower* to affirm that one concept is more precise than another. SKOS is frequently used on the semantic web to facilitate the publication and use of different knowledge organization systems like lists of subject headings, term thesauri and authority records [MIL 09].

Subject headings serve to describe the content and subjects of a book, document, manuscript, etc. These subjects are developed by experts in the field. For example, RAMEAU[19] is a directory of subject authorities developed by the DBMIST[20] and used by the BNF[21] to describe and index its collections [DIA 15]. An example of its subjects:

– French songs – 19th Century – Subjects, motifs;

– opera – Germany – 19th Century;

– religious music – France – 17th Century – History and criticism.

---

17 Simple Knowledge Organization System.
18 The World Wide Web Consortium.
19 *Répertoire d'autorité-matière encyclopédique et alphabétique unifié.*
20 *Direction des bibliothèques, des musées et de l'information scientifique et technique.*
21 *Bibliothèque Nationale de France.*

Another example of a list of subject headings is the Iconclass[22], which is specialized in the subject headings of art and iconography [ISE 14]. Regarding the thesauri of terms, they include specific terms in particular fields, and can be used for tasks that go beyond subject headings. Each term can be made up of one or more words. Among the controlled vocabularies in the heritage domain are the Getty vocabularies, the English Heritage vocabulary and the GEMET[23]. Furthermore, the authority records are used to control the names of entities like places and people to avoid errors and confusion arising when an entity has several names [STY 06].

6.2.3. *Lexical databases*

We will take Wordnet as an example of lexical databases because it is frequently used in natural language treatment (NLT) applications to perform certain tasks like text annotation, lexical disambiguation, text analysis, information extraction, semantic indexing, automatic classification, etc. [NEZ 14]. This lexical database has evolved over the course of its history and, currently, the most recent version is 3.1, available online and visually navigable. Wordnet is a thesaurus and a dictionary [IAN 03]. This database is organized like a tree and divided into three sub-databases as a function of the grammatical category, including Wordnet nouns, Wordnet verbs and Wordnet for adjectives and adverbs. Wordnet is made up of a set of meanings or concepts where each concept is represented by terms (synonyms). The concept with the representative synonyms is called a "synset". There are several semantic relationships with a lexical nature between the synsets, like, for example, synonymy, antonymy (opposing sense), hypernym (more precise meaning), etc. The semantic relationships between the synsets differ according to the grammatical category; however, the nodes originating from different grammatical categories are connected using the "*derivationally related form*" functionality. Wordnet provides a textual description for each concept containing a definition and certain examples.

6.2.4. *Ontologies*

One of the frequently cited definitions of ontology is "a formal specification of a shard conceptualization" [BOR 97]. Ontologies are explicit

---

22 http://www.iconclass.nl/home
23 General Multilingual Environmental Thesaurus.

in their conceptualizations and they provide the concepts and semantic relationships necessary for modeling knowledge in a specific domain. The relationships between the ontology's concepts are much richer than in a thesaurus because they go beyond the hierarchical nature. It is important, however, for this conceptualization to be shared by the community in a specific domain. Ontologies can be categorized according to their level of abstraction [JAR 05]. For example, there are superior ontologies and domain ontologies. Superior ontologies describe general concepts that are similar in all domains. An essential role of superior ontologies is to support semantic interoperability between diverse information systems in several domains, as they provide a very high semantic mediator at the level of conceptualization. Among these ontologies are SUMO[24] and CYC[25]. A domain ontology, on the other hand, provides a description of the concepts and properties specific to the domain. These ontologies serve to describe the knowledge of the domain in question in a pertinent way.

In the domain of cultural heritage, CIDOC CRM is a domain ontology that provides high-level classes and relationships, but ones oriented towards the heritage domain [NUS 07]. This ontology provides a chance to describe the rich knowledge that naturally exists in this domain, and it plays the role of a semantic mediator between the different sources of information in the different sub-domains of cultural heritage (museums, libraries, archives). This is an important advantage for realizing the semantic integration of heterogeneous information in the domain [CRO 11]. The current version of the ontology (Version 6.0.4)[26] is made up of 90 classes and 149 relationships explained by descriptions and illustrated with examples. This ontology offers a very large potential for describing the semantic aspects in the domain but with an elevated level of conceptual representation due to the fact that the classes and the relationships used in this ontology have a high level of abstraction, which allows this ontology to be specialized according to the sub-domain and the application.

---

24 Suggested Upper Merged Ontology.
25 The name "CYC" is derived from "enCYClopedia".
26 http://www.cidoc-crm.org/html/5.0.4/cidoc-crm.html

When two applications extend the CIDOC CRM ontology, they will be connected by the CIDOC CRM classes, and integration between their data becomes possible [BOU 10]. CIDOC CRM is developed by museum, library and archive experts as well as computer science and philosophy experts. In 2006, it was considered an ISO standard. Currently, it is frequently used to develop information systems in the heritage domain. CIDOC CRM is an event-oriented ontology because most of its semantics, like the actors and objects, are concentrated on relevant events like:

– the *E12_Production* class that represents a physical object production event;

– the *E67_Birth* class that represents a human birth event.

The following figure shows the semantic richness that we can attain with the event-oriented approach in the CIDOC CRM ontology [CRO 11].

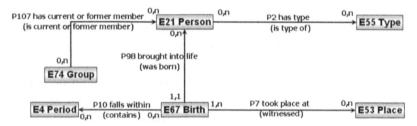

Figure 6.6. *Semantic richness/CIDOC CRM event-oriented approach*

6.3. Difficulties and possible solutions

There are several difficulties relative to knowledge management in the domain of cultural heritage. We categorize these difficulties into four main points:

– data acquisition;

– knowledge modeling;

– use;

– interoperability.

6.3.1. *Data acquisition*

In fact, data acquisition is an important stage in documenting heritage data for all cultural heritage institutions like museums, libraries and archives (GLAMS[27]). These institutions continuously perform diverse data acquisition tasks to add new objects to their collections and enrich the data on the objects that are already part of the collections. Several research projects on these heritage objects produce an enormous quantity of data that should be organized to facilitate accessibility, management and interoperability. The traditional systems for acquiring heritage data depend on the relational databases and graphic interface elements to insert data as form fields. The data on each heritage object are relative to the diverse aspects that go beyond the object itself and that includes its context, such as people, locations, events and other objects linked to its history.

In a general way, the data on a cultural heritage object can be classed into two main categories [HOH 12]:

– data concerning the identification of the object, like its username, title, creator, etc.;

– data concerning its documentation, like its history, production, conservation, archaeological digs, etc. These data, focused on the events relative to the object, are richer and more difficult to model than the identification data.

The use of semantic web technology for data acquisition is an interesting approach because it provides, from the beginning, a rich ontological description, an elevated level of interoperability, machine readability, better automatic processing and conformity with the standards of the semantic web without additional effort. Furthermore, the nature of the information needs in the field of cultural heritage is very complex because the events, locations, people and material and immaterial objects must be described. The semantic web offers techniques and resources that would allow this complexity to be dealt with.

There are, however, several issues to consider concerning the use of semantic web technology for data acquisition, e.g. data entry by experts in a domain (cultural heritage) by means of a form-type web interface is very

---

27 Galleries, Libraries, Archives, and Museums.

frequent and also makes the use of a system easier than direct access to the complexity of the knowledge base [SCH 12].

Experts in the field do not have to be directly exposed to the complexity of the ontologies and technologies of knowledge representation [MAZ 12]. The users are more comfortable with the informal and implicit semantics used within the graphic interface, such as the labels attached to form fields [HOH 12], the grouping and order in which these labels are used, and the connections between forms.

The following characteristics describe the interaction between the users and knowledge management systems:

– context helps the users understand the semantics desired by labels, for example, by associating certain labels with a particular subject, idea, or semantic aspect. [EPP 06];

– there is no separation between concepts and instances [SAR 07];

– there is a tendency to use the concrete instances and concepts associated with the clear images in the user's mind [SCH 11, SAR 07];

– there is a tendency to use complementary resources like URLs[28], images, colors, etc. [SIO 11];

– users are not able to think in terms of the explicit semantics that we find in ontologies [EPP 06].

In fact, the semantic web is based on the externalization of implicit knowledge in an explicit and formal way, which is very clear in the definition of the ontology [BOR 97]. Consequently, a direct link must be created between the implicit and explicit semantics. This link corresponds to a pathway inside the ontology [NUS 07]. An ontological pathway is a sequence of classes and properties organized in a certain way to represent certain semantics explicitly [AMA 15].

Returning to the example of the Mona Lisa, an ontological pathway to represent a painter (Leonardo da Vinci) who made a painting (the Mona Lisa) is clarified with classes, properties and the following order:

---

28 Uniform Resource Locator.

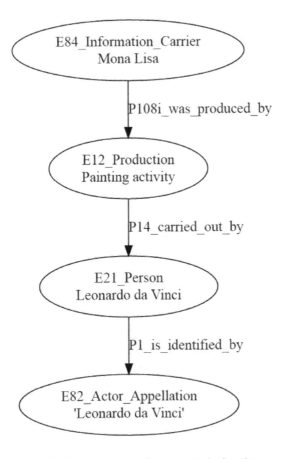

Figure 6.7. *An example of an ontological pathway*

NOTE.– This ontological pathway offers much richer and more precise semantics than *<dc:creator>* because by using this pathway, it becomes evident that we are representing the creator of the physical painting and not the creator of a digital representation of the painting. The elements of Dublin Core are not capable of making such a distinction.

The CIDOC CRM ontology is structured into several functional divisions that facilitate knowledge modeling and the creation of ontological pathways. The following example shows the ontological pathways from the functional division "*Material and Technical Information*" [CRO 11].

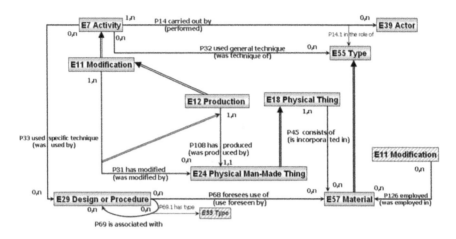

Figure 6.8. *Example of functional divisions and ontological pathways*

Certain research projects [FRI 12, VRA 14] allow users to insert data using form fields that are associated with explicit semantics using object-oriented ontologies and metadata schemata. These systems, however, are not aimed at data acquisition using event-oriented ontologies like CIDOC CRM, especially in a rich and complex field like cultural heritage, where each form field must be linked to an ontological pathway. To use these systems with ontologies like CIDOC CRM, several technical adaptations must be made [KIM 15].

[SCH 12] is a research project that allows ontological pathways to be defined by an administrator who has sufficient knowledge of semantic technologies and ontological modeling. In such an environment, each form field is associated with an ontological pathway predefined by the administrator. The inserted data become instances for the classes used in each ontological pathway.

In the framework of our research, we give the user the chance to participate in knowledge externalization using a tool that we developed and call "Path Finder" to add and structure cultural heritage data, which gives him the chance to represent his information needs dynamically.

The user interacts with the tool without being directly exposed to the ontology through the use of an intuitive terminology that we automatically classified according to the CIDOM CRM ontology and that we use as an entry for our graph traversal algorithm [AMA 15]. The tool automatically generates the ontological pathway that represents the semantics desired by the user and also creates the new form field that becomes associated with this pathway.

As we saw earlier in this chapter, users are more comfortable with the object-oriented approach, and for this reason, we ask the user to specify the object he is describing (the first concept on the pathway) and the characteristic of this object that interests him (the final concept on the pathway) using intuitive vocabularies (concrete concepts or even instances) that we provide using domain vocabularies and external knowledge bases.

For example, using a special form field, the user can search in real time (using Ajax technology) the concept of "painting" (recovered using Wordnet) or even the instance "Mona Lisa" (recovered using DBpedia), and our automatic classification algorithm [AMA 15], which we describe briefly in section 6.3.2.1, classifies this choice under the appropriate class in the CIDOC CRM ontology. For the last concept, the user can choose "painter" or even "Leonardo da Vinci". The pathway produced, however, only includes the corresponding classes from the CIDOC CRM ontology to be generalizable for all instances that are semantically compatible.

Our tool calculates all the intermediary elements of the pathway (including concepts like events and relationships between its concepts). The following figure shows part of the tool's graphic interface.

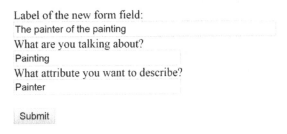

Figure 6.9. *Graphic interface of the "Path Finder" tool*

Technically speaking, our recursive algorithm proceeds from the current concept towards all those possible relationships (where the current concept is *rdfs:domain*), including those inherited from its parents, and then towards all the possible concepts of these relationships (where the concept is *rdfs:range*). We continue recursively repeating the same procedure until we find all the possible pathways that do not exceed a predefined length. Throughout the procedure, we filter the pathways so that we do not accept the pathways that enter a loop.

To disambiguate the pathways in order to choose the pathway desired by the user, we use the intermediary concepts as a key for semantic disambiguation. As illustrated in the example below, we ask the user if he is talking about the "Production" or the "Modification" of the painting. This method of creating ontological pathways, guided by programming, is both more intuitive and more efficient than the manual method.

The idea of ontological pathways is used in several data acquisition systems, such as in the BRICKS project [NUS 07], where there was a need for mapping between an object-oriented metadata schema and the CIDOC CRM ontology to ensure better semantic interoperability with other systems in the domain. In this project, mapping in CIDOC CRM was always an ontological pathway that includes certain classes and properties in a particular order corresponding to a specific element in an old schema. Furthermore, it was necessary to make several technical adaptations because the old schema was intended for a relational database, unlike the CIDOC CRM ontology that is better adapted to the semantic web and the RDF graph model.

The two kinds of users capable of providing semantic data for a heritage knowledge base are experts in the domain and hobbyists [SMI 12]. The domain experts are historians, curators, archivists, librarians, etc. The hobbyists are interested users like antique collectors. The kind of user must be taken into consideration when conceptualizing the heritage information system. We discuss this aspect in section 6.3.3.

It is important to distinguish real objects from their digital representations, such as photos, scanned versions, audio files, videos, etc. These files are normally stored using physical supports like computer hard drives. Furthermore, heritage objects can be collected, studied and analyzed by individuals and institutions, which produces a large amount of knowledge on these objects.

This knowledge may reside in the minds of individuals or even be documented in a structured, semi-structured or unstructured way in several resources like books, scientific publications, databases, documentations, manuals, websites, etc.

The extraction of structured information from a text can be realized using various natural language processing (NLP) technologies and machine learning [AKK 11]. Furthermore, ontology-based information extraction uses ontologies to guide the various information-extraction tasks. These tasks include named-entity recognition (NER), the extraction of relationships between entities, and domain vocabulary extraction using textual literature from the field.

The extracted vocabulary includes the representative terms from a specific domain. This stage is important for associating the instances and terms from a domain with the general concepts from the domain. [VLA 12] is a doctoral thesis that exploits natural language processing technologies and terminological resources in the domain of cultural heritage to automatically annotate words and phrases mentioned in the text with certain concepts.

The text chosen to test the system comes from the domain of archaeology, and the semantic annotation is based on the CIDOC CRM ontology and its CRM-EH[29] extension for the domain of archaeology. Technically speaking, the annotation task uses the JAPE[30] rules that are manually predefined. JAPE is an annotation system that uses specific rules provided by GATE software. These rules are combined with domain terms found in the EH (*English Heritage*) thesaurus as well as mechanisms for the detection of negation and lexical disambiguation.

The system allows the text to be annotated with certain CIDOC CRM classes like *E19_Physical Object, E49_Time_Appellation, E53_Place* and *E57_Material*, and certain CRM-EH extension classes like *EHE0007_ Context* (the location where the archaeological object was found), *EHE0009_Context_Find* (the object found) and *EHE0030_Context_Find_ Material* (the material observed in the object found). This search is part of the STAR[31]project that aims to integrate heterogeneous information from various resources in the archaeological domain.

---

29 Conceptual Reference Model – English Heritage.
30 Java Annotation Patterns Engine.
31 Semantic Technologies for Archaeological Resources.

[HER 08] is another example of data acquisition, but using structured and semi-structured sources like websites that include semantic descriptions, databases, Excel files and library data described with the MARC 21, DC and EAD schemata. This data acquisition task aims to automatically fill the ontology with instances from these sources in a traceable and reproducible way. Two stages are essential to achieve this goal:

– the interpretation and extraction of data: with the help of XML rules to describe the meaning of each element in the source schemata. These XML rules offer mapping with certain CIDOC CRM ontology classes or with an ontological pathway according to the semantics and functionality of each element. This stage achieves the identification and extraction of data described by the source schemata;

– the insertion of instances into the ontology: in this stage, the data extracted during the previous stage are inserted into the ontology as instances. Domain experts can verify, complete and modify the data inserted.

6.3.1.1. *The acquisition of data from different sources*

When acquiring data from different sources, two essential problems must be taken into consideration:

6.3.1.1.1. Data enrichment and fusion

Several information sources are frequently used in data acquisition and as a result, there must be a mechanism to recognize the same instances, which is important for fusing data from various sources but describing the same instance. For example, a source could provide information on the identity of an artist and another source provides detailed information on his works.

Being able to recognize that the two sources are talking about the same artist is an essential step for data fusion and providing a comprehensive representation of this artist. This identification problem is evoked by CIDOC CRM as a data integration problem where an entity can have different names. For example, Mona Lista and Giaconda, Yalta and Jalta, etc. CIDOC CRM allows several identities to be associated with the same resource using the class *E41_Appelation* and its subclasses, like *E82_Actor_Appelation* and *E44_Place_Appelation*.

Names:
    Yalta (**preferred**,C,V)
    Jalta (C,V)

Hierarchical Position:
    World (facet)
    .... Europe (continent) (P)
    .... Ukraine (nation) (P)
    .... Krym, Avtonomna Respublika (autonomous republic) (P)
    .... Yalta (inhabited place) (P)

Place Types:
    inhabited place (**preferred**, C)
    city (C)

Sources and Contributors:
    Jalta.......... [VP]
    .... Rand McNally Atlas (1989) I-81
    Yalta.......... [BHA, VP Preferred]
    .... Encyclopaedia Britannica (1988) XII, 808
    .... Times Atlas of the World (1994) 218

Figure 6.10. *An extract of the detailed*
information on YALTA in the TGN thesaurus

Furthermore, CIDOC CRM allows external knowledge sources like TGN (*Thesaurus of Geographic Names*) and ULAN (*Union List of Artist Names*) that provide detailed identification information on instances like an author or a location to be used, including the preferred and alternate names in different languages.

The semantic web also offers mechanisms to resolve this problem. For example, OWL (*Web Ontology Language*) provides the property *owl:sameAs* to explicitly confirm that two resources are really the same instance. It is possible to automate this task through the use of several techniques like machine learning, ontology alignment, semantic similarity, etc.

In fact, more and more data are being published according to linked data norms, which is very useful because the data in different knowledge bases are tied to one another and are accessible by programmatic methods. For example, a SPARQL query on DBpedia produces a result that includes links to resources on Yago, which in turn refer to other resources on Wordnet, and so on and so forth.

We have established dynamic mapping between the CIDOC CRM ontology and the knowledge in various knowledge bases using our automatic classification approach, which we briefly described in section 6.3.2.1.

This is very useful for the enrichment and interconnection of local data with external knowledge in a harmonized way, which creates a rich semantic network that can be exploited by various semantic web technologies.

As an example, a user wishing to add information on the painter of the Mona Lisa in our local knowledge base could start typing the name Leonardo da Vinci in the "Painter name" form field to obtain a list of artist names extracted dynamically from various external knowledge bases [AMA 16].

We only propose the names of artists for this form field, which means that the user obtains semantically disambiguated propositions classified according to the CIDOC CRM ontology used in our knowledge base.

6.3.1.1.2. Contradictory data and multiple perspectives

Various sources can include contradictory data values [DIF 10]. For example, various research projects in the domain of cultural heritage can provide contradictory data concerning the completion date of the Mona Lisa because each project has different arguments.

It is possible to accept all of these contradictory data and provide references to the data providers. This allows domain experts to choose the most correct value based on their research. In addition to contradictory views on data, there could be multiple perspectives on the data because each source of knowledge is focused on a different aspect and uses different conventions to name and describe data.

The semantic web provides a solution to this problem through the use of a named graph, which is a mechanism that makes it possible to identify a set of RDF declarations by a unique URI to add specific descriptions about this set, like metadata concerning the language, creator, content, provenance, etc.

Europeana has a different solution to associate a certain point of view on data with a particular source using the *edm:proxy* mechanism [EUR 13]. Each *edm:proxy* element provides a particular view on the data with different metadata values on the same resource. The reason why Europeana uses the *edm:proxy* mechanism and not the named graph is the lack of technical support for named graphs by the RDF standard.

6.3.2. *Information modeling*

There are several types of institutions in the heritage domain, including galleries, libraries, archives and museums (GLAMS) [OOM 11]. Each of these subdomains presents specific characteristics because it includes specific knowledge that has its own ontological representation.

Despite the fact that the CIDOC CRM ontology has certain influence from the museum domain [HER 08], its high conceptualization level makes it an appropriate general model for the different subdomains of cultural heritage. This is thanks to its objective of facilitating interoperability and semantic mediation between different information sources in the domain of cultural heritage, especially so that all the subdomains of cultural heritage share common points at a high level of conceptualisation.

For example, FRBR[32] is a conceptual model that traces its roots to the library domain. This model is developed by the IFLA[33] to improve access to library catalogues and databases [ZHA 10]. The idea of harmonizing the CIDOC CRM ontology and the FRBR model has been developing since 2000, as this harmonization brings numerous advantages for communities of museums and libraries.

The concrete realization of this idea started with the FRBR/CRM work group in 2003 with the goal of producing an object-oriented extension based on CIDOC CRM for the library domain by representing the original FRBR model through the use of classes, properties, and modeling techniques provided by the CIDOC CRM ontology [CRO 11].

This harmonization between the two models improves interoperability between library and museum systems. The classes and properties in the new extension, which is called FRBRoo, are based on the classes and properties of CIDOC CRM.

---

32 Functional Requirements for Bibliographic Records.
33 International Federation of Library Associations and Institutions.

Ontological modeling in the domain of cultural heritage should consider the specificities of each subdomain and application in order to choose the correct model that responds to the demands of knowledge representation and semantic interoperability with other projects in the domain.

CIDOC CRM can respond to general needs of modeling heritage knowledge, but as a function of this knowledge, various complementary conceptual models can be used to describe particular semantic aspects. For example, the ontology that describes the cultural heritage of Cantabria in Spain uses CIDOC CRM as a base ontology, as well as FRBRoo and Dublin Core as complementary models [HER 08].

FRBRoo has been used to model bibliographic information, which is an important source for the project. Dublin Core has been used for metadata harvesting, management of old data, and administrative description concerning the creation of the ontology.

Furthermore, the Cantabrian cultural heritage project has added its own extension of CIDOC CRM by specializing the CIDOC CRM classes and properties to describe the desired semantics on the application level.

The resulting ontology was generic enough to be used on other relatively similar projects, but it was also able to represent the specific semantics of its particular context. For example, queries like "all visits to Cantabria by foreign artists in the 19th Century" can be resolved using the classes and properties defined by the project as the class *Visit*, which was defined as a subclass of the *E5_Event* class of the CIDOC CRM ontology.

Nevertheless, queries on a higher level that are not aimed at the specific semantics defined by the project, like "all events in Cantabria in the 19th Century", can also be resolved.

Another example of the extension of the CIDOC CRM is the CRM-EH extension that was developed by the STAR project in cooperation with EH (*English Heritage*) to model the activities, procedures and concepts of archaeological digs. The need for such an extension was brought about by teams who work in the archaeological department of EH to improve the integration of information between various archaeological projects and to standardize conceptual modeling in the archaeological domain [TUD 13].

CRM-EH extends different classes and properties from the CIDOC CRM ontology. For example, the *EHE2007_SurveyEvent* class in CRM-EH is defined as *rdfs:subClassOf* the class *E65_Creation* because it has a specific meaning based on the class *E65_Creation* made up of events capable of creating immaterial objects like poems, texts, music, images, laws, reports, etc.

The following example shows how the *EHE2007_SurveyEvent* class creates an immaterial object (dataset).

Figure 6.11. *En example of the extension of CIDOC CRM by CRM-EH*

The *EHE2007_SurveyEvent* class is an event in which the archaeological teams carry out on-site research in a specific location to collect and record certain data in order to produce a report or a dataset. This event can be classed into different types, such as geochemical studies, topographical studies, geophysical studies, etc. It is not, however, the role of the ontology to carry these types, because they are on the terminological level and not the ontological.

These types are instances of the *EHE2007_SurveyEvent* class. This class has a high level of abstraction, and for this reason, its instances can be considered subclasses and can also have types (types of types). We can continue with this reflection until we attain the level of data, for example, as the GeophysicalSurvey_001 instance, which refers to a specific geophysical study defined by time and place.

CIDOC CRM provides a special class called *E55_Type* to carry these typologies taxonomically. The SKOS norm is generally used as a mechanism to organize such a hierarchy. It is recommended to define a specialized class of the *E55_Type* class for each class that needs to be detailed with these types.

For example, the *EHE0097_ContextFindIntendedUse* was defined by the CRM-EH extension as *rdfs:subClassOf* the *E55_Type* class from the CIDOC CRM ontology in order to document the intentional use of an archaeological object that was found during a dig. CIDOC CRM provides the

P103_was_intended_for property, which connects the *E71_Man-Made_ Thing* class to the *E55_Type* class.

EHE0009_ContextFind (the object found during the dig) is a subclass of the *E19_Physical_Object* class, which has subclasses that can also be subclasses of the *E71_Man-Made_Thing class*. Consequently, the *P103_was_intended_for* relation can be used to connect the *EHE0009_ContextFind* class to its original use.

Concerning the types of the found object, EH (*English Heritage*) uses a controlled glossary list for the possible types, such as animal bones, coins, building materials, etc. This is also connected to a thesaurus to give a more precise classification concerning these domain terms.

There are other classes defined by the CRM-EH extension like the *EHE0018_ContextSample* class (archaeological sample), which expands on the *E18_Physical_Thing* class; the *EHE0049_ContextSampleMeasure* class (sample measurement), which expands on the *E54_Dimension* class; the *EHE0017_RecordPhotograph* class, which expands on the *E38_Image* class; the *EHE0086_ResponsibleAgent* class, which extends on the *E39_Actor* class, and so on.

The addition of new classes allows the documentation process to have more precise semantics and consequently to respond to more precise research queries and questions. For example, if the new classes had not been added by the CRM-EH extension, the search for archaeological samples would be effected through the use of the *E18_Physical_Thing* class, which brings back many results, including physical objects other than archaeological samples, which means weakness in the system as a result of lacking precision. In this situation, all tasks that interact with the knowledge base would suffer from this problem of imprecision.

However, with this link between *EHE0018_ContextSample* and *E18_Physical_Thing*, if a non-expert user wanted to research all the physical objects without previous knowledge in the domain of archaeology, he would obtain a result that includes all physical objects, including archaeological samples, which is very useful for the discovery and exploration of data by non-specialized users.

There are two new classes added by the CRM-EH extension that are very important in archaeological documentation. The first is the *EHE0007_Context* class, which is a subclass of the *E53_Place* class and refers to an archaeological context, which is the place where a particular process of archaeological digs takes place. The class is called *Context* because the importance of the object found (*EHE0009_ContextFind*) depends on the surrounding context, like other objects found nearby.

The second is the *EHE1001_ContextEvent* class, which helps in the documentation of information concerning the activities and natural processes that take place in the archaeological context, like natural modification events, including saturation and chemical leaching.

Moreover, this class allows reasoning on the order in which the events took place in the archaeological context, which contributes to the acquisition of comprehensive understanding of archaeological dig sites.

6.3.2.1. Domain terms

A domain's vocabulary (terminology) is very important in modeling this domain. In section 6.2, we described different thesauri that can be used in the domain of cultural heritage.

It is nevertheless important to note that the CIDOC CRM ontology does not contain these terminologies. This is due to its ontological nature, which has a high level of abstraction so as to be extendible into different contexts that use different terminologies.

For instance, an enumeration of the types of physical objects in a museum specialized in natural life is different from that of a museum of art history or Egyptology [VLA 12].

Furthermore, the same enumeration can be classed differently according to the aspects and criteria used for the classification. It is recommended that existing classifications be used if they are appropriate for the modeling task before thinking of creating a classification. In the following illustration with the example of the Mona Lisa, the values in *italics* are domain terms that we can control:

Domain	*painting*
Denomination	*picture*
Title	Portrait of Mona Lisa (1479 – 1528) aka La Giaconda
Author/performer	*Leonardo da Vinci*
Author/performer details	Vinci, 1452; Amboise, 1519
School	*Italy*

Table 6.3. *An example of domain terms*

In many cases, however, there would not be such an existing terminology that corresponds to a particular class, either because the nature of the class requires intellectual involvement to find these types or because the class is too general, such as the *E70_Thing* that includes all material and immaterial entities.

Creating a connection between a class and its terminology is useful for numerous tasks that require prior knowledge, such as the recognition of named entities, the extraction of information based on ontologies, semantic indexing, etc. Certain classes, however, are not appropriate for the recognition of named entities, such as *E5_Event*, because it describes events that are phenomena in time and space and not material or immaterial entities.

Linking the ontological and terminological level has been investigated in various studies. For example, [SAN 05] is a study that creates links between the ontological (conceptual) level and the terminological level of Wordnet. The ontological level is made up of high-level synsets (concepts) in Wordnet, while the terminological level is made up of lower-level synsets.

The determination of the level of abstraction is based on the methodology of Resnik [RES 95]. The idea is that the probability of finding an instance of a particular concept increases when the concept is more elevated in the concept hierarchy. The informative character of the concept, on the other hand, increases when this probability decreases. This link between the two levels allows for the training of a classifier using the Semcor corpus, which is a text corpus annotated by human experts using Wordnet synsets.

The goal of this classifier is to perform the task of Word Sense Disambiguation (WSD[34]) and semantic annotation based on the ontological level of Wordnet. This task had become possible through the connection between the two levels thanks to the fact that the terms in the text (the terminology) are associated with the ontological level (the concepts), which makes their disambiguation and annotation possible.

The authors explain how the creation of a connection between the terms appearing in the text and the ontology's classes is a difficult task. The ontologies do not contain an exhaustive list of instances for each of its classes. The authors think it is imperative for lexical resources like lexicons, gazetteers and thesauri to be attached to the ontology in order to automate the ontological annotation process so that a term can be associated with an ontological class.

[IAN 03] carries out mapping between the superior ontology SUMO and Wordnet. What makes this mapping possible is the fact that the two ontologies contain general concepts. The author nevertheless observed that at a lower level of abstraction, semantic conflicts are more frequent.

In the domain of cultural heritage, the first example that we present of the connection between the ontological and terminological levels is the doctoral thesis [VLA 12] aiming to perform semantic indexing based on the CIDOC CRM ontology. This indexing is performed after creating links between certain classes of the CIDOC CRM ontology and thesauri in the cultural heritage domain as well as the use of lexical rules.

The second example is [SCH 13], who carries out mapping between the CIDOC CRM event classes and certain corresponding concepts in Wordnet. The goal of this study is to detect events in the text. The main hypothesis is that when a Wordnet synset corresponds to a class in the CIDOC CRM ontology, its sub-synsets are also valid subclasses for this CIDOC CRM class.

In the framework of our research, we have created a dynamic mapping between external knowledge, which is located in knowledge bases and thesauri, and the CIDOC CRM ontology. The realization of this mapping is based on the automatic connection that we created between the CIDOC

---

34 Word Sense Disambiguation.

CRM ontology and the Wordnet lexicon. To create this connection, we first effected a semantic disambiguation of the instances that are provided by the CIDOC CRM ontology as examples of each of its classes.

We use the result of this semantic disambiguation, which makes up a set of Wordnet synsets, to form a supervised machine-learning classifier capable of automatically classifying new instances according to the CIDOC CRM ontology's classes [AMA 15].

Concerning semantic disambiguation, we adapt the JIGSAW algorithm [BAS 07], which is an unsupervised semantic disambiguation algorithm based on graph theory. The algorithm uses Wordnet as a lexical knowledge base to disambiguate each word in the text and perform target word sense disambiguation after the analysis of its context.

Furthermore, the algorithm defines a function that calculates a confidence score in the range [0, 1] using three strategies based on grammatical categories: one strategy for nouns, one for verbs and one for adjectives and adverbs.

To adapt the algorithm and improve our task's precision, we used an Ngram entity detection, which gives us the chance to detect terms made up of a sequence of N-words.

This detection improves the precision of sense disambiguation, which is very important for detecting the names of people, places, objects and events, which are abundant in cultural heritage texts.

We also adapted the context dimension, which means the number of contextual words to the left and right of the target word. We configured this dimension dynamically in the limits of the sentence as a function of the word's position and the sentence's length.

Moreover, we increased the weight that gives more importance to common synsets according to the ZIPF law. We also increased the Gaussian factor, which gives more weight to contextual words that are closer to the target word in terms of distance.

Our classification approach for new instances using the CIDOC CRM ontology has an F-measure of 86.6667%, which is better than the classic approach that can be found in the literature, such as in [MAT 11]. In the following table, we present the result of the evaluation of our approach for a sample of classes from the CIDOC CRM ontology.

Class	Precision	Recall	F-Measure
Information Carrier	1.000	0.800	0.889
Physical Man-Made Thing	0.667	0.667	0.667
Physical Feature	0.833	1.000	0.909
Actor	1.000	1.000	1.000

Table 6.4. *The result of evaluation measurements for a sample of classes*

Furthermore, we use semantic disambiguation and our automatic classification algorithm to semantically index cultural heritage documents. First, a word sense disambiguation is executed; then, our algorithm is used to classify the disambiguated terms.

Our classification algorithm calculates a semantic similarity score between the disambiguated terms and the synsets of instances of the classes from the CIDOC CRM ontology that we used to train our classifier, as explained above. The semantic similarity measurements that we use are explained in [LIN 08].

A text fragment is then classified into the class that maximizes this semantic similarity score. For example, "Church of the Nativity" is classified into the *E22_Man-Made_Object* class and "destruction of the church" is classified into the *E6_Destruction* class, and so on and so forth.

For the weight of each concept, we use a modified version of TF-IDF because we are operating on the conceptual level. Consequently, we calculate the CF-IDF that is based on the frequency of the concept in a document and the inverse frequency of the documents that include the concept in the whole corpus.

We also perform semantic text annotation by highlighting the fragments of the text that we semantically classified according to the CIDOC CRM ontology with different colors. Each color corresponds to a particular class in order to visually distinguish the class of each classified term.

The user can verify or improve our automatic results by using the candidate classes that we propose (sorted by similarity score) for each term. For this task, we improve a classic text editor through the use of semantic technologies to give the user the chance to complete our automatic preprocessing [AMA 16].

In fact, the association that we performed between the terminological and conceptual levels produces a semantic network that we use not only to create ontological pathways, but also for other tasks, like information searches, automatic classification and data enrichment.

The advantages of the connection between the two levels can be summarized in the following points [BHA 11]:

– the ontology's formal specifications and its axioms can be applied on the term level;

– the improvement of the ontology and the verification of its completeness, which is determined by its ability to contain the terms;

– the domain terms of different languages can be linked;

– the ontologies from different domains can be linked.

When the taxonomy of the terms from a particular domain is not available, it is possible to create it automatically or semi-automatically through the creation of ontologies from the text (*Ontology Learning*).

There are different methods for realizing this task. Certain techniques, however, are frequently used [WAN 12], such as:

– lexical expansion and vocabulary analysis using Wordnet;

– semantic similarity algorithms [LIN 08, BIG 12];

– searching texts to explore the literature of a particular domain;

– TF-IDF and automatic text classification algorithms like SVM.

The detailed description of these techniques, however, is not among this chapter's objectives.

6.3.3. *Use*

It is important to consider the profile of the users of an information system in the domain of cultural heritage, because this affects the decisions for coming up with such a system. For instance, to acquire data, it is important to use the object-oriented approach for metadata labels and organize the data acquisition forms according to their subjects or semantic aspects, which corresponds to the users' data insertion habits.

6.3.3.1. *The user's level of knowledge on the semantic web*

Certain information systems based on semantic technologies allow direct interaction between users and the knowledge models of the semantic web, without an intermediary level that hides all the complexity of these models.

For example, Wikidata can be used by ordinary users, but many of its functionalities are aimed at people with knowledge management skills, such as the proposition of a concept or a property [VRA 14].

[KIM 15] is another research project concerning the creation of a knowledge base on growing Korean tea. The authors have added an extension of the CIDOC CRM ontology and used Ontowiki to collect data on growing Korean tea.

Ontowiki is a knowledge acquisition system with numerous functionalities, and one that requires certain semantic web skills to take advantage of all its functionalities. For example, navigation between the instances follows the internal structure of the knowledge models used, which is not easy for an ordinary user. Moreover, certain elements of these models are not concealed from the user, such as the classes and properties used [HEP 05].

Domain experts can participate in such an environment, but they need the appropriate tools that respect certain principles in order to be in a position to do this [PAR 13, OOM 11]. For instance, as we saw earlier in this chapter, we developed a tool that allows users to participate in the structuration of cultural heritage data in the context of the semantic web [AMA 15, AMA 16].

6.3.3.2. *The user's level of prior knowledge in the domain*

If the user possesses prior knowledge in the domain, this affects certain aspects in the technical solution proposed, such as the accessibility of digital content during searches and browsing. Generally, domain experts use the content search functionality to respond to a particular search question, while non-expert users have a tendency to browse in order to learn more about the domain without having a particular need for information [HER 08].

Consequently, as a function of the user's profile, certain accessibility mechanisms can be used, like interactive maps, timelines, tag clouds and contextual suggestions of content like places or events relevant to the historic person.

In addition to the mechanisms that we have identified in our review of the literature, we added the possibility of searching and browsing within multimedia resources like text, audio, images, animation and videos by using classes from the CIDOC CRM ontology and other concepts that we have semantically associated with this ontology in an automatic way.

We use the textual information from these resources like the content, subject headings, markers and descriptions that we index semantically, as explained in section 6.3.2.1, which provides better precision than classical indexing based on keywords [VLA 12]. This means that resources are automatically structured according to the classes of the CIDOC CRM ontology and the domain vocabulary [AMA 16].

The presentation of the content, however, should not follow the ontology's structure, because this structure is not intended for content presentation but rather for conceptual modeling. Improved content presentation can be applied manually to the system or realized dynamically as in the Cantabria project where a visualization ontology was used by the system [HER 08].

This visualization ontology is specifically conceived to present the content in a way better adapted to the users' profile; it is capable of determining which instances to show and in what context. The result of this mechanism is the separation of the ontological structure and the presentation.

It is also possible to browse through the content thematically, according to the subjects represented in this content. Each subject can include several classes from the ontology used in the system. For example, we can use the classification Iconclass to browse the knowledge base.

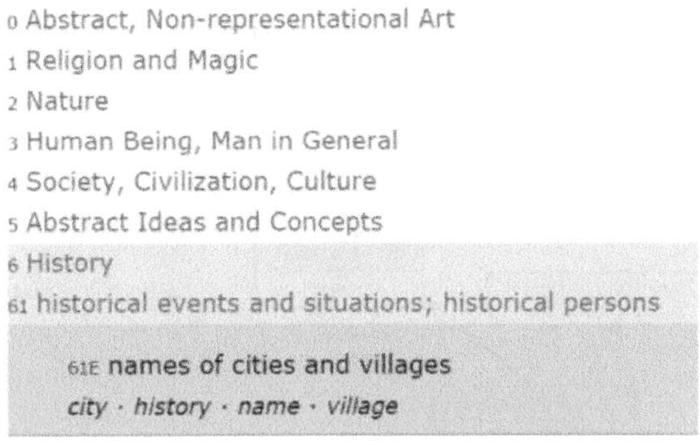

0 Abstract, Non-representational Art
1 Religion and Magic
2 Nature
3 Human Being, Man in General
4 Society, Civilization, Culture
5 Abstract Ideas and Concepts
6 History
61 historical events and situations; historical persons

61E names of cities and villages
city · history · name · village

Figure 6.12. *An example of the Iconclass classification for thematic browsing*

The description of a resource's subject can be realized using different properties, such as Dublin Core's *dcterms:subject* or CIDOC CRM's *P129_is_about*. These properties create a link between a resource and a list of subject headings. As a result, the resources that discuss the same subject can be browsed together [ZAB 12].

6.3.3.3. *The nature of the terminology that will be used in the system*

The terminology that was often used to describe cultural heritage objects was added by experts who work in different heritage institutions [PAR 13].

This has created a conflict, however, between the terminology used by the general public and the professional terminology used by professionals like curators, librarians and archivists. This highlights the importance of the participation of ordinary users to add their own descriptions of cultural heritage objects, like adding metadata and marker elements.

6.3.4. *Interoperability*

The semantic web not only describes data semantically, but also tries to attain a high level of interoperability between the different information sources. Data interoperability depends on several factors, like the way of structuring the data.

This means that the classes and properties used as well as their order create particular semantics that depend on the aspects and perspectives that we wish to consider. For example, the following figure shows two different methods of modeling the material of an artistic work and the production method [TUD 13, NUS 07].

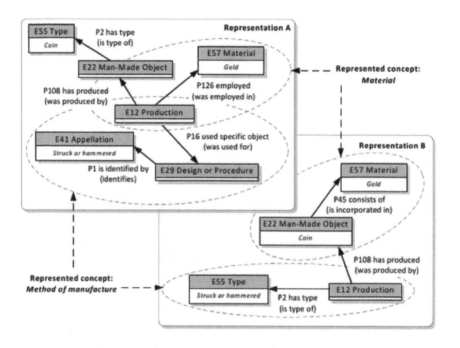

Figure 6.13. *An example of several correct models of the same ideas*

In representation A, the modeling of the artistic work's material is done by means of an ontological pathway:

E22_Man-Made_Object → P108i_was_produed_by → E12_Production
E12_Production → P126_employed → E57_Material

Frame 6.1. *Modeling of the artistic work's material/representation A*

Whereas in representation B,

```
E22_Man-Made_Object → P45_consists_of → E57_Material
```

Frame 6.2. *Modeling of the artistic work's material/representation B*

We can see that the first pathway underlined the event of producing the artistic work and the material that was used in this event, which may (or may not) become a composite of the produced object. The second pathway directly describes the material that was observed in the artistic work produced.

Likewise, in representation A, the modeling of the production method is done by means of an ontological pathway:

```
E22_Man-Made_Object → P108i_was_produced_by → E12_Production

E12_Prodction → P12_used_specific_object → E29_Design_or_Procedure

E29_Design_or_Procedure → P1_is_identified_by → E41_Appellation
```

Frame 6.3. *Modeling of the production method/representation A*

Whereas in representation B,

```
E22_Man-Made_Object → P108i_was_produced_by → E12_Production

E12_Production → P2_has_type → E55_Type
```

Frame 6.4. *Modeling of the production method/representation B*

In each case, the two representations are correct; they try to say the same thing, but in different ways or from different perspectives. However, this affects interoperability between different systems that use different representations. This problem can be reduced by using semantic web mechanisms that allow the creation of mapping between the different models [TUD 13].

Another solution is the use of metadata norms that are shared by specific communities to exchange data between different systems. For instance, in the museum domain, the metadata norm LIDO is frequently used to share metadata between the different documentation systems used by various museums. Despite the fact that the LIDO norm is based on CIDOC CRM, it was not thought up to represent very rich semantics, but rather to represent the base semantics in museum documentation in order to offer a high level of interoperability. We can see that the increase in interoperability is likely to bring about a certain loss in semantic richness.

Furthermore, modeling a single concept can be different. For example, high relief can be modeled as *E29_Design_or_Procedure* if it is considered a sculpting technique, while certain people consider it a type of sculpture.

This depends on the context, and it can be explained using informal semantics in an explanatory note. For example, the British Museum clarifies in an explanatory note that it modeled the concept "Nation" as a subclass of the *E74_Group* class of the CIDOC CRM ontology. This explanatory note helps others understand the modeling choice.

There are mappings that were performed on different knowledge models to improve interoperability. For example, there is a mapping between Dublin Core and CIDOC CRM, which enriches the description of DC because the CIDOC CRM ontology is richer.

There is also the CRM-IDA schema, which aims to associate LIDO with CIDOC CRM elements. It is important to note that mapping an event-oriented model like CIDOC CRM to the object-oriented model causes certain semantics to be lost [ZAB 12].

Computer science experts and domain experts should participate in ontological modeling, and it is always important to have an exchange of experiences with other, similar projects through workshops, colloquia, learning days, etc.

Concerning interoperability at the level of metadata harvesting, metadata harvesting institutions use knowledge models with a high level of conceptualization to describe data coming from different providers who use different local schemata. For example, Europeana uses the EDM (Europeana Data Model) to perform metadata harvesting using the OAI-PMH protocol [EUR 13].

Finally, there are different elements on the semantic web for improving interoperability between different systems, such as *owl:sameAs* for the same instances and *owl:equivalentClass* for the same concepts. Furthermore, aligning ontologies is an active research subject that aims to create mappings between two ontologies in an automatic or semi-automatic way [LIN 08].

6.4. Conclusion

As we have seen, there are various knowledge resources that can be used in the conservation and promotion of cultural heritage in the context of the semantic web.

The reuse of these preexisting resources increases data quality and improves interoperability with other projects. Several factors determine the way in which these resources must be used in the proposed solution. For example, the level of detail that should be represented in the context of a project, the questions that the project needs to respond to, the level of interaction with other projects in the domain, the user's level of expertise and his information needs, the nature of the domain, and the terminology used.

There are certain general principles, however, that can be considered to ensure a better solution. For instance, concealing the complexity and ontological structure, using concrete instances and concepts instead of abstract semantics, domain experts and computer scientists participating in the proposed solution, using informal semantics to explain modeling decisions, and exchanging experiences and results with the community in the domain in question.

In combination with these principles, there are several techniques in the context of the semantic web that should be taken into consideration to guarantee a state-of-the-art solution, such as natural language processing, information extraction, semantic similarity and ontology alignment.

The extension of cultural heritage ontologies to represent specific semantics in the context of the project is essential for the improvement of interoperability, the satisfaction of the user's information needs, and the contextual, spatial and temporal enrichment of data. This contributes greatly to the conservation and promotion of cultural heritage in the context of the semantic web.

6.5. Bibliography

[AKK 11] AKKER C., LORA M., OOMEN J., "Digital hermeneutics: agora and the online understanding of cultural heritage", *ACM Web Science Conference*, Koblenz, Germany, June 2011.

[AMA 15] AMAD A., "User participation in the structuring of cultural heritage data in a collaborative knowledge base", *H2PTM International Conference*, Paris, France, 2015.

[AMA 16] AMAD A., BOUHAI N., ZREIK K., "Data acquisition and enrichment in the context of poorly documented cultural heritage", *HIS3 International Conference*, Kerkennah, Tunisia, 2016.

[BAS 07] BASILE P., DEGEMMIS M., GENTILE A.L. *et al.*, "JIGSAW: an algorithm for word sense disambiguation", *Proceedings of the 4th International Workshop on Semantic Evaluations (SemEval-2007)*, Prague, Czech Republic, 2007.

[BHA 11] BHATT B., BHATTACHARYYA P., "IndoWordNet and its linking with ontology", *ICON-2011*, Chennai, India, 2011.

[BIG 12] BIGGINS S., MOHAMMED S., OAKLEY S. *et al.*, "Two approaches to semantic text similarity", *First Joint Conference on Lexical and Computational Semantics*, Montréal, Canada, June 2012.

[BIZ 09] BIZIMANA B., Interopérabilité des éléments de métadonnées: vers une approche sémantique, Thesis, University of Quebec, 2009.

[BOR 97] BORST W., Construction of engineering ontologies for knowledge sharing and reuse, PhD Thesis, University of Twente, 1997.

[BOU 10] BOUNTOURI L., PAPATHEODOROU C., GERGATSOULIS M., "Modelling the public sector information through CIDOC conceptual reference model", *International Conference on On the Move to Meaningful Internet Systems*, Crete, Greece, 2010.

[CRO 11] CROFTS E., DOERR M., GILL T. *et al.*, Definition of the CIDOC conceptual reference model, Report, ICOM, 2011.

[DIA 15] DIAKITÉ M., MARKHOFF B., "Construction semi-automatique d'une ontologie sur des manuscrits ouest sahariens", *Ingénierie des Connaissances 2015*, Rennes, France, 2015.

[DIF 10] DIFRANZO D., DING L., ERICKSON J. *et al.*, "TWC LOGD: a portal for linking open government data", *International Semantic Web Conference*, Shangai, China, 2010.

[DOE 06] DOERR M., KRITSOTAKI A., "Documenting events in metadata", *The 7th International Symposium on Virtual Reality, Archaeology and Cultural Heritag*, Nicosia, Cyprus, 2006.

[EPP 06] EPPLER M., "A comparison between concept maps, mind maps, conceptual diagrams, and visual metaphors as complementary tools for knowledge construction and sharing", *Information Visualization Journal*, vol. 5, pp. 202–210, 2006.

[EUR 13] EUROPEANA, "Europeana data model primer", Report, Europeana, 2013.

[FRI 12] FRISCHMUTH P., MARTIN M., TRAMP S. *et al.*, "OntoWiki – an authoring, publication and visualization interface for the Data Web", *Semantic Web Journal – Interoperability, Usability, Applicability*, vol. 1, no. 5, pp. 1–25, 2012.

[HEP 05] HEPP M., BACHLECHNER D., SIORPAES K., "Community-driven ontology engineering and ontology usage based on Wikis", *The 2005 International Symposium on Wikis – WikiSym 2005*, San Diego, USA, 2005.

[HER 08] HERNANDEZ F., RODRIGO L., CONTRERAS J., "Building a cultural heritage ontology for Cantabria", *The Annual Conference of CIDOC*, Athens, Greece, 2008.

[HOH 12] HOHMANN G., FICHTNER M., "Embedding an ontology in form fields on the web", *Semantic Web Journal – Interoperability, Usability, Applicability*, vol. 3, no. 4, pp. 1–9, 2012.

[IAN 03] IAN N., "Linking lexicons and ontologies: mapping WordNet to the suggested upper merged ontology", *The 2003 International Conference on Information and Knowledge Engineering*, Las Vegas, USA, 2003.

[ICO 05] ICOMOS, "Definition of cultural heritage", Report, International Council on Monuments and Sites, 2005.

[ISE 14] ISEMANN D., AHMAD K., "Ontological access to images of fine art", *ACM Journal on Computing and Cultural Heritage*, vol. 7, no. 1, pp. 1–26, 2014.

[JAR 05] JARRAR M., Towards methodological principles for ontology engineering, PhD Thesis, Free University of Brussels, 2005.

[KIM 15] KIM H., SUH J., AHN J., "Constructing a semantic wiki for living cultural heritage: case study of Korean tea culture", *International Conference on Ubiquitous Information Management and Communication – IMCOM 2015*, Bali, Indonesia, 2015.

[LIN 08] LIN F., SANDKUHL K., "A survey of exploiting WordNet in ontology matching", *Artificial Intelligence in Theory and Practice II*, vol. 276, pp. 341–350, 2008.

[MAT 11] MATALLAH H., Classification automatique de textes: approche orientée agent, Dissertation, University of Abou Bekr Belkaïd, 2011.

[MAZ 12] MAZUREK C., SIELSKI K., WALKOWSKA J. *et al.*, "Applicability of CIDOC CRM in digital libraries", Rapport, ICOM CIDOC, 2012.

[MER 12] MERTI G., Roman necropolis: an ontology for the semantic web, Thesis, University of Patras, 2012.

[MIL 09] MILES A., BECHHOFER S., "Simple knowledge organization system reference", Report, W3C, 2009.

[NEZ 14] NEZREG H., LEHBAB H., BELBACHIR H., "Conceptual representation using WordNet for text categorization", *International Journal of Computer and Communication Engineering*, vol. 3, no. 1, pp. 27–30, 2014.

[NUS 07] NUSSBAUMER P., HASLHOFER B., "Putting the CIDOC CRM into practice", Report, University of Vienna, 2007.

[OOM 11] OOMEN J., AROYO L., "Crowdsourcing in the cultural heritage domain: opportunities and challenges", *The 5th International Conference on Communities and Technologies*, Brisbane, Australia, 2011.

[PAR 13] PARASCHAKIS D., Crowdsourcing cultural heritage metadata through social media gaming, Thesis, University of Malmö, 2013.

[RES 95] RESNIK P., "Using information content to evaluate semantic similarity in a taxonomy", *The 14th International Joint Conference on Artificial Intelligence*, Montréal, Canada, 1995.

[SAN 05] SANFILIPPO A., TRATZ S., GREGORY M. *et al.*, "Ontological annotation with WordNet", *The 4rd International Semantic Web Conference ISWC*, Galway, Ireland, 2005.

[SAR 07] SARKER B., WALLACE P., GILL W., "Some observations on mind map and ontology building tools for knowledge management", *World Conference on E-Learning – E-Learn 2007*, Québec, Canada, 2007.

[SCH 11] SCHOPENHAUER A., *Le vouloir-vivre. L'art et la sagesse*, Presses universitaires de France, Paris, 2011.

[SCH 12] SCHOLZ M., GOERZ G., "WissKI: a virtual research environment for cultural heritage", *Frontiers in Artificial Intelligence and Applications*, vol. 242, pp. 1017–1018, 2012.

[SCH 13] SCHOLZ M., "A mapping of CIDOC CRM events to German Wordnet for event detection in texts", *Practical Experiences with CIDOC CRM and its Extensions*, Valletta, Malta, 2013.

[SIO 11] SIOCHOS V., PAPATHEODOROU C., "Developing a formal model for mind maps", *The First Workshop on Digital Information Management*, Corfou, Greece, 2011.

[SMI 12] SMITH K., "Social metadata for libraries, archives, and museums", Report, OCLC Research, 2012.

[STY 06] STYLTSVIG H., Ontology-based information retrieval, PhD Thesis, University of Roskilde, 2006.

[TUD 13] TUDHOPE D., BINDING C., MAY K. *et al.*, "Pattern based mapping and extraction via the CIDOC CRM", *Practical Experiences with CIDOC CRM and its Extensions*, Valletta, Malta, 2013.

[UNE 15] UNESCO, "What is meant by cultural heritage?", available at: www. unesco.org, UNESCO, 2015.

[VLA 12] VLACHIDIS A., Semantic indexing via knowledge organization systems: applying the CIDOC-CRM to archaeological grey literature, PhD Thesis, University of Glamorgan, 2012.

[VRA 14] VRANDECIC D., KROTZSCH M., "Wikidata: free collaborative knowledgebase", *Communications of the ACM*, vol. 57, no. 10, pp. 78–85, 2014.

[WAN 12] WANG Q., GAUCH S., HIEP L., "Ontology learning using Word Net lexical expansion and text mining", in S. SAKURAI (ed.), *Theory and Applications for Advanced Text Mining*, InTech, Rijeka, 2012.

[WEL 10] WELLER K., *Knowledge Representation in the Social Semantic Web*, De Gruyter, Berlin, 2010.

[ZAB 12] ZABADOS A., LETRICOT R., "L'ontologie CIDOC CRM appliquée aux objets du patrimoine antique", *3ème Journée d'Informatique et Archéologie de Paris JIAP*, Paris, France, 2012.

[ZER 11] ZERVANOU K., KORKONTZELOS I., BOSCH A. *et al.*, "Enrichment and structuring of archival description metadata", *The 5th ACL-HLT Workshop*, Portland, USA, 2011.

[ZHA 10] ZHANG Y., SALABA A., ZENG M. *et al.*, "FRBR implementation and user research", *ASIST 2010*, Pittsburgh, USA, 2010.

7

On Knowledge Organization and Management for Innovation: Modeling with the Strategic Observation Approach in Material Science

7.1. General introduction

This contribution joins an information system (IS) construction work aimed at promotion and innovation in nanosciences [SID 14a, SID 14b] and particularly in material sciences in a large French laboratory. It involves an interdisciplinary approach to natural language processing (NLP) and knowledge organization (KO) and its management (KM) with an aim to develop an approach of technological cooperation between two highly technological areas: research laboratories and the industrial world.

The Jean Lamour Institute (IJL) in Nancy (France), one of the largest mixed research units, is made up of several centers of expertise dedicated to material analysis. One of these centers, the Technology and Knowledge Transfer Office, aims to bring fundamental research and the socio-economic world together through a technological cooperation program. Being able to identify and structure the Institute's expertise, the laboratory's skills and know-how in order to offer exhaustive skills in its regional, national or international environment therefore lie at the heart of the work of this center of expertise.

Chapter written by Sahbi SIDHOM and Philippe LAMBERT.

The main aim of our research is to have a method that allows the semi-automatic extraction (man–machine) of scientific and technological information to establish a cartography of the IJL's expertise with the final goal of developing the innovation approach between the IJL and manufacturers.

The laboratory has a heterogeneous, corpus, taking an inventory of the research activities of different teams and the activities of centers of expertise. There are more than 250 researchers and educators – researchers who are split into four departments on several sites (Nancy, Metz and Epinal), with significant tacit knowledge possessed by researchers that is difficult for scientific communities (regional or national) to identify and exploit.

The working hypothesis that underlies our proposition is that the creation of a tree view of classes bringing together and belonging to a study domain ontology [BUI 05] would allow our project of offering expertise in material science to be structured and to explicitly bring out the Institute's best domains of expertise.

The national evaluation policy that French research laboratories must follow produces a series of documents (reports, analyses, questionnaires, promotions, AERES/www.aeres-evaluation.fr for evaluation reports, etc.). This volume of documents remains relatively significant and complex in its processing, but it allows contributions to be made to the analysis of our issue. The application of our approach in the trilogy (skills to be promoted, corpus of activities, ontology for promotion and innovation in material science) aims to give governmental (or state) instances or decision makers (university presidents) a "cliché" of laboratory activities (in terms of skills, know-how, technical knowledge, etc.). In time (occasionally) and for a given period (4–5 years), the instances may respond to international requests for proposals or recommendations in technological "challenges" for innovation.

Study of the corpus reproduced the "Cognitive Redaction Model" [SID 02]. This revelation in language structures actually hides a stability of writing in the evaluation texts that we use to implement a hierarchy of classes (see Figure 7.1). A rigorous methodology in KM depending on the use of NLP technologies allows specific information (or knowledge entity) extraction processes to be set in motion with an aim to define the laboratory's operational fields.

Therefore, the chapter outline that remains in tune with the adopted methodology is subdivided into three large processes. The first step consists in adapting the KM approach (or MASK) to our logical sequence of harnessing different heritage elements of the IJL to establish a book (or dictionary) of the organization's knowledge. This becomes an indispensable reference work for the innovation approach. The second step concerns TAL technologies, particularly the *ad hoc* creation of resources for exploiting our corpus and value-added information extraction processes (see Figure 7.1). The third step lies in the formalization and structuration of information in a hierarchy class of knowledge to structure skill offers in our IS.

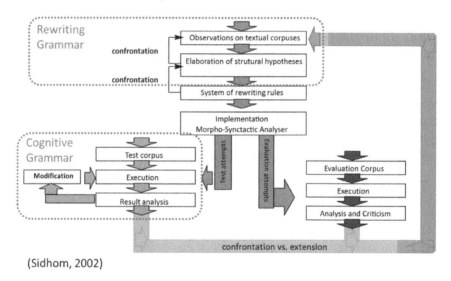

(Sidhom, 2002)

Figure 7.1. *Identification of a cognitive writing grammar [SID 02]*

In the research outline provided, it will be a matter of demonstrating that the adopted methodology will allow satisfying results to be provided and a robust indexing structure to be had for identifiable skills; also that the class hierarchy of knowledge (or the innovative material domain ontology) will allow the scientific evolution of the laboratory to be followed and the laboratory to be repositioned in a larger group gathering scientific communities in the domain; and lastly, that a developed conceptual cartography will serve the technological observation processes [LAM 11] in order to respond to recommendation subjects in a strategic development process.

7.2. Research context: KM and innovation process

7.2.1. *Jean Lamour Institute*

Since January 1, 2009, the primary research laboratories in Lorraine in the domain of material science and nanotechnologies have come together to form the Jean Lamour Institute (IJL), named after the famous 18th Century blacksmith, ornamental ironworker, and creator of the iron gates in the Place Stanislas in Nancy.

The IJL is a Mixed Research Unit (or UMR in French) with a staff of approximately 550 researchers from the University of Lorraine and the CNRS, its two administrative overseers. It is one of the best European centers in the domains of material science and engineering.

The IJL aims to practice fundamental research activities and ensure the spread of their results. Like all MRUs, the IJL also performs technology transfer activities, which allows it to allocate funds to its fundamental research projects. In this way, the IJL perfectly matches the definition of a research organization made in the RDI framework (article 2.2.d).

The IJL essentially develops four large research domains:

– Surface engineering, particularly for those of the most fundamental concepts, on the one hand, and for what affects clean, safe elaboration, preparation and surface coating procedures, on the other hand;

– The nanosciences relevant to electronics, information and communication technologies, catalysis, or clean energy generation, and those whose study calls on solid physics and chemistry as well as crystallography;

– Metallurgy, which gathers studies involving structure materials and studies of procedure engineering, of mechanics, and of the physical chemistry of complex inorganic materials, in terms of both surface and volume;

– Thermonuclear fusion sciences (plasma turbulence, plasma-wall interaction and reactor structure), plasma applications, for example, spatially.

A fifth domain is currently emerging: materials from biomasses or elaborated and/or functionalized for living organisms.

The IJL also concentrates on scientific challenges concerning structure materials, their elaboration and treatment processes, microstructures and properties, all while integrating sustainable development. These challenges fall under material physics and chemistry as well as the elaboration and study of innovative materials and products.

Furthermore, the gathering of the institute's forces offers a unique chance to open the field of research to new subjects that appear in the future on the horizon of 2020: materials under extreme conditions, biology–matter interface (molecular grafting, nanodevices for bio-informatics, bio-inspired materials, etc.), architecture of carbon compounds, intensive use of digital calculations for predictive metallurgy, application of metallurgical processes for sustainable development issues, etc.

7.2.2. Technology and Knowledge Transfer Office (or CC-VIT)

The CC-VIT is a component of the IJL promoting the transfer of technology between the IJL's research teams and actors in the socio-economic world (PME, PMI, TPE, TPI, etc.). Its goals are twofold: on the one hand, it acts to bring issues to research times; on the other hand, it acts to manage innovative projects and allows industries know what is being done within different teams at the Institute in terms of fundamental research.

The Institute's administration wanted to structure the promotion of its scientific activities through a KM process (KM-p), allowing the optimization of innovation processes and technological cooperation between teams. The roadmap approved by this administration is broken up into three distinct stages: (1) the creation of a cartography of the Institute's know-how, skills and instrumental heritage; (2) the implementation of an IS that would allow the previously mentioned and created cartography to be presented; (3) the projection of the thereby motivated KM dynamics to the outside to develop innovative projects, thanks to the active involvement of companies and industries.

The stakes of this process allow the creation of value through technological cooperation projects, incremental innovation projects, or separation, by accumulating knowledge at the heart of transfer activities.

A precondition is being able to formalize explicit knowledge in a pertinent way in order to transform them into intelligent (informational and documentary) resources that, in our project, take the shape of an IS with particular functionalities for content indexing, knowledge representation, mapping, etc. One dimension, which we will not deal with in this chapter, falls under information confidentiality, its spread, and, more generally, the economic security policy inherent to the protection of immaterial heritage (data, information, knowledge) that this KM-p assumes.

However, seeing the KM-p as a simple inventory devoid of all dynamics would make the practice of accumulating knowledge useless: inventorying knowledge without putting it to use for a company's profit, without creating added value for the laboratory. Moreover, the promotion of tacit knowledge can be foreseen in a much more dynamic form after becoming more oriented towards contacts, interactions and exchanges between laboratory actors, rather than towards the formalization of their knowledge. This will allow the permanent evaluation of knowledge to update and enrich it by returning experience and feedback and creating new knowledge.

7.3. Methodological approach

7.3.1. *Observation and accumulation of knowledge for innovation*

7.3.1.1. *MASK*

In the course of this better mastery of internal information, it was decided that a process of accumulating knowledge through the MASK method (Modeling, Analysis and Structuring of Knowledge) would be implemented. This method is based on previous work [ERM 93] and was first applied at CEA (Center for Atomic Energy, France). According to Ermine, "MASK is a method based on modeling knowledge, which responds to the characteristics of this kind of method and which allows for compensation of the limits of methods based on transcription". The MASK system is made up of a set of knowledge in six fundamental perspectives, namely: (1) fundamental knowledge, (2) activities, (3) historic context, (4) know-how, (5) concepts, (6) history of solutions and their justification (see, for example, Figure 7.2).

The main difficulty of implementing this strategy through the MASK method lay in the fact that the field of information and KO and its management was then non-existent within the IJL. MASK required strong interaction with experts in the target structure to transform their tacit knowledge into explicit knowledge, the goal being to create the Book of Knowledge, a collection assembling all knowledge of the structure to be promoted.

Tacit knowledge is a notion created by the Hungarian philosopher M. Polanyi in the mid-1960s [POL 09]. Keeping in mind that not all knowledge can be expressed solely through texts, his adage, "we can know more than we can tell", is very widespread, underlying the idea that tacit knowledge is difficult to express in words or by other means of communication due to its subjectivity and its personal character. The notion was then taken back up in the domain of international innovation [GIL 10a, GIL 10b] in a more practical logical sequence for organizations [NON 95] going from tacit to implicit knowledge in the framework of intra-company group exchanges.

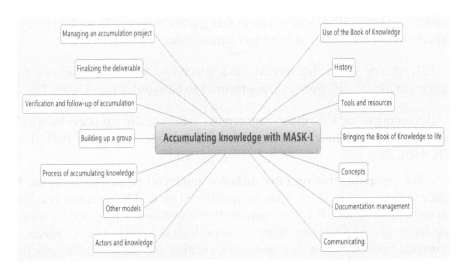

Figure 7.2. *MASK method structuring (source: http://aries.serge.free.fr)*

7.3.1.2. *C-K theory*

Understanding the information necessary to start an innovation process is difficult for several reasons. The first is its nature, hence our orientation towards the C-K theory of innovation based on the principle of expansion.

The C-K theory [AGO 13] formalizes the creative conception approach. This methodology has been well established in the methodologies of innovation for more than 10 years now. In fact, it was developed in collaboration with large industrial groups and enjoys increasing renown.

The approach's synthetic schema is made up of a K space (the heritage of Knowledge) and a C space for Concepts, which can be understood as the space of (innovative) ideas, which have not yet been verified. The C-K process is a loop between these two spaces.

C-K theory models conception as the coevolution of these two spaces [AGO 13]: the concept (C) space and the knowledge (K) space. With four operators that interact within as well as outside of these two spaces, innovative conception will evolve little by little into an expansive logical sequence. The two C-K spaces can in fact gradually spread from the creative process that should respond to an innovation issue.

C-K theory offers interpretive and generative power that allows the restrictive hypotheses from existing theories to be avoided (see Figure 7.3).

According to the C-K theory, conception is the cognitive process by which a concept will generate other concepts and become knowledge [GIL 10a, GIL 10b]:

– K-C operator: this operator adds (or subtracts) properties from the K space to the C space. The C space is partitioned by K. This operator is called semantic disjunction. It is the operator that transforms a proposition with a logical status into a proposition without logical status. The C space is expanded upon by K; it is a matter of creating the unknown through the known.

– C-K operator: this operator gives a logical status to a concept. In other words, when the creator is faced with a concept like "car missing a tire", for example, this will activate his knowledge to truly create a "car missing a tire". This production of knowledge aims to verify a concept; this can be proved, for instance, by laboratory experiments. The K space is expanded upon by C.

– C-C operator: this operator designates the trace of the object to be conceived, that is, the series of properties that make it up. It is also this operator that allows concepts to be created from other concepts. It is particularly what is done when, during the creativity process, new ideas (absent in the domain) are stumbled upon.

– K-K operator: this operator corresponds to the production of knowledge (be it new to the creator or not) from other knowledge. This expansion is made possible by logical inferences like induction, deduction and abduction.

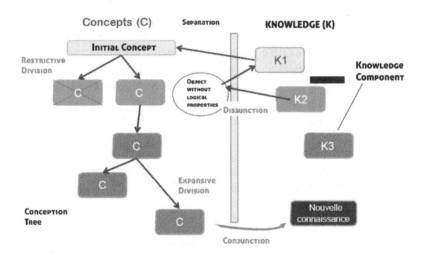

Figure 7.3. *Schema of the C-K theory K [SOU 10]*

7.3.2. *Strategic observation and extraction of knowledge: towards an ontological approach*

7.3.2.1. *Corpus analysis strategy*

In his research work, [SID 02] elaborated a morphosyntactic analysis platform for information retrieval (IR) and automatic indexing. It is made up of an indexing core (i.e. indexing process) that uses the model of noun phrases (NPs) (or SN, "nominal syntagma", in French) as descriptors (i.e. indexing concept) of textual information. To use Michel Le Guern's definition of a NP [LEG 89], placing the word from the lexicon in a discourse universe that places it, *de facto*, in an extensional logical sequence gives the NP a referential status, segment of the reality that is associated with it. In our context, the NP shows itself to be a carrier of a semantic load that makes it a central element, pertinent for the analysis of informational contents and the identification and then the extraction of knowledge entities. Through this, we regard ourselves as developers of an approach in the field of KO. Our corpus analyses are oriented towards these desired semantics.

Therefore, the grammar of NP recognition is articulated on three logical levels, which are: (1) the intensional level (i.e. properties of the language) is represented by the level N: the considered units are free predicates, simple (i.e. the properties of the noun) or complex (i.e. the properties of the noun modified by other elements: adjectives A', prepositional expansions (PE), verbs V-inf, etc.); (2) the intermediary level or N' level (i.e. the consideration of the discourse universe in question) is the transition from the intensional to the extensional; (3) the extensional level or N'' level (i.e. the NP and its complexity) is the closing operation by means of a quantifier that selects a precise element in the N class of nouns. These are the world's existing objects, those referred to, or those constructed by thought.

Corpus experiments to verify a NP grammar in its regularity and to consider an interoperable exploitation, if possible, have led us to multiple fields of study: INA, health, nanosciences and material science.

7.3.2.2. *Identification of a cognitive grammar*

The goal of this work is to provide a model adaptive to the analysis of the language in open resources: from documentary corpuses (closed or semi-closed) to web corpuses, web-use corpuses and opinion corpuses (open). Thus, this study focused on discourse through its textual materiality and was oriented towards the organic units that make it up on the intensional as well as the extensional level [SID 02, BAC 04] in the language and its description [MAN 93, SID 02].

In the creation of this study, which remains complex, we will report the different experiments allowing a cognitive grammar to be established:

7.3.2.2.1. *INA corpus*

In an initial corpus study through indexing, the principal stages of the process consist in collecting bibliographic records incorporating content summaries from providers specialized in this domain. A scientific collaboration [SID 02] with specialists from the INA (i.e. *Institut national de l'audiovisuel* in Paris) revealed professional experience and acquisitions dating back to the ORTF (i.e. *Office de Radiodiffusion-Télévision Française*) in the 1950s.

The creation of summaries from documentary contents is, in certain specialized organizations like the INA (the BnF, etc.), based on formal criteria and methods acquired through experience [BRO 96, CAR 97, GUI 93]. This allows a regularity and consistency of processing realized by information analysts to be ensured. This documentary richness, once created and made exploitable according to traits attached to the content (i.e. the accumulation of information sources and associated knowledge) [CHA 10, COU 09], can be adapted to various technologies for the exploitation and diffusion of content [VAN 87, MAR 94, CAL 13].

In the INA's corpuses, we sought to study the stability of the textual details, mainly in the sections at hand in content analyses. It was a question of establishing, through a statistical analysis, the morphosyntactic components in the sentences (S) produced [SID 02]. In our study, the creation of S is articulated through four fundamental structures, namely: (1) a structure that precedes the sentence S (or introductory proposition IP); (2) the NP subject of S (in the form of a complex NP or NP_max); (3) the verbal phrase of S (or VP); (4) the optional relative clause (or REL), which remains a completive proposition or clause for NP or VP. Each of these structures is identified in its linguistic units bringing together its morphosyntactic organization [SID 02]:

$$S \rightarrow [IP] + NP + [REL_{NP}] + VP + [REN_{VP}]$$

$$[X]: \quad optional\_element$$

The model of S is determined by a cognitive grammar that defines the following structures in French:

In these examples, we use [FR] for the rule application in French and, when possible, its reuse [EN] in English.

IP	Examples
1) IP = PP = Prep + NP, ⊂ S (PP: prepositional phrase)	[FR] Pour + les 20 ans d'AIRBUS INDUSTRIE, … [EN] For + the 20 years of AIRBUS INDUSTRY, …
2) IP = PE = Prep + Noun, ⊂ S (prepositional expansion)	[FR] En parallèle, …| par hypothèse, … [EN] In parallel, … | by hypothesis, …
3) IP = EP + PP, ⊂ S	[FR] En direct + depuis l'observatoire de Meudon, … [EN] Live + from the Meudon Observatory, … [FR] En compagnie + de Marianne GRUNBERG-MANAGO, … [EN] In (the) company + of Marianne GRUNBERG-MANAGO, …
4) IP = PasP + PP, ⊂ S	[FR] Embarqués + à bord de l'astrolabe depuis l'extrême sud de l'Australie, … [EN] Sent + from the extreme south of Australia, …
5) IP = PreP + PP, ⊂ S	[FR] Proposant + un voyage à travers les sites industriels de France, … [EN] Proposing + a trip around France's industrial sites, …
6) IP = Prep(en| "in") + NPdat, ⊂ S	[FR] En juin 1986, … [EN] In June 1986, …
7) IP = Prep(en| "in") + PreP + PP, ⊂ S	[FR] En + passant + [par (la littérature)], … [EN] In + going + [through (the literature)], …
8) IP = Conj, ⊂ S	[FR] Cependant, … [EN] However, …
9) IP = Conj + Adv + PP, ⊂ S	[FR] Car + contrairement + aux Américains, … [EN] Because + similarly + to Americans, …
10) IP = en | "by" + PreP, ⊂ S	[FR] En vaccinant, [EN] By vaccinating, …

Table 7.1. *Prefixed structures to the sentence: introductory proposition*

NP	Examples
11) NP (details on NP in [21])	[FR] Le lac … ⊃ SN [EN] The lake … ⊃ NP [FR] le lac dans le nouveau Québec (…) ⊃SN [EN] The lake in New Quebec (…) ⊃ NP
12) EP ⊂ NP	[FR] Une équipe ⊃ de tournage … [EN] A team ⊃ of recorders … [FR] Un avion Hercule ⊃ de transport stratégique [EN] A Hercules aircraft ⊃ for strategic transport
13) PP ⊂ NP	[FR] La présence ⊃ d'un lac … [EN] The presence ⊃ of a lake …
14) {NP, PP, EP} ⊂ NP	[FR] L'utilisation ⊃ d'images de synthèse … [EN] The use ⊃ of synthesis images …
15) REL (explanatory relative clause) ⊂ NP	[FR] La présence d'un lac ⊃ qui se serait formé suite à la chute d'une météorite … [EN] The presence of a lake ⊃ that would have formed after a meteorite landing …
Exceptions:	
16) NP∇ = NP with no determiner	[FR] Psychologues et physiciens (se penchent sur leurs multiples facettes.) [EN] Psychologists and physicians (look at their multiple aspects.)

Table 7.2. *Noun structures in a sentence: NP*

REL	Examples
17) /REL = relP + NP/ ⊂ NP	[FR] … , qui + son père, … [EN] … , that + his father, …
18) /REL = relP + VP/ ⊂ NP	[FR] … qui + se serait formé suite à la chute d'une météorite … [EN] … that + would have formed after a meteorite landing …
19) /REL = relP + S/ ⊂ NP	[FR] a) … qu' + il a réalisé sur le même sujet en 1973. b) … dont + le pouvoir suggestif déborde largement le cadre du bâtiment lui-même. [EN] a) … that + he did on the same subject in 1973. b) … whose + suggestive power goes far beyond the limits of the vessel itself.

Table 7.3. *Relative structures in a sentence: relative clause (REL)*

VP	Examples
20) V + (Prep + V-inf) + PP	[FR] …**est** + (de récupérer) + de la matière cosmique [EN] …**is** + (to return) + from the cosmos
21) V + (Prep + V-inf) + NP	[FR] …**sont montrées** + (pour comprendre) + les difficultés techniques et économiques [EN] …**are shown** + (to understand) + the technical and economic difficulties
22) V + (V-inf) + NP	[FR] …**a pu** + (rencontrer) + AIRBUS INDUSTRIE [EN] …**could** + (meet) + AIRBUS INDUSTRIE
23) V + (V-inf) + (Prep + V-inf) + NP	[FR] …**devait** + (permettre) + (d'identifier) + le sexe [EN] …**should** + (help) + (to identify) + the sex
24) V + (PreP) + NP	[FR] …**a suivi** + (durant) + trois semaines les activités d'une équipe [EN] … **followed** + (during) + three weeks the activities of a team
25) V + NP	[FR] …**sont** + le reflet de notre société [EN] …**are** the reflection of our society
26) V + PP	[FR] … **est** + **réservée** aux avions Hercule [EN] … **is reserved** +for Hercules aircrafts
27) V + {NP, PP, EP, VP}	[FR] … **essaie** + d'expliquer le mystère de l'étoile de Bethléem [EN] … **tries** + to explain the mystery of the star of Bethlehem
28) V + (Adv) + NP	[FR] …**explique** + (comment) + les pays européens exportent des armes [EN] …**explains** + (how) + the European countries export weapons
29) V + (Adv) + V	[FR] a) …**sont** + intimement + **liées** b) …**est** + ainsi + **développé** [EN] a) …**are** + closely + **tied** b) …**is** + thus + **developed**
30) V + (Adv) + (Prep + V-inf) + NP	[FR] …**s'attache** + (plus) + (à expliquer) + la course du côté soviétique [EN] …**aims** + (further) + (to explain) + the race from the Soviet side

31) V + /EP/ + NP	[FR] ...**démontre** /en particulier/ la politique de la France à ce sujet [EN] ... **shows** +/in particular/ + the policy of France on this subject
32) V + /Conj/ + NP	[FR] ...**poursuit** /donc/ cette balade à la fois historique, sociologique et architecturale [EN] ... **continues** ..., +/thus/ + this tour at a time historical, sociological and architectural
33) V	[FR] (Ce chien) **mord** [EN] (This dog) **bites**
34) V + (Adj) + PP	[FR] ...**furent** +(découvertes) + en 1988 [EN] ...**were** +(discovered) + in 1988
35) V + {Adv, Adj}	[FR] (il) + **décide** rapidement... [EN] (he) + **decides** quickly...

Table 7.4. *Verbal structures in a sentence: VP*

We find that this model of syntagmatic grammar as a "cognitive" model of the sentence S can help us both as a language analysis tool and an automatic indexing tool, and its orientation inherently as a tool for (social) re-indexing according to uses.

7.3.2.2.2. INIST's corpus on "ChroniSanté"

After the INA's corpus and the identification of a cognitive model for writing analytical summaries, we completed our observation on a health corpus in the framework of the "*ChroniSanté*" project (i.e. Chronicity Health Society, http://chronisante.inist.fr/). For this, most of the actors of the healthcare system and, first of all, for patients, dealing with chronic illnesses come down to a medical administrative plan for long-term illnesses (LTI)[1]. LTI, called "exonérante" in French, when their effects include severity and/or chronicity, require prolonged treatment and particularly costly therapy for which user fees are removed. However LTIs, simple or "exonérantes", are almost always chronic illnesses.

---

1 LTIs are illnesses involving prolonged treatment and particularly costly therapy (Definition from the French National Authority for Health).

It is in this context that "*ChroniSanté*" was thought up and created in 2008. "*ChroniSanté*" is an IS that helps with decision-making [LAM 10], bringing together R&D aspects in the professional context of the INIST in France (i.e. Institute of Scientific and Technical Information – Unit of the CNRS for providing specialized information).

In this work, the same NP morphosyntactic grammar for INA was rewritten for the NooJ platform in two stages: first, the work consisted in reformatting the linguistic resources (dictionaries and grammars) in our possession; second, we elaborated the NP's final-stage transducer. The existing dictionary labels were harmonized to correspond to the syntactic graph of the NP. This is made up of a set of five graphs (see Figures 7.4 and 7.5), returning to the structure presented in Figure 7.1.

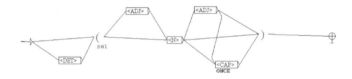

Figure 7.4. *Example of a syntactic graph in NooJ for extracting a simple NP*

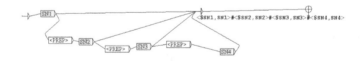

Figure 7.5. *Example of a syntactic graph in NooJ for extracting embedded NPs*

The graph proposes a system for numbering phrases, allowing the level of syntactic embedment to be identified in the results. For instance, the assertion "the existence of long-term illness management" will be coded as:

<the existence,NP1> <illness,NP2> <long-term illness,NP3> <management,NP4>.

The *ChroniSanté* system aimed to help a multidisciplinary work group from the French National Authority for Health (HCSP: www.hcsp.fr/, "Haut Conseil de la Santé Publique" in French) focusing on chronic illnesses to make a series of recommendations on healthcare reform in France[2]. This project was jointly developed by the HCSP and the INIST.

7.3.2.2.3. Nano corpus of the "Club nanoMétrologie"

In another study context, we retested the cognitive NP grammar on an opinion poll including open- and closed-ended questions in the framework of creating a themed club for nanosciences and nanotechnologies (nanoMétrologie). The Club nanoMétrologie is organized by large domain actors in France, like the National Laboratory of Metrology and Testing (LNE) and the Center in Competences in Nanosciences (C'NANO) that brings together all domain laboratories. A hypothesis made on the nature of the open text transmitted in open-ended questions is that it does not concern style or writing constraints proposed or imposed (upon respondents to the survey). For us, it is a matter of an open text to be prepared for the automatic text analysis and knowledge extraction in text processing.

In order to verify the cognitive observations presented above, we applied our process to the domains of nanoscience and nanotechnologies through an opinion poll including open- and closed-ended questions. This survey took place in the framework of a new collaborative structure, the Club nanoMétrologie, put in place by the Center in Competences in Nanosciences (C'NANO) and the National Laboratory of Metrology and Testing (LNE). The main goals of this exercise were: (1) to draw up a cartography of the Club's members; (2) to determine the reasons for their inscription; (3) to find out their expectations from this kind of collaborative structure.

A hypothesis made on the nature of the text (or the opinion work): the work is (1) open, (2) transferred through open-ended questions, and (3) no style or writing constraints are proposed or imposed. The variety of its content describes its representative nature as a document to validate our choices on the strength of the cognitive grammar implemented. The open text proposed by the respondent is proposed for automatic analysis in order to extract NP structures as knowledge and its properties.

---

2 National Authority on Health, The treatment and social protection of people suffering from chronic illnesses, report, November 2009, p. 72, (URL visited in April 2016)www.hcsp.fr/docspdf/avisrapports/hcspr20091112_prisprotchronique.pdf

In the synthesis and during the analyses on the different corpuses (INA, INIST, and nanoMétrologie), we demonstrated the reusability of the cognitive grammar model (see Figure 7.4) while varying the study contexts. The corpus changes show the stability of this grammar's properties and inherently the initially implemented language model. As it happens, in the opinion poll corpus of the Club nanoMétrologie, the identified structures and their morphosyntactic organization are translated by the following cognitive sub-grammar S':

$$S' \subseteq S$$
$$S' \rightarrow [V - \text{inf}] + NP + [REL_{NP}]$$

with: $V_{\text{inf}} \subset IP$ and $[x]$: optional_element

In the experiment, this cognitive grammar has observed implementations (see Figure 7.4) since its creation with INA corpuses [SID 02] and various checks, essentially in health domain (identification of chronic illnesses in the "ChroniSanté" project) and in the nanoscience domain with the "Club nanoMétrologie" [SID 13].

In the INA Corpus context, the S sentence structure is:

$$S \rightarrow [IP] + NP + [REL_{NP}] + VP + [REL_{VP}]$$

$[x]$: optional_element   (Sidhom, 2002)

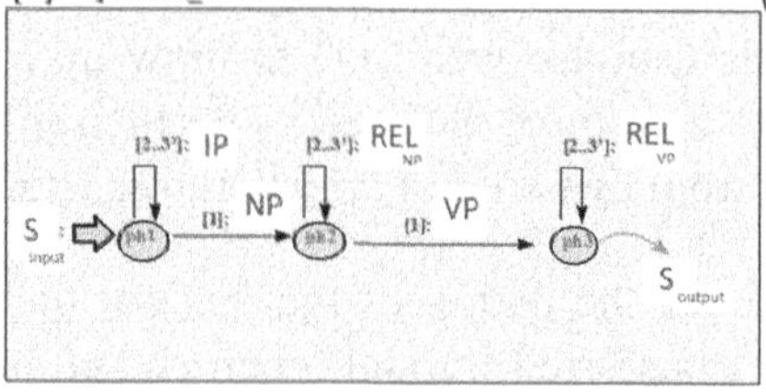

In the nanoMetrology Corpus context, the S' structure is:

$$S' \subseteq S$$
$$S' \rightarrow [V - \text{inf}] + NP + [REL_{NP}]$$

$[x]$: optional_element   (Sidhom & Lambert, 2014)

Figure 7.6. *Stability of syntagmatic and cognitive grammar on a corpus*

7.3.3. *Creation of a class hierarchy (of knowledge)*

Since the 60–70s that saw the birth of NLP, one of the largest issues has been grasping the meaning of a document automatically. Most systems intended for these tasks have shown themselves to be ill adapted due to the overly generic vision of automatic understanding. Research has thus been focused more on the issue of information extraction making semantic categories like named entities or time markers the pivot of their work. If spotting these elements in and of itself does not allow a text to be understood, it does, however, allow the primary elements of meaning to be extracted to create conceptual specifications that are very useful for ISs [ZAC 07].

Ontologies are a means of modeling a domain vocabulary [GRU 93] by identifying the terms and relationships that they contain. Applied to Artificial Intelligence (AI), ontologies not only allow for the fine extraction of date, but also for the proposition of systems based on developed knowledge [BUI 05]. For our work, we will situate ourselves in the first step before ontology creation, namely realizing a taxonomy and developing a class hierarchy, without concerning ourselves with the description of the attributes and relationships between these classes [BIE 05]. This aspect will be completed in subsequent steps with the semantic relationships that morphosyntactic structures (S, NP, SP, VP, etc.) can preserve upon being extracted from the contents.

7.4. Conceptual modeling for innovation: technological transfer

This aspect is a return on experience with the constitution of a schema for the IJL's conceptual model for technological cooperation and innovation. The main stake of this process is to have access to a conceptual reference that models every activity of the institute's research teams.

In the course of KM, having a conceptual reference is indispensible for several reasons: (1) tt reports a T_0 (i.e. time zero) instant of the state of the IJL's fundamental research to compare the evolution of the themes; (2) the tool also serves to analyze the industrial needs for R&D to determine what teams can be asked to respond to these needs; and, finally, (3) in the course of innovation, this tool allows the possibility of becoming engaged in a product innovation project to be determined, taking into account what exists internally in terms of skills and instruments, thereby allowing a feasibility prognosis to be presented. Through this, we regard ourselves as approach experimenters in the field of KM.

Our process breaks down in the following way:

1) Collection of tacit data and constitution of a cartography of the skills and instrumental heritage of the institute, established through the realization of an IS dedicated to actors outside the IJL (actors in economic development, innovation networks, scientific communities, interest groups from social networks, etc.). This IS is the result of the MASK method. The information it contains comes notably from a semi-directive questionnaire and specific interviews with the heads of different departments at the Institute. The IS represents the digital version of the Book of Knowledge, the main deliverable of the MASK method. Furthermore, it possesses indexing and re-indexing functionalities through use, allowing detailed research to be conducted (contents and user activities), which we will see later.

2) Extraction of explicit trade information through NLP. We have thus preferred to work on a corpus of homogeneous information rather than processing a heterogeneous corpus (bibliographic database from a laboratory, patents, scientific articles, etc.). The whole laboratory must undergo a national evaluation policy that analyzes the evolution of the structure over a period of 4 years. The report resulting from this obligation represents a sort of Book of Knowledge of the MASK method: this document reports advances in scientific research in a precise manner. The use of ALP tools for information extraction through this evaluation report allows a specialty class hierarchy and the associated concepts or C space to be obtained.

3) The use of NLP tools for information extraction through this evaluation report allows a specialty class hierarchy of knowledge and the associated concepts or C spaces to be obtained.

4) Reusing of the tree view obtained in (3) allows precise re-indexing complementary to the information presented in our IS, on the one hand [SID 14c] and an enrichment of the K space, on the other hand.

7.4.1. Implementations

The tool that we preferred for extracting information from our corpus is NooJ. It is an automatic NLP environment developed by Max Silberztein [SIL 04] from the University of Franche-Comté (France). NooJ is a multisystem that recognizes a large number of document formats [DON 13].

In this implementation environment, it is possible to create fully configurable local grammars (through finite-state automata to process asfinite-state machines with regular grammars) for information extraction. The NooJ resources are principally made up of dictionaries and syntax rules (or final stage transducer graphs), allowing complex extractions to be located, lemmas to be extracted and textual resources to be annotated automatically. The application makes it possible to cascade analysis processes, which allows detailed resource analysis.

Moreover, we have already used the tool in our previous works; as a result, we have linguistic resources at our disposal for processing in the nanoscience domain [SID 13c]. The strength of these linguistic resources allows us to create new extensions that can be adapted to new study contexts (see Figure 7.7).

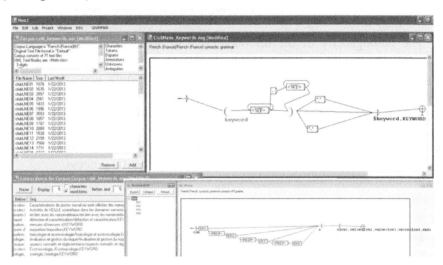

Figure 7.7. *Implementation of NooJ to extract NP from corpuses*

7.4.2. *Corpus specificities*

The corpus used for this work is an evaluation report with around 800 pages, made up of six volumes describing the scientific activities of each of the laboratory's teams, with three volumes collecting financial data, pertinent to human resources. To create the class hierarchy of knowledge, we only used the first volume of this report, amounting to 300 pages and describing the laboratory's activities for the period from 2007 to 2010.

This document was created through the contribution of each of the laboratory's teams with a common report, gathering team presentation, contractual activity and presentation of scientific themes. The advantage of this document is to present a structured text for all teams. The use of different parts will be subordinate to the informational need: the "team presentation" part can give way to a specific work on the named entities "proper nouns" and "localization", for example, while other parts can be used to extract other types of information (know-how, skills, competences, innovation needs, etc.). For our study, we chose only to use the "scientific themes" part, whose structure greatly facilitates the information extraction process.

The organization of the text with its titles and subtitles allows a relatively precise conceptual tree view to be obtained for each scientific theme provided by the teams. The information extraction process can therefore be supported by this editorial structure of the text to elaborate the hierarchy we need [SID 13a].

The homogeneity of the discourse is also an element in favor of the information extraction task. At the rhetorical level, the persuasive and argumentative character of the text can be felt strongly upon reading the report. The quality of the writing at both the grammatical level – short, simple sentences – and the lexical level – repetition of terminology particular to writing on the hard sciences – is also rather homogeneous. At the structural level, each theme follows the classical IMRD (i.e. Introduction, Materials and methods, Results and Discussion) scientific process.

7.4.3. NLP engineering applied to the corpus

For our work, we chose to work with the XML format so as to be able to process specific parts of the text. NooJ allows several document formats to be processed, including XML. As such, we must declare the nodes the ALP processes apply to. Furthermore, the software provides a file presenting the source document dealt with and the extracted pattern. By "pattern", we understand the extracted form, be it simple (token, lexeme, etc.) or complex (phrases, structures, etc.). The goal of preparing our source document is then to have a sort of Tuple (Source, Pattern) that can be reprocessed by specific scripts, notably to implement these results in a data visualization program [SID 11a, SID 11b] or for re-indexing.

All the documents have thus been transformed into a series of XML documents, thanks to a series of scripts written in Python. For each team report, an initial script recognized the title and subtitle numerations through regular expressions and then divided the text into as many parts as necessary. For a team report, a corpus was then obtained with the team name as its root and a tree view of texts numbered from 1 to n (see Figure 7.8).

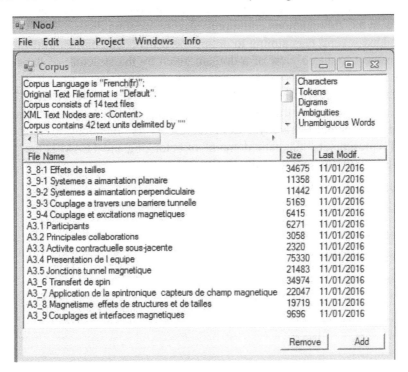

Figure 7.8. *XML corpus used to extract information*

A second script was used to transform these texts into XML files. A declaration line of the XML file was added to teach file, followed by three nodes: one node called <Entry>; another <Title>, corresponding to the title line; and a final <Content>, corresponding to the title's content.

Finally, a third Python script renamed each file with the name from the <Title> node to facilitate the reading of the output file. This is a CSV file that will first give the file's theme – Title – and then the extracted Pattern.

Thus, for each team, we obtained a corpus with an average of seven texts. These corpuses (24, in total) were processed separately by pooling the lexical resources used.

NooJ uses lexical resources like dictionaries and morphological grammars for textual labeling. In this way, we created a simplified version of a dictionary on nanoscience [SID 13b] for finding domain terminology (physics, chemistry and material science). The structure of the dictionary that we propose is made up of the lexeme, followed by its nature (N for noun, V for verb, etc.), which returns to the abbreviations commonly used by existing dictionaries. We have also added several tags aiming to define the conceptual belonging of the term with respect to a tree view of a domain given by the structure of the corpus. Each lexical entry is thus given, for example, as: <Lexical entry, NP+Lev2=XXXX+Lev1=XXX+DOM=SPINTRONIC+TEAM=XXX+UNAMB>, where NP labels the result as a "noun phrase", Lev2 represents the level of the "conceptual hierarchy", Lev1 represents its "hierarchy level at n+1", DOM represents its "thematic domain" of belonging and TEAM is the "team" that deals with this subject at the IJL Institute.

Figure 7.9. *Example of the NooJ class dictionary*

The grammars we created allow complex NPs and chemical formulas to be extracted (see Figure 7.9). The first grammar allows NPs (NP_max) from level 1 (i.e. common nouns) to level 3 (a nesting of three nouns juxtaposed or separated by different lexemes) to be extracted. The grammar will identify, for example, terms like "spintronic", "magnetic moments" or even "states of quantum sinks at ambient temperature". The grammatical graph presented in Figure 7.7, and implemented in Figure 7.8, allows these elements to be extracted.

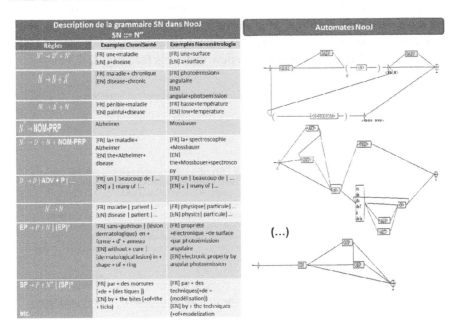

Figure 7.10. *NooJ syntactical graphs for extracting NPs (NP or N")*

The pattern – i.e. nesting series – is condensed into a variable noted with $()$ that can then be reused to create dictionary entries or label the text. The output variable will then be attributed a grammatical category that will thereby create a dictionary entry. The iteration of this grammar on the whole text allows thematic dictionaries to be created quickly. This is also the case with NooJ's "locate" function, which allows the unknown terms to be found with the <UKWN> tag. We then reworked the series of unknown terms to attribute to each of them a grammatical category and descriptive elements with previously defined tags (see Figure 7.10).

The second type of information that we wanted to extract concerns the chemical formulas dealt with in the report. This element is actually very important in the framework of a technological or scientific observation process [LAM 11], because the use and combination of particular chemical elements constitute the excellence of the research. They are therefore determining elements that seemed just as important for us to study as the extracted NPs and patterns. Dictionaries and grammars referring to these chemical structures can be reused at a later time for a weak signal (WS) detection task [SID 11a, SID 11b] on new materials (see Figure 7.11).

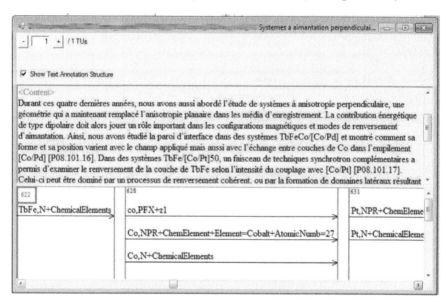

Figure 7.11. *Labeling chemical formulas present in a specialized text*

7.4.4. *"Polyfunctionalities" favoring strategic observation*

As we mentioned in the general introduction of this chapter, the linguistic resources and their associated processes (indexing and KO and representation using NP structures) created to build the domain class hierarchy of knowledge tend to serve several ISs to optimize strategic observation. Thus, by considering this class hierarchy to be a reference work in the domain, this tool can be used in several ways:

– In KM, it offers a state of knowledge and the advances in the research task from an instant, T, that can then be compared to T+1 in evaluation logic systems. The differential that exists between this reference work and the new scientific or technological branches that are added to this also allow the evolution of the laboratory to be determined and indicators to be given to the structure's administrative organizations;

– In innovation process (IP), our method makes a dynamic tool available that identifies the know-how and skills in the framework of innovative projets. It can therefore respond to questions of R&D project feasibility by defining the laboratory's field of action in terms of both the knowledge it possesses and the know-how and equipment when resolving complex problems. Finally, it helps identify the missing skills and can thus increase the aim for external, supplementary skills in the process of creating a chain of partner value;

– Finally, in strategic observation (SO), the linguistic resources, cognitive grammars and their associated processes implemented specifically for this study allow the detection and treatment of weak signals (WS) of a theme in material science. Dictionaries and grammars can actually be applied quite easily to the analysis of reference works (bibliographies, open resources, opinion polls, etc.) in order to determine the new fields of scientific research in a given sub-theme.

7.5. Conclusion: principal results and recommendations

The results of extracting information from a corpus presented, on average, 150 specialized NPs for each research team in the IJL. The process is still being evaluated and perfected. This work intrinsically joins a multidisciplinary domain calling on NLP to create content indexing databases and encourage KO and its KM in professional networks.

As new extractions were made, the information was reinjected into the IJL IS dedicated to the Technology and Knowledge Transfer Office. It is a developed web module made up of specific skill cards for each team at the Institute that presents its scientific specificities in a logical system of knowledge processing and mutualization. It is worth noting that each card includes two fields for content indexing: (1) for key concepts (tied to key words) reserved for the front-end of the application and appearing when the card is displayed and (2) indexing concepts (tied to simple and complex NP concepts of knowledge) that include patterns from the information extraction process from the bibliographic resources of the Web of Science (WoS).

The information extracted by these processes is complementary to that from bibliographic data extraction and that presented by teams during interviews in the scope of the MASK method. They contribute to improving the pertinence of search engines in our IS when queries are sent by a user expressing informational needs to find scientific skills in his area, competences in a chain of partner value, skills needed in an innovative process, etc.

NooJ's linguistic resources created specifically for this project also allow the IJL's skills to be identified more easily during industrial demands. In fact, when analyzing industrial needs systematically, the need must be formulated scientifically. For instance, to demand the optimization of an industrial process, it will be necessary to identify the existing process in all those forms to start an innovation task. Thanks to this tool implemented in the IS, we can thus propose the use of NooJ to analyze the problem expressed in terms of new information needs. By basing ourselves on the dictionary structure and in an attempt to develop a specialized knowledge database, the tool will then specify if the subject is dealt within the framework of the IJL, if the team that deals with the subject has skills or innovations, and how it fits into the class hierarchy.

Finally, the class hierarchy of knowledge created from the results of our processing allows a tree view to be displayed (see Figure 7.12) in the scope of conception–innovation workshops using the C-K theory. This visualization allows a Research–Innovation–Development task to be conducted with a specific team from the IJL in order to determine the existence of such a resource or, on the contrary, to figure out whether elements are missing and must be the focus of an innovative work. The methodology developed in this way also allows the internal structure's skills and those of its network to be diagnosed with the detection of the heterogeneous nature: the network's skills and actors in innovation domain. We conclude, and it is not the end of this research work; these heterogeneous elements will be focused on in a future study applying the detection and analysis of WS in the dynamics of innovation processes (IP).

KNOWLEDGE: scientific skills

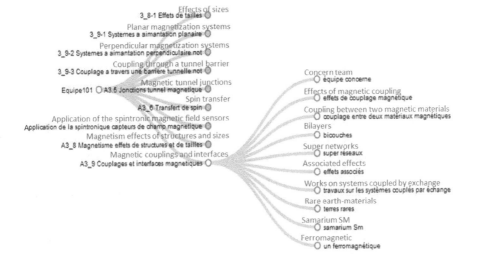

Figure 7.12. *Example of a K tree view for the innovative creation of the "spintronic"*

7.6. Bibliography

[AGO 13] AGOGUÉ M., ARNOUX F., BROWN I. *et al.*, *Introduction à la conception innovante: éléments théoriques et pratiques de la théorie C-K*, available at: https://books.google.com/books?hl=fr&lr=&id=7KchUKyxN1UC&pgis=1, 2013.

[BAC 04] BACHIMONT B., "Signes formels et computation numérique: entre intuition et formalisme", in SCHRAMM H., SCHWARTE L., LAZARDZIG J. (eds), *Instrumente in Kunst und Wissenschaft – Zur Architektonik kultureller Grenzen im 17*, Walter de Gruyter Verlag, Jahrhundert, Berlin, 2004.

[BIE 05] BIEMANN C., "Ontology learning from text: a survey of methods", *LDV-Forum 2005 – Band*, vol. 20, no. 2, pp. 75–93, 2005.

[BRO 96] BROWNE G., "Automatic indexing and abstracting", *Indexing in Electronic Age Conference*, Robertson, NSW, 20–21 April 1996, Australian Society of Indexers, p. 8, 1996.

[BUI 05] BUITELAAR P., "Ontology learning from text: methods, evaluation and applications", in BUITELAAR P., CIMIANO P., MAGNINI B. (eds), *Computational Linguistics*, vol. 32, no. 4, 2005.

[CAL 13] CALMET J., MARET P., "Toward a trust model for knowledge-based communities", *WIMS 2013*, 47, 2013.

[CAR 97] CARBONELL J.G., YANG Y,. FREDERKING R.E. *et al.*, "Translingual information retrieval: a comparative evaluation", *Proceedings of IJCAI-97*, Nagoya, Japan, 1997.

[CHA 10] CHAUDIRON S., IHADJADENE M., "Electronic information access devices: crossed approaches and new boundaries", in PAPY F. (ed.), *Information Science*, ISTE, London and John Wiley & Sons, New York, 2010.

[COU 09] COUZINET V., "Complexité et document: l'hybridation des médiations dans les zones en rupture, RECIIS", *Electronic Journal of Communication Information and Innovation in Health*, vol. 3, no. 3, pp. 10–16, 2009.

[DON 13] DONABÉDIAN A., KHASKARIAN V., SILBERZTEIN M., "NooJ computational devices", *Formalising Natural Languages with NooJ*, Cambridge Scholars Publishing, Cambridge, 2013.

[GIL 10a] GILLIER T., Comprendre la génération des objets de coopération interentreprises par une théorie des co-raisonnements de conception: vers une nouvelle ingénierie des partenariats d'exploration technologique, Institut National Polytechnique de Lorraine, available at: https://tel.archives-ouvertes.fr/tel-00493563/, 26 May 2010.

[GIL 10b] GILLIER T., PIAT G., ROUSSEL B. *et al.*, "Managing innovation fields in a cross-industry exploratory partnership with C-K design theory", *Journal of Product Innovation Management*, vol. 27, no. 6, pp. 883–896, 2010.

[GRU 93] GRUBER T.R., "A translation approach to portable ontology specifications", *Knowledge Acquisition*, vol. 5, no. 2, pp. 199–220, 1993.

[GUI 93] GUIMIER-SORBETS A.-M., "Des textes aux images: accès aux informations multimédias par le langage naturel", *Documentaliste – Sciences de l'information*, vol. 30, no. 3, pp. 127–134, 1993.

[LAM 10] LAMBERT P., SIDHOM S., "Extraction des connaissances et visualisation: cas d'application sur un corpus du projet ChroniSanté en France", *Proceedings SIIE'2010 International Conference*, February 2010 (Sousse), IHE Edition 2010, 2010.

[LAM 11] LAMBERT P., SIDHOM S., "Problématique de la veille informationnelle en contexte interculturel: étude de cas d'un processus d'identification d'experts vietnamiens", *Concepts et outils pour le management de la connaissance – ISKO-Maghreb 2011*, May 2011, Hammamet, 2011.

[MAN 93] Maniez J., "L'évolution des langages documentaires", *Documentaliste et Sciences de l'information*, vol. 30, nos 4–5, pp. 254–259, 1993.

[MAR 94] Maret P., Pinon J.-M., Martin D., "Capitalisation of consultants' experience in document drafting", *Conference Proceedings RIAO 1994*, Paris France, pp. 113–118, 1994.

[SER 11] Serrano L., "Modélisation d'une ontologie de domaine et des outils d'extraction de l'information associés pour l'anglais et le français", *Linguistics*, available at: http://dumas.ccsd.cnrs.fr/dumas-00569002, 2011.

[SID 02] Sidhom S., Plate-forme d'analyse morpho-syntaxique pour l'indexation automatique et la recherche d'information: de l'écrit vers la gestion des connaissances, Doctoral Thesis, University Claude Bernard-Lyon I, 2002.

[SID 11a] Sidhom S., Lambert P., "Information design for "Weak Signal" detection and processing in economic intelligence: a case study on health resources", *Journal of Intelligence Studies in Business (JISIB)*, vol. 1, pp. 40–48, 2011, available at: https://ojs.hh.se/index.php/JISIB/article/view/13/pdf>.

[SID 11b] Sidhom S., Lambert P., "Information Design" for "Weak Signal" detection and processing in Economic Intelligence: A case study on Health resources", *4th International Conference on Information Systems and Economic Intelligence – SIIE'2011*, Marrakech, pp. 315–321, February 2011.

[SID 13a] Sidhom S., Lambert P., Validations informationnelles pour l'organisation des connaissances sur le Community Manager: contexte d'étude en nano-sciences et -technologies. IUFM – IDEKI – Didactiques et Métiers de l'Humain; Nancy, October 2013.

[SID 13b] Sidhom S., Lambert P., "Project management within economic intelligence: using NooJ as diagnostic tool for nanometrology cluster. The Language Technology Lab of the German Research Center for Artificial Intelligence (DFKI GmbH)", *NooJ 2013 International Conference*, Saarbrücken, 1 June 2013.

[SID 13c] Sidhom S., Lambert P., Management (by concepts and processes) in Economic Intelligence: nanoMetrology cluster Project. IMSIE Alger et ESAA Alger. Colloque international de l'Institut de Management Stratégique et d'Intelligence Economique (IMSIE) d'Alger – Algeria. June 2013.

[SID 13d] Sidhom S., Lambert P., Traitement de l'information scientifique et technique dans un contexte de veille: plateforme d'apprentissage multilingue. *Cinquième journée Technopolice spécialisée*, Paris, September 2013.

[SID 14a] Sidhom S., Lambert P., Le "Community Manager" dans un contexte d'étude en nanosciences et nanotechnologies: de la validation informationnelle à l'organisation des connaissances, *IDÉKI nouvel espace et nouveaux enjeux pour construire et innover en didactiques*, 1, L'Harmattan, 2014.

[SID 14b] SIDHOM S., LAMBERT P., "Project management in economic intelligence: NooJ as diagnostic tool for nanometrology cluster", *Formalising Natural Languages with NooJ 2013: Selected Papers from the NooJ 2013 International Conference*, vol. 1, Cambridge Scholars Publishing 250, 2014.

[SID 14c] SIDHOM S., LAMBERT P., "Modèle d'analyse pour l'activité en Community Management: de la ré-indexation sociale à l'organisation des connaissances en nanosciences". University of Bordeaux. 1st International Conference *"Connaissances et Informations en Action: Transfert et organisation des connaissances en contexte", May 2014*, Bordeaux, p. 20, 2014, available at: http://gccpa.espe-aquitaine.fr/index.php/colloques-cia. May 2014.

[SOU 10] SOULIGNAC V., ERMINE, J.-L., PARIS, J.-L. *et al.*, Un serveur de connaissances pour l'agriculture biologique. In *Colloque SFER "Conseil en agriculture: acteurs, marchés, mutations"*, 14 and 15 October 2010 – AgroSup Dijon, 26 boulevard Docteur Petitjean 21079 DIJON, France.

[VAN 87] VAN SLYPE G., "Les langages d'indexation: conception, construction et utilisation", *Systèmes d'information et de documentation*, Editions d'Organisation, Paris, 1987.

[ZAK 07] ZACKLAD M., Classification, thésaurus, ontologies, folksonomies: comparaisons du point de vue de la recherche ouverte d'information (ROI). CAIS/ACSI 2007, *35e Congrès annuel de l'Association Canadienne des Sciences de l'Information. Partage de l'information dans un monde fragmenté: Franchir les frontières*, Montreal, May 2007.

List of Authors

Ashraf AMAD
Paragraphe
University of Paris 8
Paris
France

Mathieu ANDRO
Paragraphe
University of Paris 8
DIST Institut National de la
Recherche Agronomique
Paris
France

Abdelkrim BELOUED
Institut National de l'Audiovisuel
Paris
France

Nasreddine BOUHAÏ
Paragraphe
University of Paris 8
Paris
France

Steffen LALANDE
Institut National de l'Audiovisuel
Paris
France

Philippe LAMBERT
Institut Jean Lamour
University of Lorraine
Nancy
France

Lénaïk LEYOUDEC
COSTECH
UTC
Compiègne
France

Muriel LOUÂPRE
CERILAC
University of Paris 7
Paris
France

Imad SALEH
Paragraphe
University of Paris 8
Paris
France

Sahbi SIDHOM
LORIA Lab
University of Lorraine
Nancy
France

Peter STOCKINGER
Institut National des Langues et
Civilisations Orientales
(INALCO)
Paris
France

Samuel SZONIECKY
Paragraphe
University of Paris 8
Paris
France

Index

Other titles from

in

Information Systems, Web and Pervasive Computing

2016

BEN CHOUIKHA Mona
Organizational Design for Knowledge Management

BERTOLO David
Interactions on Digital Tablets in the Context of 3D Geometry Learning
(Human-Machine Interaction Set – Volume 2)

BOUVARD Patricia, SUZANNE Hervé
Collective Intelligence Development in Business

DAUPHINÉ André
Geographical Models in Mathematica

EL FALLAH SEGHROUCHNI Amal, ISHIKAWA Fuyuki, HÉRAULT Laurent,
TOKUDA Hideyuki
Enablers for Smart Cities

FABRE Renaud, in collaboration with MESSERSCHMIDT-MARIET Quentin,
HOLVOET Margot
New Challenges for Knowledge

GAUDIELLO Ilaria, ZIBETTI Elisabetta
Learning Robotics, with Robotics, by Robotics
(Human-Machine Interaction Set – Volume 3)

2014

STOCKINGER Peter
Introduction to Audiovisual Archives

STOCKINGER Peter
Digital Audiovisual Archives

VENTRE Daniel
Cyberwar and Information Warfare

2010

BONNET Pierre
Enterprise Data Governance

BRUNET Roger
Sustainable Geography

CARREGA Pierre
Geographical Information and Climatology

CAUVIN Colette, ESCOBAR Francisco, SERRADJ Aziz
Thematic Cartography – 3-volume series
Thematic Cartography and Transformations – volume 1
Cartography and the Impact of the Quantitative Revolution – volume 2
New Approaches in Thematic Cartography – volume 3

LANGLOIS Patrice
Simulation of Complex Systems in GIS

MATHIS Philippe
Graphs and Networks – 2nd edition

THERIAULT Marius, DES ROSIERS François
Modeling Urban Dynamics

2009

BONNET Pierre, DETAVERNIER Jean-Michel, VAUQUIER Dominique
Sustainable IT Architecture: the Progressive Way of Overhauling
Information Systems with SOA

PAPY Fabrice
Information Science

RIVARD François, ABOU HARB Georges, MERET Philippe
The Transverse Information System

ROCHE Stéphane, CARON Claude
Organizational Facets of GIS

2008

BRUGNOT Gérard
Spatial Management of Risks

FINKE Gerd
Operations Research and Networks

GUERMOND Yves
Modeling Process in Geography

KANEVSKI Michael
Advanced Mapping of Environmental Data

MANOUVRIER Bernard, LAURENT Ménard
Application Integration: EAI, B2B, BPM and SOA

PAPY Fabrice
Digital Libraries

2007

DOBESCH Hartwig, DUMOLARD Pierre, DYRAS Izabela
Spatial Interpolation for Climate Data

SANDERS Lena
Models in Spatial Analysis

2006

Printed and bound by CPI Group (UK) Ltd, Croydon, CR0 4YY

27/10/2024

14580725-0001